Twayne's English Authors Series

Thomas Nashe

TEAS 317

Pierce Penilesse his

Supplication to the *Diuell.*

Defcribing the ouer-fpreading of
Vice, and fuppreffion of
Vertue.

Pleafantly interlac'd with variable delights: and pathetically intermixt
with conceipted reproofes.

Written by *Thomas Nafh* Gentleman.

LONDON,
Imprinted by *Richard Ihones,* dwelling at
the Signe of the Rofe and Crowne,
nere Holburne Bridge.
1592.

THOMAS NASHE

By DONALD J. McGINN
Georgian Court College

TWAYNE PUBLISHERS
A DIVISION OF G. K. HALL & CO., BOSTON

Library of Congress Cataloging in Publication Data

McGinn, Donald Joseph.
Thomas Nashe.

(Twayne's English authors series ; TEAS 317)
Bibliography: p. 183–88
Includes index.
1. Nash, Thomas, 1567–1601—Criticism and
interpretation.
PR2727.M3   828'.309   80–19760
ISBN 0-8057-6807-6

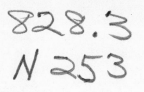

To My Grandchildren

Contents

About the Author

Born in Indian Lake, New York, Donald J. McGinn received his A.B., M.A., and Ph.D. from Cornell University. Former head of the English Department of the Rutgers Preparatory School, he became a member of the department of English of Rutgers University, from which he retired as professor emeritus in 1973. At Rutgers he taught undergraduate courses in Shakespeare, modern drama, the novel, and the correlation of the fine arts. He also taught graduate courses in Shakespeare and sixteenth-century nondramatic literature. He is presently professor of English at Georgian Court College, Lakewood, New Jersey. His publications include *Shakespeare's Influence on the Drama of his Age, The Admonition Controversy, Literature as a Fine Art, John Penry and the Marprelate Controversy,* and numerous critical essays and reviews. Dr. McGinn has been a member of the College Council on English in the Central Atlantic States, the Shakespeare Association of America, the Renaissance Society of America, and the Catholic Commission on Intellectual and Cultural Affairs. He is a life member of the Modern Language Association of America and of Phi Beta Kappa. He is listed in *Who's Who in the East*, the *Directory of American Scholars*, and *Contemporary Authors*.

Preface

During the 1590s in Elizabethan England many aspiring young writers were striving to outdo one another in composing tragedies, romances or sonnet cycles. A notable exception was Thomas Nashe, fresh from Cambridge University, who decided not to follow the crowd but to make a name for himself primarily as a pamphleteer. Instead of recounting the intrigues of kings, the adventures of knights and ladies, and the agonies and ecstasies of courtly love, Nashe for his literary material sought the crowded streets, shops, and taverns of the London of his own day. In his pamphlets he portrays the various types of middle-class Londoners—their appearance, their manners, and their customs.

Two major works on this highly original writer have appeared during the present century: Ronald B. McKerrow's edition in five volumes of the writings generally assigned to Nashe (1903–10) and George R. Hibbard's *Thomas Nashe: A Critical Introduction* (1962). McKerrow's edition is a landmark in Elizabethan scholarship. Yet he states in the preface to his final volume that he has made no attempt whatever at a description or an appreciation of Nashe's compositions. The second study, as its subtitle indicates, supplements McKerrow in these areas. In order both to avoid an excessive number of notes and also to enable the reader to check my main sources at once, I have included in parentheses within my text all references to McKerrow and Hibbard, whom I frequently quote. Since McKerrow's work covers several volumes, I have indicated the particular volume, page, and, wherever possible, lines. My references to Hibbard are to pages only.

A third, more recent scholar than either of these, to whom all students of Nashe are greatly indebted, is Mr. C. G. Harlow. His two excellent articles in the *Review of English Studies* have corrected the chronology of Nashe's activities between 1592 and 1594, when he composed some of his most important pamphlets, and have thereby solved several perplexing problems.

In order that the reader may be fully aware of the originality of Nashe's genius, I am giving fairly detailed summaries of each of the pamphlets published under his name and also of the anti-Martinist

pamphlet *An Almond for a Parrat,* which he wrote under a pseudonym. My aim in preparing these summaries is not to discourage the
reading of the original text but rather to provide a supplement to that
text.

Needless to add, my greatest debt is to McKerrow, from whom I
have derived the main facts in my chapters of Nashe's life and on his
reputation among his contemporaries. In the progress of my research
of over forty years' duration I have been aided by numerous grants
from the Rutgers University Research Council. These have enabled me
to purchase microfilms from libraries in this country and abroad and
to defray the incidental expenses of secretarial assistance. I also wish to
thank Sister Anita Talar, the librarian of Georgian Court College, and
her very able staff, who have assisted me in the final stages of the preparation of my manuscript.

DONALD J. MCGINN

Georgian Court College

Chronology

1567 November, Thomas Nashe born, third son of William Nashe, "minester," and second wife, Margaret.

1573 Family moves from Lowestoft to West Harling, Norfolk.

1582 October 13, matriculation as sizar of St. John's College, Cambridge.

1584 Appointed as scholar of Lady Margaret Foundation of the university.

1586 Awarded degree of Bachelor of Arts but continues at the university.

1587 Father dies.

1588 Listed as resident in Cambridge. Early autumn, leaves Cambridge for London. September 19, registration of *The Anatomie of Absurditie*.

1589 August 23, registration of preface to Robert Greene's romance, *Menaphon*. October 23, registration of Richard Harvey's *A Theologicall Discourse of the Lamb of God and His Enemies* with the attack on Nashe leading to the Nashe-Harvey controversy. December 2, Nashe's mother dies.

1590 March or April, publication of anti-Martinist pamphlet, *An Almond for a Parrat*, and of *The Anatomie of Absurditie*.

1591 Publication of edition of Sir Philip Sidney's *Astrophel and Stella* with short preface by Nashe.

1592 July 20, registration of Robert Greene's *A Quippe for an Upstart Courtier* with first attack on the Harveys, possibly written by Nashe. August 8, registration of *Pierce Penilesse, His Supplication to the Divell*. September or October, the performance of *A Pleasant Comedie, called Summer's Last Will and Testament* at the palace of Archbishop John Whitgift, Croydon. December, publication of *Strange Newes of the Intercepting Certaine Letters* (first reply to Gabriel Harvey).

1593 January 12, registration of *Strange Newes*. February, visits at a house in the fenlands, probably that of Robert Cotton at Conington near Huntingdon. From March until June works as corrector of the press or literary adviser in London with the printer

John Danter. June 30, registration of *The Terrors of the Night*. September 8, registration of *Christ's Teares Over Jerusalem*. September 17, registration of *The Unfortunate Traveller*. October, at Windsor introduced to Sir George Carey, captain-general of the Isle of Wight. October or November, publication of *Christ's Teares* dedicated to Lady Elizabeth Carey. December, action taken against Nashe by the London City Council. Released through intervention of Carey and taken with Carey family to Isle of Wight.

1594   Remains in Isle of Wight until February. Returns to London. Publication of *The Unfortunate Traveller* (date unknown). Publication of second issue of *Christ's Teares*. October 25, second registration of *The Terrors of the Night*. Publication without official registration of *The Tragedie of Dido Queene of Carthage* as "written by Christopher Marlowe and Thomas Nashe."

1596   Publication without registration of final reply to Harvey, *Have with You to Saffron-Walden*.

1597   About July 28, production of satirical play *The Isle of Dogs* (now lost), begun by Nashe and completed by Ben Jonson. Reaction in governmental circles forcing Nashe to flee to Yarmouth. October 11, registration of pamphlet attacking Nashe entitled *The Trimming of Thomas Nashe, Gentleman* under name of Don Richardo de Medico Campo, professing to be pseudonym of Richard Lichfield, barber at Trinity College, Cambridge.

1598   January 11, registration of *Nashe's Lenten Stuffe*.

1599   June 1, orders from Archbishop John Whitgift and Bishop Richard Bancroft to call in "all Nasshes bookes and Doctor Harvyes bookes."

1601   Reference in Charles Fitzgeffrey's *Affaniae* to Nashe as deceased.

CHAPTER 1

A Brief Biographical Sketch

I Birth and Education

THOMAS Nashe was born in the autumn of 1567 in Lowestoft, Suffolk, the third son by the second wife of William Nashe, who is described as a "minester" of that community. McKerrow points out, however, that the elder Nashe, who apparently was not a university graduate, was never formally instituted as vicar of Lowestoft (V, 3 n.). John Blomvile had resigned this vicarage in 1555 and had been succeeded by Thomas Downing, who died in 1559. McKerrow speculates that the vicarage of Lowestoft may have been returned to Blomvile at Downing's death and that since Blomvile could not take care of both the vicarage in Rollesby, Norfolk, to which he had been transferred, and his former one in Lowestoft, he may have appointed William Nashe as a stipendiary curate. Although on the title page of the younger Nashe's popular pamphlet *Pierce Penilesse, His Supplication to the Divell* the author is referred to as "Thomas Nash Gentleman" (I, 149), he himself in a later pamphlet modestly brushes aside this title and denies any claim to gentle birth (I, 312, 1–3).

In 1573, when Thomas was six years old, his father moved from Lowestoft to a living in West Harling, Norfolk, where he was rector until his death in 1587. Nashe probably spent the remainder of his childhood until his departure to the university with his family in West Harling. Since the nearest school of any size was at Thetford, seven miles away across a heath, Nashe may have received his early education from his father. After the elder Nashe's death his wife returned to Lowestoft, where she died on December 2, 1589.

Of Thomas's early years there is no record. The first that is heard of him is the entry in the Cambridge University Register, which records his matriculation as sizar of St. John's College on October 13, 1582. By November 1584 he had become a scholar of the Lady Margaret Foundation. In March 1586 he graduated Bachelor of Arts and continued on toward the degree of Master of Arts. Among the undergraduate and graduate students listed as residing in Cambridge in 1588 his name again appears. McKerrow assumes that since such lists as these were usually drawn up at the beginning of the academic year Nashe was probably attending Cambridge until the summer of 1588 (V, 8). Then he suddenly withdrew without completing the work for his final degree.

In his last pamphlet, *Nashe's Lenten Stuffe*, he himself states that he was a member of St. John's College, Cambridge, "for seuen yere together lacking a quarter" (III, 181, 24–25). But McKerrow points out that the period from the date of his matriculation in October 1582 to October 1588 would be only six years (V, 8). Yet the author of a mock biography of Nashe, entered in the Stationers' Register on October 11, 1597, *The Trimming of Thomas Nashe, Gentleman*, states that at the time of severing connections with the university Nashe was a "Batchelor of the third yere,"[1] which could include any date between March 1588 and March 1589. In order to reconcile Nashe's statement with that in the so-called biography McKerrow postulates that Nashe had entered the university "early in 1582 or even in 1581" (V, 8). Moreover, since *The Anatomie of Absurditie* was entered in the Stationers' Register (the Elizabethan counterpart of our modern copyright listings) in London in September 1588, the date of his departure from Cambridge seems to have been in September of that year.

Although Nashe completed his career at the university without obtaining the coveted degree of Master of Arts, he evidently left of his own free will. In his second reply to Gabriel Harvey, *Have with You to Saffron-Walden*, he states that it was general knowledge that had he wanted to continue at St. John's College he could have become a fellow there (III, 127, 33–34). Furthermore, had he been expelled, the anonymous author of *The Trimming of Thomas Nashe, Gentleman* would certainly have seized upon that fact. In this satirical biography Nashe is depicted as what today would be regarded as a "student revolutionary" participating in the riots between town and gown and taking part in a scurrilous play, *Terminus & non terminus*, for which his partner was expelled.[2] But his biographer merely implies that Nashe left the university in order to avoid getting into further trouble.[3]

Even though in the epistle to the reader prefacing the second issue of *Christ's Teares Over Jerusalem* Nashe professes his high regard for "a number of excellent wel conceipted learned men" in Cambridge (II, 182, 34–35), he probably was not always comfortable in his particular college. In his first printed essay, his preface to Robert Greene's romance, *Menaphon*, entered in the Stationers' Register on August 23,

1589, and published in the early autumn of that year, he paid a glowing tribute to St. John's College as it had flourished at the beginning of the century: "that most famous and fortunate Nurse of all learning, Saint *Iohns* in *Cambridge*, that at that time was an Vniuersity within it selfe, shining so farre aboue all other houses, Halles, and hospitals whatsoeuer, that no Colledge in the Towne was able to compare with the tithe of her Students . . ." (III, 317, 9–14). Then, after naming the famous graduates of St. John's in the early sixteenth century, Nashe laments the changes when that college became the center of Puritan activity, which Nashe abhorred. St. John's, indeed, had been strongly Puritanical since the early 1570s, when the eminent Puritan preacher and polemicist Thomas Cartwright was on its faculty. Later the Puritan and Separatist John Penry received much of his religious bias there.

II *Early Literary Activity*

Perhaps the real reason for Nashe's hasty departure from Cambridge was his lack of funds stemming from his father's death early in 1587. In *Have with You* he admits that his father had helped to support him at the university (III, 127, 29–34). McKerrow suggests that his money may have run out (V, 11). In his *Anatomie of Absurditie* he seems to be expressing his own feelings when he writes as follows:

When as wits of more towardnes shal haue spent some time in the Vniuersitie, and haue as it were tasted the elements of Arte, and laide the foundation of knowledge, if by the death of some friend they shoulde be withdrawne from theyr studies, as yet altogether raw, and so consequently vnfitte for any calling in the Common wealth, where should they finde a friend to be vnto them in steed of a father, or one to perfit that which their deceased parents begun. (I, 37, 13–21)

Thus forced to fend for himself, he decided to join the small group of professional writers, now referred to as the University Wits—graduates of Oxford and Cambridge who for want of other sources of income had decided to make their livings by their pens.

Upon his arrival in London he proceeded to enter in the Stationers' Register his first literary venture, *The Anatomie of Absurditie*. As he himself states in his opening paragraph, it had been written during a "vacation," when "hauing laide aside" his "grauer studies for a season," he had been "idle in the Countrey"—probably the preceding summer of 1587 (I, 9, 16–18).

Although this pamphlet was his earliest literary effort, his first actual publication was his preface to Greene's *Menaphon*. McKerrow suggests that Nashe's invitation to introduce this romance was the result of having "already won some reputation as a wit" (V, 15). His need for money, as well as his ambition for literary fame, would make doubly welcome an opportunity to appear in print with this distinguished author. In the preface, in which he writes as a literary critic, he includes the name of the Cambridge scholar Gabriel Harvey in his list of England's foremost writers (III, 320, 28). For this youthful presumption he was immediately censured by Harvey's brother Richard in a pamphlet entitled *A Theologicall Discourse of the Lamb of God and His Enemies*. Richard's sarcastic remarks were to rankle in Nashe's mind until Gabriel in *Foure Letters and Certaine Sonnets* would add insult to injury by a second attack and thereby open the Nashe-Harvey controversy.

Nashe's eagerness for controversy appeared early in his career. Harvey in *Foure Letters* alludes to a quarrel with Thomas Churchyard, not denied by Nashe, about which nothing else has come down to us.[4] His preliminary training in literary combat occurred in his participation in anti-Martinist pamphleteering. In Martin Marprelate's pamphlets, indeed, he discovered a satirical style most compatible with his own talents. Martin's first pamphlet, *Oh read ouer D. Iohn Bridges for it is a worthy worke*, commonly known as the *Epistle*, represents an experiment in the dissemination of printed matter in colloquial English for the purpose of informing and influencing public opinion—what today would be labeled journalism. It was primarily intended as a reply to Dean John Bridges's extremely long, scholarly, and—it must be confessed—dull *Defence of the Church of England*. In order to acquaint the reading public with the Puritan criticism of the episcopacy, Martin Marprelate hit upon the idea of playing the buffoon in print. In a sort of monologue consisting of simple words and short sentences Martin mingles seemingly good-humored raillery with scandalous gossip about various prominent clergymen of the Established Church. With this device to arouse and to maintain the interest of his readers he attacks the basic ecclesiastical organization.

The immediate popularity of the Martinist pamphlets is described by Nashe in his preface to *Menaphon* as follows:

... those and these are so affectionate to dogged detracting, as the most poysonous *Pasquil* any durty mouthed *Martin* or *Momus* euer composed is gathered vp with greedinesse before it fall to the ground, and bought at the dearest, though they smell of the friplers lauender halfe a yeere after. (III, 315, 1–6)

The alarm of the high officials of both church and state at the appearence of this new literary weapon is evident from their haste to counterattack. At first they tried long theological treatises which would appeal only to the intellectual. Then, recognizing the popularity of Martin's jests and innuendos, they turned to the theaters. The plays written for propaganda, however, proved offensive to public taste. It is not at all impossible that Nashe with his previous dramatic experience at Cambridge may have attempted to write some of these unsuccessful plays, none of which is extant. Before the bishops could assemble their forces Martin had published a second pamphlet with another derisive title several sentences in length, usually abbreviated as the *Epitome.* The first serious attempt at rebuttal, Bishop Thomas Cooper's *Admonition to the People of England,* though not as lengthy and tedious as Bridges's *Defence,* was immediately knocked down at one blow by Martin's *Hay any worke for Cooper.* This third Martinist pamphlet, containing somewhat more earnest matter than the first two, was written in a similarly racy idiom.

Martin did not meet his match, indeed, until Nashe, imitating the style of the Martinist pamphlets, published *An Almond for a Parrat.* This pamphlet J. Dover Wilson calls "the last shot fired on the Marprelate battlefield."[5] Although he finds it "much more closely reasoned and well-informed than any other anti-Martinist production," Wilson complains that "its literary merits are small."[6] Contrary to Wilson's estimate, however, the literary, as well as the historical, merits of *An Almond* are by no means small, either to the student of the Marprelate controversy or to the critic of Nashe. Historically this pamphlet contains the first credible account of the conspirators involved in the controversy. Moreover, in it Nashe specifically names John Penry as Martin (III, 365, 25 ff.). In newspaper jargon today this announcement would be termed a scoop; here for the first time Martin Marprelate is publicly identified.

What is more important to an understanding of Nashe's literary development, *An Almond* was the only anti-Martinist pamphlet to produce a successful imitation of Martin's invective. In Nashe's later pamphlets, beginning with his attack on Richard Harvey in *Pierce Penilesse* and continuing through his final pamphlet, *Lenten Stuffe,*

Nashe perfected this borrowed style and finally made it his own. Because *An Almond* turns all of Martin's verbal ammunition back upon him, it has won Nashe credit for—as Archbishop John Whitgift expressed it—stopping "Martin's and his fellows' mouths" (V, 44 n.). For the student of English literature it provides the stylistic link between Nashe's early publications and his successful *Pierce Penilesse* and thus enables us to understand how he came to discard the ornate euphuism displayed in *The Anatomie of Absurditie* in favor of the colloquial style characteristic of his later writings from *Pierce Penilesse* on.

A few months after the publication of the preface to *Menaphon* and about the same time as the publication of *An Almond*, Nashe's *The Anatomie of Absurditie* appeared. It was dedicated to Sir Charles Blount, then busily engaged in the wars in the Low Countries, who probably had little time to acknowledge this compliment even if he had known of it. At any rate, since Nashe never thereafter mentions Blount, this first attempt to find a patron came to naught. Through such rebuffs as this he was to come to realize that he must abandon the convention of the patronized writer who dedicated his masterpiece to a nobleman with the hope of receiving a monetary reward. Instead he gradually began to recognize that he must depend for his bread and butter upon his popularity with the reading public. His only other publication before *Pierce Penilesse* was a short preface to an edition of Sir Philip Sidney's sonnet cycle *Astrophel and Stella*, which appeared in 1591.

III   *Nashe's First Important Success*

Gabriel Harvey in *Foure Letters* provides the next direct news of Nashe's activities in London, namely, his presence at a banquet of pickled herring and Rhenish wine in the company of Robert Greene and a certain Will Monox, about whom little else is known. According to Harvey, Greene's final illness, which resulted in his death on September 2 or 3, 1592, was due to his excesses on this occasion.[7] Nashe's four years in London previous to this event would have given him plenty of opportunity to observe and record the life and ways of its citizens which were to become the source of material for his subsequent writing.

During the summer he had managed to complete *Pierce Penilesse*, which McKerrow terms "the most popular of his books, and the one which perhaps first brought him into general notice" (V, 18). It was entered in the Stationers' Register on August 13, 1592, and was dedicated to "Amyntas," probably Ferdinando Stanley, the Earl of Derby. While Nashe was in London, perhaps consulting with his printer, he dined with Greene and Monox. In *Pierce Penilesse* he published his first reply under his own name to Richard Harvey's depreciatory remarks about him in the *Lamb of God*.

A few weeks before the publication of *Pierce Penilesse*, however, an attack on the Harvey family, written in Nashe's satirical vein or in a very good imitation of it, had appeared in a short passage in Greene's *A Quippe for an Upstart Courtier*, entered in the Stationers' Register on July 20, 1592, and immediately published. But since the offending passage was deleted from the pamphlet in the process of being printed, only one copy containing the original passage is extant. When McKerrow published his edition, he had not seen this copy, which now is in the Huntington Library. Nevertheless from remarks made both by Nashe and Harvey in the course of their controversy McKerrow accurately surmised the substance of the attack (V, 77). Though Nashe could not savor the vindictive pleasure of having the satire on the Harvey family published under his own name, its insulting tone succeeded in goading the Cambridge scholar into entering the ring, as it were, and issuing the opening challenge.

Not having read the passage in the *Quippe* McKerrow naturally assumed that Greene had written the entire pamphlet himself. Yet he uneasily notes that the section dealing with Richard Harvey in *Pierce Penilesse*, which is little more than an expansion of the original deleted passage, seems "to bear strong traces of having been added as an afterthought" (V, 78). Undoubtedly it was.[8] In other words, Nashe may have hoped that the Harveys would be properly scored in the *Quippe* so that he could get on with his work on his own pamphlet. McKerrow concludes that " . . . Nashe apparently regarded the reference to the Harveys in the *Quippe* as a direct reply to the *Lamb of God*" (V, 77 n.). But when that attack was deleted, he had to insert another in his *Pierce Penilesse*.

Shortly afterward Greene became ill and within a few days died. In the meantime, however, Nashe returned from the plague-ridden city to take refuge in the country where he had been spending the summer. In a "priuate Epistle of the Author to the Printer" prefixed to the second edition of *Pierce Penilesse*, published, McKerrow believes, in the middle of October (IV, 78–79), he explains his absence as follows: " . . . the feare of infection detained mee with my Lord in the Countrey" (I, 153, 21–22). At this country retreat Nashe composed *Strange*

Newes of the Intercepting Certaine Letters, his first reply to Gabriel Harvey's attack on him in *Foure Letters*. According to C. G. Harlow's revised chronology for Nashe's activities between 1592 and 1594, this pamphlet could not have been begun before the end of September.[9] It was entered in the Stationers' Register on January 12, 1592–93. In *Strange Newes* Nashe writes that he was living "in a house of credit, as well gouerned as any Colledge, where there bee more rare qualified and selected good Schollers than in any Noblemans house" in England (I, 329, 22–25). Harlow considers this a perfect description of Archbishop Whitgift's palace at Croydon, particularly since in the next sentence Nashe refers to his host as "my Lorde."[10] Both McKerrow (V, 20) and Hibbard (p. 88) agree that "my Lorde" was Whitgift. And McKerrow adds that the archbishop may have invited Nashe to Croydon in order to reward him for his contribution in the campaign against Martin Marprelate (V, 21).

As a result Nashe was absent from London when Greene died and when *Pierce Penilesse* was published. McKerrow further presumes that Nashe composed his play *A Pleasant Comedie, Called Summer's Last Will and Testament* for immediate performance at Croydon during September or October 1592, although it was not published until 1600 (IV, 418; V, 34).

IV   *Noncontroversial Pamphlets of 1593*

As Harlow assembles the pieces of the puzzle, Nashe remained at Croydon until December and perhaps even later.[11] However, in February 1592–93, when he wrote the first draft of *The Terrors of the Night*, he was visiting in a house in the fenlands, probably that of Robert Cotton at Conington, near Huntingdon.[12] Harlow postulates that after a brief stay here Nashe returned to London, where from March until June he worked with John Danter, the printer, probably in the capacity of corrector of the press or literary adviser.[13] Before June 30 he had completed an early version of *The Terrors of the Night* for the press and sold it. It was entered in the Stationers' Register as of June 1593, but was not published until 1594. He probably was not in the city during July and August, the worst months of the plague. In spite of his work in the printer's house the period between February and September was one of concentrated literary activity. On September 8 his *Christ's Teares* was registered and a few days later, on September 17, *The Unfortunate Traveller*.

The publication of *Christ's Teares* immediately made trouble for Nashe. Among his satirical comments on London life in *Pierce Penilesse* he had included a political-religious allegory concerning a "Beare" and a "Foxe." Similarly in *Christ's Teares* he attacks the greed of London merchants and also makes thinly veiled charges about the misappropriation of public funds and the taking of bribes by civic authorities in charge of these funds (II, 158, 4 ff.). The ensuing uproar resulting from his broad insinuations forced him to revise his remarks and, in issuing the unsold sheets of the first edition, to print a denial that he was directing his criticism at any particular individual.

A second important episode associated with the publication of *Christ's Teares* was an attempt on the part of certain friends made during the preceding summer to reconcile Nashe and Harvey. As a result of their efforts Nashe, in his first epistle to the pamphlet, generously apologizes to Harvey (II, 12, 13 ff.). This apology appeared in the first edition published toward the end of September 1593. A few days later, about the middle of October, in *A New Letter of Notable Contents* Harvey attacked Nashe as though unaware of the proffered olive branch.[14] McKerrow attributes Harvey's seeming obduracy to an unfortunate accident for which he was not responsible, namely, that his two pamphlets—his earlier reply to Nashe, probably completed the previous April, *Pierce's Supererogation or a New Prayse of the Old Asse,* and the later *New Letter*—bound as one were published by his printer, John Wolfe, without the author's knowledge (V, 103–105).

Hibbard, however, disagrees with McKerrow's extenuation for what on the surface seems a lack of forgiveness on Harvey's part: "For one who had never seen it [Nashe's apology] he certainly knows a great deal about it" (pp. 215–16). The more recent biographer notes that Harvey in his *New Letter* expresses suspicion of Nashe's good intentions. Consequently Hibbard believes that after reading the apology Harvey permitted his hostile feelings to get the better of "his more rational intention to behave generously." Hibbard therefore concludes that Harvey himself authorized the publication of his two-part attack on Nashe, published under the inclusive title of *Pierce's Supererogation,* because he "was proud of it, because he thought it would put the seal on his victory over Nashe, and because he wished it to be published." In other words, Harvey's own journalistic instinct got the better of him. For, as Hibbard also points out, "nothing is more typical of the man than the high value he set on his own writings and the strong desire he felt to see himself in print." At any rate, realizing that his overtures of peace had fallen on deaf ears, Nashe in his epistle to the reader written for the second issue of *Christ's Teares* again lashes out at his opponent.

V   *Nashe and the Careys*

Contrary to McKerrow and Hibbard, Harlow convincingly argues that Nashe first became acquainted with the family of Sir George Carey, a cousin of the queen, knight marshal, and governor of the Isle of Wight, late in the year 1593. In October of that year Sir George was stopping in Windsor because the queen and her court were there. Harlow suggests that Nashe, "sheltering from the plague," may have been among the "hangers-on and would-be courtiers" in the lodging houses in the town and thus may have been introduced into the Carey circle.[15] Consequently, when *Christ's Teares* was published in October or November, it was dedicated to Lady Carey. Nashe's satirical remarks about simony in the city government provoked the lord mayor and aldermen of London. Harvey, seeing his adversary at a disadvantage, took this opportunity to "incense" the lord mayor still further. As a result, when Nashe returned to London at the beginning of December, the city council took action against him. Only through the intervention of Carey was he released and taken off with the Carey family to Carisbrooke Castle on the Isle of Wight, where he remained until February 1594.

From Nashe's description of the career of a conjurer in *The Terrors of the Night*, which closely resembles the evidence made public at the trial of Dr. Ruy Lopez, the queen's physician, beginning in February 1593–94, Harlow assumes that Nashe was back in London at that time.[16] Also in 1594, *The Unfortunate Traveller*, which had been completed on June 27, 1593, and registered on September 17, was published. Harlow attributes the delay in publication to the direct result of Nashe's persecution by the city authorities followed by his absence in the Isle of Wight. The narrative appeared before the second issue of *Christ's Teares* with its new preface taking back his apology to Harvey.

On October 25, 1594, *The Terrors of the Night* was entered for the second time in the Stationers' Register. As Harlow points out, a second entry of the same work is "very unusual."[17] He suspects that since Nashe alludes to a case of witchcraft near where he was writing his pamphlet the Stationers' Company may have delayed publication until the matter was settled. Then, in the fifteen or sixteen months before the second entry, Nashe added enough new material to require reregistration: for example, the dedication to Elizabeth Carey, a section in praise of the Careys, the allusion to the Lopez conspiracy, and perhaps more.[18]

VI *More Controversy along with Some Dramatic Composition*

Between the publication of *The Terrors of the Night* in late November 1594, as Harlow dates it,[19] and the summer of 1595, Nashe worked on his second lengthy reply to Harvey, *Have with You*. During this same interval he may have made his additions to Marlowe's *Tragedie of Dido Queene of Carthage*. And in a letter to William Cotton written about September 1596 he says that he had for some time been trying his hand at dramatic composition with little or no success (V, 194).

After the publication of *Have with You* Nashe began work on a comedy entitled *The Isle of Dogs*, of which no trace remains. Upon its presentation on the stage he found himself in more trouble than ever. Apparently his distinguishing literary attribute, his satirical vein, again caused him to lash out at the vices and follies of the political leaders of the day. The play was declared seditious. Nashe's lodgings were searched by order of the Privy Council, and his papers seized and submitted to Richard Topcliffe, the chief agent for the government in prosecuting acts suspected of treason.

Nashe himself admitted to composing only a small section of the play, namely, the "induction" and the "first act." The remaining "foure acts," he maintains, "by the players were supplied" without his consent (III, 154). Pointing out that the sale of an incomplete play was "not uncommon," Hibbard adds that this particular play was completed by Ben Jonson and put on "some time in the summer of 1597 before 28 July, when the theaters were closed" (pp. 234–35). Although Nashe may have been ordered to prison, he apparently was able to avoid punishment by fleeing to Yarmouth, where he arrived "in the latter ende of Autumne" 1597 (III, 154, 19–20).

The only suggestion that he might have spent some time in prison appears in *The Trimming of Thomas Nashe, Gentleman*, which contains a sketch of him in irons.[20] But the author of that scurrilous tract never specifically declares that Nashe was imprisoned. On the contrary, in discussing what he terms "that most infamous, most dunsicall

and thrice opprobrious worke *The Ile of Dogs*," he makes much of
Nashe's excape from the authorities.[21] Certainly, had Nashe been
imprisoned, as much space or more would have been given to his
disgrace.

VII   *Nashe's Final Pamphlet*

At Yarmouth, where he was hospitably treated, Nashe remained for
six weeks during the late autumn of 1597. After departing, during Lent
1598 he wrote *Lenten Stuffe* (III, 151, 10–11). In this pamphlet he
complains that "here in the countrey" he is "bereaued" of his "notebooks and all books else" (III, 175, 34 ff.). But from his epistle to the
reader it is evident that he returned to London in order to be on hand
while the pamphlet was being printed (III, 152, 16–19). In the opening
paragraph of its main text he announces that he has "a pamphlet hot
a brooding that shall be called the *Barbers warming panne*" (III, 153,
24–25)—in other words, his reply to his self-styled biographer.
Although he promised to publish it during the following Easter term,
it never appeared.

On June 1, 1599, Whitgift and Bishop Bancroft issued the order that
"all Nasshes bookes and Doctor Harvyes bookes be taken wheresoeuer
they maye be found and that none of theire bookes bee euer printed
hereafter" (V, 110). In 1600 the last product of Nashe's pen, *Summer's
Last Will and Testament*, written eight years earlier, appeared in
print. McKerrow suggests that it may even have been posthumously
published (V, 34). Thus this brilliant satirist who had shocked and
delighted literary London with his mordant wit quietly disappeared
from the scene. In Charles Fitzgeffrey's *Affaniae* (1601) he is referred
to as already deceased. When and where he died and where he is buried are unknown.

CHAPTER 2

Four Early Literary Exercises

I The Anatomie of Absurditie

*T*HE *Anatomie of Absurditie*, with the subtitle "Contayning a
breefe confutation of the slender imputed prayses to feminine perfection, with a short description of the seuerall practises of youth, and
sundry follies of our licentious times," is the work of a novice with
ambitions to become a literary critic. In its dedication to Sir Charles
Blount Nashe's reference to his first writing as "satyricall" (I, 5, 20)
indicates that from the beginning of his career he knew where his talents lay. The first target of his satirical pen is the inconstancy of all
women—all, that is, except the queen, whom he praises with the customary hyperboles. In a similarly conventional vein he terms Sir Philip
Sidney the English counterpart of Castiglione's Courtier. He concludes
with an exaggerated compliment to Sir Charles, along with a modest
disclaimer of his own ability.

In the opening lines of his main text it soon becomes evident that his
denunciation of women in his dedication is not so much antifeminism
as a criticism of the popular romances of the day. He considers it his
mission to debunk these imitators of the medieval writers, "those exiled
Abbie-lubbers, from whose idle pens proceeded those worn out impressions of the feyned no where acts, of Arthur of the rounde table, Arthur
of litle Brittaine, sir Tristram," and so on (I, 11, 6–11). Exhibiting his
skill at euphuism he asks his reader to cast aside the idealized creation
of these writers and to look at a real woman. Obviously imitating John
Lyly, the master of this balanced alliterative style, he comments as
follows:

Neuer remembring, that as there was a loyall *Lucretia*, so there was a light
a loue *Lais*, that as there was a modest *Medullina*, so there was a mischiuous
Medea, that as there was a stedfast *Timoclea*, so there was a trayterous *Tar-
peya*, that as there was a sober *Sulpitia*, so there was a deceitful *Scylla*, that
as there was a chaste *Claudia*, so there was a wanton *Clodia*. (I, 11, 22–28)

25

As if these examples were not sufficient to prove his point, he continues with a long list of contrasting figures from classical literature intended to impress his reader with his erudition. Then he cites the antifeminist comments of the "ancient Philosophers, as touching the Femall sexe" (I, 12, 11 ff.). With particular emphasis on women's inconstancy he concludes his diatribe with more examples from mythology and history.

Turning next to the pamphlet, another literary form becoming popular, he condemns the intolerance and unscholarliness of writers pretending "to anatomize abuses and stubbe vp sin by the rootes" (I, 20, 3–4)—a punning allusion to Philip Stubbes's *Anatomy of Abuses.* Since a zeal for reforming society was especially typical of the Puritan pamphleteers, Nashe seizes this opportunity to lash out at their alleged hypocrisy.

Though he exonerates from pretence the writers of astrological pamphlets, he believes that their concern with improbabilities also should be condemned. They succeed only in deluding the simple and ignorant. Along with these authors of almanacs he classes the composers of ballads, songs, and sonnets who will tell any lie whatsoever as long as it fits the rhyme and meter of their poems.

At this point Nashe assures his reader that he himself is a friend of pure poetry, which he defines as a branch of philosophy teaching good manners and morals. Mere rhyming is not poetry. While conceding that some profitable knowledge may be extracted from erotic poetry, he urges that it be restricted to mature readers. Nevertheless he does not recommend public censorship. Like Milton he is convinced that a truly evil man will find evil even in the Bible.

Only through age or adversity will young men learn to obey their elders who urge them to study. Instead, thriftless sons will spend the fortunes accumulated by their parents on fine clothing and dissipation. The true wealth is wisdom, which enables poor men to equal princes. Frequently a poor man by thrift may build a fortune. His sons, as ignorant as their father, will then apply for a coat of arms and appear in court as gentlemen. In the old days both men and women sought education. At the present time, however, ignorance is the enemy of learning. The upstarts who have enriched themselves with the wealth of the monasteries now covet the land owned by the universities. On the contrary, the educated man without a fortune finds no position open to him. If a university student is interrupted in his studies by a lack of funds, he must become either a tradesman or a preacher like the clergymen now attacking the Established Church. Learning is essential in every profession. Everyone can learn from the lives of the great philosophers, all of whom cared more for study than for rich food and drink. Although Sir Thomas Elyot questioned diversity of diet, he probably did not condemn it. Nashe quotes many arguments to prove that a diverse diet is not harmful.

Rather than spend time discussing food for the body, however, he decides to concentrate on mental nourishment. In his opinion the student should guard against negligence of important things (or sloth), want of wisdom (or no method in reading), and fortune (or external accident interrupting studies). Nashe gives a series of warnings about how, what, and why to read. He also condemns conceited scholars who cultivate newfangled studies in order to impress other people: for example, scholars who prefer Ramus to Aristotle.

Of all the arts rhetoric is the most admirable, for without eloquence the other arts are ineffective. Knowledge of the arts, however, is not enough but must be qualified by experience. Young students tend to be distracted by irrelevancies in classical learning and unnecessary speculations in philosophy.

In closing, Nashe recommends Ascham's *Schoolmaster* as an excellent reference for the study of classical authors. Finally he warns against the danger of letting Aristotle and the "lighter studies" (I, 48, 31 ff.), by which he seems to mean poetry, interfere with the practice of religion for the salvation of one's soul.

II   *Critical Commentary*

Since *The Anatomie of Absurditie* was entered in the Stationers Register on September 19, 1588, McKerrow presumes that it was already completed by that date (IV, 1). Its euphuistic style indicates that it was an early work, probably written while Nashe was still at the university. As he himself later admits, he was then a great admirer of Lyly's *Euphues* (I, 319, 15–19). Although McKerrow surmises that this pamphlet was originally intended as an attack on the female sex (IV, 1), he observes that Nashe's criticism of women seems actually "a protest against the revival of worn-out, old-fashioned literature" (IV, 9) and hence may have been only incidental to his literary criticism. Then, after concluding his satire on the romantic heroine, Nashe apparently decided to throw in whatever else he had on his desk— brief fragments on education, other literary forms, diet, and so on.

McKerrow terms it "a patchwork of scraps from others, containing little, if any, original matter" (IV, 2).

Hibbard is in general agreement with McKerrow. He describes this pamphlet as "very much a young man's work" with "little literary merit" (p. 10). Consequently it aroused no interest when it first appeared or since. By echoing the title of Stubbes's *Anatomy of Abuses*, Nashe, according to Hibbard, is reminding his reader that his main purpose in writing was to produce an "anti-satire" defending poetry and the arts against the Puritan pamphleteers who during the past ten years had been satirizing poetry, the stage, and popular entertainment of any kind (pp. 12–13).

Perhaps its two main attractions to the student of Nashe are its foreshadowing of ideas to be developed in later writings and its realistic point of view that makes its author the most modern of the Elizabethans. Nashe's distaste for romance was its failure to depict life as it really is. This "obvious preference for realism," as Hibbard expresses it (p. 16), is what distinguishes Nashe from his fellow writers. In his prefatory epistle he terms this first work a "pamphlet" (I, 8, 17). Everything that he afterward wrote except his play and his unpublished erotic poem might well be thus classified. *The Anatomie of Absurditie* marks the debut of an Elizabethan journalist.

III   *The Preface to Greene's* Menaphon

Nashe opens his epistle entitled "To the Gentlemen Students of Both Universities," to which McKerrow refers as the preface to *Menaphon*, with a request for courteous treatment. He expresses his awareness that the uneducated person ("euery mechanicall mate"—III, 311, 15) is using eloquent language learned from the playwrights, who pride themselves on their bombastic blank verse. Some of these playwrights with only a grammar-school education must depend on translations for their subject matter. Robert Greene's *Menaphon* is far more eloquent than anything taken over from the Italian. After all, if a writer requires seven years or borrows from the classics, he should be able to produce a masterpiece. Nashe himself prefers the "extemporall veine" (III, 312, 25). Furthermore, too many writers derive their themes, vocabulary, and ideas from Italian and French writers.

Instead of reading pamphlets only for relaxation from serious literature, most people will sooner buy a pamphlet about a popular event than a poem by Tasso. Everyone enjoys reading scurrilous pamphlets like the Marprelate tracts which attack people in high positions. Here Nashe's concession that "in scholler-like matters of controuersie a quicker stile may passe as commendable" (III, 315, 10–12) reflects his almost unwilling admiration for Martin's style, which at the time he was learning to imitate. Nevertheless, as if he feels bound to censure Martin's lack of respect for his superiors, he complains that "the irregular Ideot," presumably Martin or any other pamphleteer attacking either the Established Church or the queen as its head, is too immature and too inexperienced to be truly critical.

Unfortunately many clerks, insufficiently educated, abandon their trade for a literary career. Instead of composing original works they depend upon English translations of the classics, particularly of Seneca, whom they slavishly imitate. Or they turn to translating from the Italian for the same purpose. Using these translations as models, they put together plays in their leisure moments. For a bit of recreation they give a little time to perusing French translations. Perhaps feeling that he has been too harsh, Nashe commends certain translators, especially Erasmus, who translated Greek works into Latin. With them he includes English writers and orators noted for their fluency in Latin and Greek. But altogether too many people nowadays, Nashe complains, rush into the pulpit before completing their education. Instead of mastering Priscian and Aristotle, they waste their time on epitomes. Indeed, it has become the fashion to make "abbreuiations of Arts" (III, 318, 11)—presumably compendiums[1]—and contractions of every sort, even to writing the Our Father on a penny.

Returning to the subject of translation, he adds more names to his list of learned translators of the past. Today, however, all that are left are Thomas Newton, Gabriel Harvey, and two or three others. Nashe attributes this scarcity of translators and of English writers of poetry in Latin and Greek to the Puritan clergy, who condemn poetry as vain and impious. On the contrary, Nashe insists, unless a man is a poet he is not a scholar. Yet he ridicules those poets who believe that they must drink wine or ale in order to compose. He also is impatient with the Italianate Englishmen who stress the inferiority of the native poets as compared with those of other countries. Patriotically Nashe would place Chaucer, Lydgate, and Gower above them all. The court and the city, too, have many able poets and playwrights, the greatest of whom by far is Spenser. After him come Roydon, Achlow, and particularly Peele, whom he calls "the chief supporter of pleasance now liuing, the *Atlas* of Poetrie, and *primus verborum Artifex*," whose play *The*

Arraignement of Paris "goeth a steppe beyond all that write" (III, 323, 26–31).

This reference to a play reminds Nashe that many other fine playwrights are supplying plays for the actors, who would otherwise be living in poverty. Every actor each morning therefore should pray for his benefactor, the playwright, but for whom he would be traveling in the country. In conclusion, Nashe begs the good opinion of his readers and promises them his *Anatomie of Absurditie* in the near future.

IV   *Critical Commentary*

Nashe's preface to *Menaphon*, although not his first composition, was his first published work. Hibbard describes it as "the *Anatomy of Absurditie* boiled down and brightened up" (p. 32). It differs from that work, however, in that it more closely resembles a challenging news article than the earlier one and clearly forecasts the road that the young journalist will travel. Several of its "items" are still of lively interest to scholars. As Hibbard puts it, "it has attracted more attention and been discussed in greater detail than anything else Nashe ever wrote" (p. 28). Hibbard adds that "it appears to be full of promising allusions, which if they could only be interpreted properly, would throw much light on the literary scene as it was in 1589."

The first of these allusions complains of the "seruile imitation" by "euery mechanicall mate" of "vaine glorious Tragedians, who contend not so seriously to excell in action, as to embowell the cloudes in a speech of comparison, thinking themselves more then initiated in Poets immortality, if they but once get *Boreas* by the beard and the heauenly Bull by the deaw-lap." And even more reprehensible than these "Tragedians," he continues, are "their ideot Art-masters, that intrude themselues to our eares as the Alcumists of eloquence, who (mounted on the stage of arrogance) thinke to out-braue better pennes with the swelling bumbast of bragging blanke verse" (III, 311, 14–29).

At first glance it might appear that Nashe is attacking playwrights guilty of corrupting the language. But as McKerrow explains, "Tragedians" could also mean actors or even writers in general. Hence he doubts that the phrase "bragging blanke verse" is aimed especially at Marlowe, whose "mighty line" has become a cliché of literary criticism. In McKerrow's words, "though we may now recognize the superiority of his [Marlowe's] blank verse to that of other writers of the day, this is by no means the same thing as showing that he was the leader of the movement (IV, 445–46). Hibbard, on the contrary, reiterates the earlier theory that this passage is an attack on Marlowe on the ground that in it Nashe is attempting to curry favor with Greene, who on occasions had made slighting remarks about Marlowe (pp. 34–35).

A second possible target for Nashe's criticism is Thomas Kyd, who also wrote tragedies in blank verse. Moreover, three or four pages further on in the preface is Nashe's reference to the "nouerint-maker," or scrivener, who has written "whole Hamlets." This statement, immediately followed by the celebrated allusion to the "Kid in *Aesop*," is regarded by many Shakespearean scholars as evidence of Kyd's authorship of the Ur-Hamlet (III, 315, 25 ff.). Since Kyd was the son of a scrivener, to whose occupation, according to McKerrow, Nashe always refers "as if representative of the lowest class of work connected with the pen" (IV, 450), Nashe might consider him one of the "mechanicall mates" who imitated the "vaine glorious Tragedians."

A third possibility is the author of the very romance to which Nashe is writing his preface, namely, Robert Greene himself. Why such a young unknown writer as Nashe would have been asked to contribute a prefatory epistle to a romance by a distinguished author is, in Hibbard's opinion, "the first problem posed by the *Preface*" (p. 29). Although Nashe's scathing attack on romances and writers of romances in *The Anatomie of Absurditie* had not yet appeared, it is highly improbable that he had changed his mind about them. On the contrary he seems to be using this opportunity to contrast the sprightliness of his newly discovered martinizing style with Greene's more formal rhetoric (III, 312, 24–29; 313, 26 ff.; see also Hibbard, pp. 29–30).

Summing up these mysterious allusions in the preface, the only positive comment to make upon them is that any interpretation is largely a matter of personal opinion. These ambiguities force the conclusion that the preface to *Menaphon* is not a well-written piece of work. As Hibbard expresses it, it is merely "a pot-boiler, a work put together, probably in a hurry, for a particular occasion" (p. 33). While Stanley Wells concedes that it may include passages referring to literary events "undoubtedly satirical in import," he terms these "so privately expressed that they remain totally and maddeningly incomprehensible."[2] Wells attributes this "unintelligibility" to "over-particularity" in Nashe's use of satire.

V   *Preface to Sir Philip Sidney's* Astrophel and Stella

Nashe's brief preface to *Astrophel and Stella* is casually entitled "Somewhat to reade for them that list." He warns his readers that they are about to witness "the tragicommody of loue," the chief actor in which is Melpomene, the "argument" cruel chastity, the prologue hope, the epilogue despair (III, 329, 14 ff.). It will be performed on a "paper stage streud with pearle, an artificial heau'n to ouershadow the faire frame, & christal wals."

After this elaborate introduction Nashe, writing in what critics now call his "high style," announces that in this edition of the sonnets Astrophel, or Philip Sidney, "Englands Sunne," will reappear to expel the darkness on the literary scene, where now only inferior writers show their deceiving flames (III, 330, 14). Astrophel has received the ivory harp of Apollo. Although like Orpheus he must remain in the Elysian Fields, in these sonnets the ashes of his love will live again like the fabled Phoenix.

Nashe compliments Sidney's sister, the Countess of Pembroke, as a "second Minerua" (III, 331, 23). Then he apologizes for his style which he fears might be construed as mere flattery. He admits that it is "somewhat heauie gated" (III, 332, 2). Although not a light or foolish style, it is not as fresh as "the Almond leape verse" (III, 332, 6). Merely because a writer fills his pages with euphuism or classical allusions, he is not necessarily learned. Just as the ass in spite of his wise appearance has certain imperfections preventing him from becoming a magistrate, so these writers because of their frequent publication are admired by certain critics.

VI   *Critical Commentary*

Hibbard dismisses the preface to *Astrophel and Stella* as "an undistinguished bit of hack work" (p. 49), suggesting that Nashe at the time of writing was in serious financial straits. Only one minor passage seems worthy of comment, namely, his complaint that his prose lacks "any skill to imitate the Almond leape verse." Quoting Gregory Smith's definition of "Almond" as "Almain," that is, German, McKerrow doubts any connection between Nashe's "Almond" and the dance known as the Almain, "a slow and stately measure" (IV, 459–60). Instead this allusion sounds like a typical pun, similar to the "Kid in Aesop" in the preface to *Menaphon*. Between the publication of *An Almond* and of *Pierce Penilesse* Nashe was probably working on the Martinist style, which he was to forge into a new style of his own. And, as Hibbard suggests, in this second preface "the 'extemporall veyne' eludes him" (p. 50).

VII   An Almond for a Parrat

While Nashe was working on his first piece to be published, his preface to Greene's *Menaphon*, which appeared in 1589, the bishops of the Established Church, reeling under the first onslaught of Martin's satirical pen, assembled a group of anti-Martinist writers, chief among whom was Nashe. In his preface he expresses a grudging admiration for the railing style of the Puritan writers in general and of Cartwright and Martin Marprelate in particular. In *An Almond* he reveals how carefully he has studied Martin's use of epithets, colloquialisms, and character assassination.

In dedicating *An Almond* to the celebrated clown Will Kempe, who after Tarlton's death in 1588 succeeded him in popularity as the leading clown in London, Nashe indicates his awareness that part of Martin's appeal lay in his assumption of the guise of a jester. Echoing Martin's signature of his *Epistle*, "by your learned and worthy Brother, Martin Marprelate,"[3] Nashe signs his preface, "Thine in the way of brotherhood, Cutbert Curry-knaue" (III, 343, 14–15).

In the main section of *An Almond* Nashe immediately begins by singling out prominent Puritans for ridicule. First he selects the "long tongd doctresse Dame *Law*" (Margaret Lawson), the "honest citizens wife," as Martin once called her.[4] Since nothing more has been heard of her, Nashe concludes that she "must haue beene faine (in spite of insperation) to haue giuen ouer speaking in the congregation, and employ her Parrats tong in stead of a winde-clapper to scarre the crowes" from Martin's "carrion" (III, 344, 9–12). From this passage it seems likely that Nashe in his title is alluding to her as the "Parrat" whom he intends to pacify with his "Almond," or pamphlet.

Having thus disposed of Dame Lawson, he next sketches the humble backgrounds of the Puritan ministers for the purpose of contrasting their illiteracy with the university training of the ministers of the

Church of England. In the midst of his tirade, as though fascinated by Martin's railing, he pauses to repeat all of his opponent's epithets for the bishops. With this tribute to Martin's invective as an overture Nashe makes his triumphant announcement of the recent arrest of the Martinist printers and the capture of their press.

As if to maintain suspense, however, he does not at once disclose the names of the culprits but returns to cite specific examples of antiintellectualism among the Puritan ministry. Almost ready to reveal his big news, which is the identity of Martin Marprelate, he arouses his reader's curiosity by referring to the mysterious figure as "his welchnes" (III, 355, 10 ff.). Leading up to the disclosure he first announces that government pursuivants have captured the Martinist printers John Hodgkins, Arthur Tomlyn, and Valentine Symmes, who had disguised themsleves as "saltpetermen." Their denial of any crime—in other words, their perjury, Nashe insists—is typical of Puritan morality. This accusation permits him to digress with a few more examples of immoral, ignorant Puritan leaders, including Philip Stubbes and Cartwright.

After thus building up suspense Nashe suddenly names John Penry, the Welshman, as Martin Marprelate (III, 365, 25–31). Evidently from whatever evidence had been made available to Nashe he had no doubt but that Martin and Penry were identical. He then presents a mock-biographical sketch of Penry, who "as he was begotten in adultery and conceiued in the heat of lust, so was he brought into the world on a tempestuous daie, & borne in that houre when all planets wer opposite" (III, 365, 36 ff.). Insinuating that Penry originally had been a Roman Catholic, a charge designed to infuriate him and his followers, Nashe traces his conversions from papist, to Brownist, to anabaptist, and finally to Martinist.

His mock-biography completed, he pauses a moment to exult in his newly discovered style. Then he turns to deal with the Puritan-inspired rumor that the bishops have refused to grant the Puritans a disputation. He stresses the absurdity of such a confrontation as this because of the difficulty of finding a suitable place for it. Furthermore it would be impossible to select authorities and moderators acceptable to both sides. In addition, he shows that in view of the present supply of qualified preachers Martin's demand for a preacher in every church in England and in Wales could never be satisfied. Back on the subject of Puritan preachers Nashe scornfully suggests a list of possible candidates for the vacant parishes—another opportunity for character assassination.

Finally, with a threat to publish his "blacke booke" containing many more stories, he ends with an exhortation to Martin to mend his ways and no longer to deceive the simple and ignorant.

VIII *Critical Commentary*

In spite of its lack of form the general plan of *An Almond* follows that of Martin's *Epistle*—a series of accounts of the shortcomings and absurdities of particular clergymen interlaced with an occasional brief reply to the most damaging elements of Puritan propaganda. The main significance of this pamphlet to the student of Nashe is that it furnishes the stylistic link between his early publications and his successful *Pierce Penilesse* and later pamphlets. Accepting my identification of the anonymous *An Almond* as the work of Nashe,[5] Hibbard agrees that this pamphlet is "the bridge between the laboured, imitative quality of the *Anatomy of Absurdity* and the confident assurance of *Pierce Penilesse*" (pp. 37–38).

CHAPTER 3

Pierce Penilesse, His Supplication to the Divell

I *Introduction*

THE name "Pierce Penilesse," given by Nashe to the persona of his first literary success, reveals the author's natural inclination for punning. In spite of McKerrow's doubts about the similarity in pronunciation between *Pierce* and *purse*, the evidence that he presents from the notes of H. G. Hart, along with Pierce's own complaint of poverty in his opening lines, would verify this play on words (IV, 86). And as both McKerrow and Hibbard (p. 64) point out, the name Pierce also is intended to recall the plain-spoken country fellow in Langland's *Piers Plowman*.

After briefly lamenting his penniless state, first in prose and then in poetry, Pierce recalls all the ignorant laborers who have become wealthy. Even scriveners and pamphleteers who have "set foorth a Pamphlet of the praise of Pudding-pricks" or who "write a Treatise of *Tom Thumme,* or the exployts of *Vntrusse*" are paid better than scholars for the "best Poeme" they can make (I, 159, 2–6). Sir Philip Sidney, a scholar himself and a patron of scholars, now is dead and has left no successor. Pierce complains of the indifference of patrons, "men of great calling" to whom a pamphlet is dedicated, who merely "put it vp in their sleeues, and scarce giue him thankes that presents it (I, 159, 22–26). While scholars starve, upstart young gallants from the country spend their hard-earned patrimonies on high living in the city.

In the face of this economic injustice Pierce, with no money whatsoever, decides to send a supplication to the Devil. Recalling that his Satanic Majesty has frequently been seen hobnobbing with lawyers, Pierce first visits Westminster Hall. Not finding him there he visits the Royal Exchange, the financial center of London, where he meets an old usurer who says that a friend of his, a broker, had informed him that the Devil was at home suffering from gout and would not be spo-

ken with for far more than Pierce could afford to pay him. Pierce
finally goes to St. Paul's Cathedral, where he meets a "knight of the
Post," a "fellowe that will sweare you any thing for twelue pence" (I,
164, 8–10). This unsavory character agrees to deliver his supplication
to the Devil.

II   *The Contents of the Supplication*

Pierce's first request in this document is that gold, imprisoned by
Greedinesse and his wife, Dame Niggardize, be set free. These "two
Earthwormes" (I, 167, 21–22), hoarding everything that they can get
their hands on, live in a house spacious and strongly built in every room
except the kitchen and buttery, where even the rats, mice, and insects
starve to death. Pierce's lament over the sad condition of gold introduces a pageant of the Elizabethan London counterpart of the medieval Seven Deadly Sins.

Beginning with the sin of Pride, "the peruerter of all Vertue" (I,
168, 29), Pierce describes a typical young son of a prosperous country
squire who has come to London to spend what his father had toiled to
earn. Pretending to be of noble birth, he plays at writing sonnets and
affects foreign accents and mannerisms. Or he might assume the
appearance of an important politician and go about shrouded in mystery with his garters untied and his hat pulled down over his eyes. Even
though he may be starving most of the time, he will manage to make
a rare appearance at an expensive restaurant so that he may be seen in
the best society. Sometimes this young gallant spends all of his money
at the Inns of Court or in the City and then runs off to sea where he
anticipates winning a fortune by plundering Spanish ships. All that he
gets, however, is a bad case of seasickness.

Turning from these spendthrifts to nonconformists in religion,
Pierce comments on the pride of scholars like Martin Marprelate,
Henry Barrow, and John Greenwood, who, dissatisfied with the Estab-
lished Church, seek to form new sects to be named after them.

After singling out these few examples of what he terms "the sub-
urbes" of Pride (I, 172, 31), Pierce surveys the city itself. First, he calls
attention to the "base Artificer" (I, 173, 1), in this instance a tailor, who
attires himself like a gentleman. Next he mentions the merchant's wife,
who eats only the most expensive foods, struts about, and speaks with
absurd affectation. Then he describes the pride of the newly rich
upstarts—formerly scullions, brewers, vintners, dung-farmers, hostlers,

apothecaries, colliers, butchers, hackney men—all "raised from the plough to be checkmate with Princes" (I, 173, 23). What troubles Pierce is not that these workmen are prosperous but that they are better rewarded than men of learning. Here Pierce warns noblemen not to trust these social climbers.

Lest the reader think pride to be the besetting sin only of Englishmen, Pierce for the moment leaves London for the Continent. The overweening pride of the Spaniard is shown in his boasting. The Italian is less obvious and, in fact, affects a deceptive humility. Effusive in hospitable offers, he does not expect them to be accepted and is quick to resent a real or fancied insult. The Frenchman, although outwardly courteous, thinks only of himself. Pierce scoffs at the traditional French levee, the attendance at which is supposed to be a mark of royal favor. The Danes are a stupid, military nation of barbarians who give more attention to outward appearance and rank than to merit. They are more interested in drinking than in poetry.

Back in England Pierce cites as further evidence of the ravages of Pride the many painted faces of English women. An allusion to their use of false hair evokes a warning to both men and women of the threat of baldness resulting from syphilis. He concludes his account of Pride by scoffing at persons interested only in the past who are deceived by false claims of antiquarians into purchasing "guegawes and toyes" (I, 183, 1–2).

Next in Pierce's catalogue of sin is Envy, who, he maintains, has been improperly represented by the poets. They usually picture him as a "leane, gag-toothed Beldam, with hollow eyes, pale cheeks, and snakie haire," whereas he really is a "iolly, lusty, old Gentleman, that will winke, and laugh, and ieast drily, as if he were the honestest of a thousand" (I, 183, 20–24). The adopted son of Pride, Envy pretends to be sympathetic but in reality will do his best to prevent another man from getting anything.

As the first example of Envy, Pierce cites Philip of Spain, who, having won the new world, now wants both France and Belgium. But England was a match for him and defeated his Armada. Courtiers cultivating pride, riot, and whoredom are always envious of their fellows favored by the Prince or better dressed than they. However, they conceal their hatred in smiles. Envy is inevitably accompanied by murder. In Italy, the "Academie of man-slaughter" (I, 186, 22), the envious man has cultivated the art of poisoning. Every five years, indeed, the papal chair is "washt" with poison. Pierce reports the rumor that Philip of Spain has recently poisoned Sixtus V.

Although Envy generally is directed at some one better than oneself, the third of the Deadly Sins, Wrath, attacks anyone, great and small. If the wrathful man is a judge or a justice, he will condemn everyone coming under his jurisdiction. Like his companion Avarice, Wrath is an old man and must be bribed with money or women. People become angry for various inconsequential reasons. As a result the law courts are filled with contentious men that fall out over nothing.

The chief cause of wrath is drunkenness. When a man gets drunk, he loses his senses, his words become confused, and he quarrels with everyone. Railing is akin to drunkenness: not only railing at people, but also railing at the arts, especially poetry. Pierce discloses that on one occasion he himself was the victim of railing. A stupid clergyman, whose dull sermons were a patchwork of the writings of Calvinist theologians, was the culprit. Such a clergyman as this could not appreciate any exquisite poem.

Here Pierce digresses to discuss poetry, which he terms the art "to describe discontented thoughts and youthfull desires" (I, 192, 27–28). The example of "siluer tongu'd" Henry Smith, who began as a poet, proves the value of poetry to a preacher. Poets benefit the state by improving our language and by inspiring men to virtue. England owes a debt to Sir Philip Sidney, Sir Nicholas Bacon, Sir Thomas More, and Chaucer, the "chiefe pillers of our english speech" (I, 194, 3). The poet is superior to the historian, who is merely a recorder of political leaders and events and possesses no critical judgement whatsoever. Pierce boasts that his education has prepared him as a poet to honor any generous patron. His sense of gratitude would enable him to outdo himself in order to praise a benefactor. Yet if any man were to slight him in word or deed, he has "tearmes . . . laid in steepe in *Aquafortis*, & Gunpowder, that shall rattle through the Skyes, and make an Earthquake in a Pesants eares" (I, 195, 20–23).

In order to display his skill at railing he will apply some of these terms to a man who recently attacked him in print for lack of learning. Turning his artillery upon this man, the son of a ropemaker, Pierce accuses him of having been refused his bachelor's degree for ridiculing Aristotle. Although he does not mention his persecutor by name, Cambridge men, as McKerrow points out (IV, 120), would recognize him to be Richard Harvey, who preferred the philosophy of Ramus to that of Aristotle. Pierce calls Harvey a "student in Almanackes" (I, 196, 11), one of which was published under his brother's name. Since Pierce immediately ridicules Richard Harvey's *Astrologicall Discourse upon the Conjunction of Saturn and Jupiter*, McKerrow assumes that

Pierce's reference is to the *Astrologicall Addition* to this almanac (IV, 121). When the prophecies in it came to nothing, the author was publicly ridiculed.

Next Pierce asks his detractor, a vicar, why he had compared him to Martin and had abused him for praising outstanding scholars. Furthermore, in confusing him with Thomas Nash, the master butler of Pembroke Hall, Harvey has likewise injured a third party, Pierce's friend. Finally, jeering at Harvey's *Lamb of God* and threatening him with a counterattack from Paphatchet (John Lyly), Pierce bids him go "trusse vp" his life in the string of his sancebell (the bell rung at the service).

After impudently asking his reader to note the "extemporall" quality of his railing (I, 199, 6), he proceeds to the Deadly Sin of Gluttony. First he compares the London gluttons to the Roman emperors after Augustus. The variety of meats on the English dinner table scandalizes visitors from other countries. As a contrast Pierce mentions the abstinence of two distinguished Spanish friars, who by their control over their appetites would put the English gluttons to shame. The only advantage of English gluttony, Pierce wryly comments, is to kill off the wealthy so that their hoarded treasures can be passed on to unthrifts who will liberate it.

Another form of Gluttony which England has learned from its alliance with the Low Countries is Drunkenness. Pierce defines and describes each of its various forms, eight in all: ape drunk, lion drunk, swine drunk, sheep drunk, maudlin drunk, martin drunk, goat drunk, fox drunk.

The nurse of drunkenness, as of all other evils, is Sloth or Idleness:

Men, when they are idle, and know not what to do, saith one, let vs goe to the Stilliard, and drinke Rhenish wine. Nay, if a man knew where a good whorhouse were, saith another, it were somwhat like. Nay, saith the third, let vs goe to a dicing-house or a bowling alley, and there we shall haue some sport for our money. (I, 208, 29–34)

As the living image of Sloth, Pierce describes a certain stationer whom he knows who is too lazy even to speak to his customers but instead uses a boy as an interpreter. Only at meal time does he come alive.

Pierce believes that of the two, the glutton and the unthrift, the latter is the superior. Whereas the glutton achieves nothing but illness, the unthrift exercises his body at the various places of recreation, which he, in turn, enriches. What he loses in gambling, he wins in sharpening his wits. Best of all, he attends the theater, cultivates the acquaintance of poets, and improves his manners by courting beautiful women. The slothful man, on the contrary, is despised by his companions. The only cure for this evil is a well-tempered sense of emulation to inspire a person to set up as an ideal a virtuous man and then to try to outdo him in virtue. Likewise in state affairs, a nation will be stronger when it is kept alert by the threat of invasion. One of the values of a foreign war is that it eliminates useless people, who otherwise would cause trouble at home.

Another way of combating Sloth is to attend plays, preferably English historical plays. Pierce specifically recommends those that feature the English heroes Talbot and King Henry V. To critics objecting that plays corrupt youth and interfere with business Pierce replies that instead they portray the inevitable punishment of evil deeds and thus combat crime. Furthermore the English actors are the best that have ever lived.

Finally Pierce comes to Lechery, the child of Sloth, which he disposes of in little more than a page. He charges that London is filled with prostitution and venereal disease. As proof he points at Shoreditch, Southwark, and the suburbs in general. He concludes his supplication with "your Diuelships bounden execrator" and his signature (I, 217, 11–12).

III   *Devils and Other Spirits*

With some amazement the Knight of the Post calls it the maddest supplication that he has ever seen. However, he doubts that the Devil will be grateful for it. Pierce expresses indifference at its reception. Changing the subject, he asks his companion to tell him something about Hell and its inhabitants, whether it is a place of torment as tradition has it or whether it is nonexistent. The Knight begins his description by saying that it is a place where the souls of evil men are imprisoned until the Resurrection. It is governed by spirits attendant upon their "Lieftenaunt Generall" Lucifer (I, 219, 5). From every part of Hell the damned are able to gaze into Heaven, the sight of which causes them great anguish.

In order to describe the Devil, the Knight begins his discourse with demons, which some people believe to be only personifications of abstractions representing human inclinations to "vanitie, villanie, or

monstrous hypocrisie" (I, 220, 8). Each of these evils the Knight defines
but devotes most of his attention to hypocrisy, under which he includes
"all Machiauilisme, puritanisme, and outward gloasing with a mans
enemie, and protesting friendship to him that I hate and meane to
harme, all vnder-hand cloaking of bad actions with Common-wealth
pretences" and "all Italionate conueyances" (I, 220, 14–19). In the
midst of his discussion of hypocrisy he digresses to recount what sounds
like a prank played by college students, perhaps one in which Nashe
himself may have participated: the theft of chickens from a Cambridge miller, who for precaution kept his poultry at his bedside.

As a more serious and more pertinent example of hypocrisy, the
Knight tells an allegory of a hypocritical Bear, the "chiefe Burgomaster
of all the Beasts vnder the Lyon" (I, 221, 15–16). Having sampled all
of the animals of the Forest except the Horse, he approached a large
"Cammell," or horse, to demand homage. Nothing daunted, the Horse
replied with a kick that knocked the Bear over. Infuriated the Bear
consulted with the Ape. Although naturally disliking the Bear because
of his noble rank, the Ape advised him to dig a pit for the Horse. By
this means the Bear killed the Horse. Then the "hungrie Vsurper"
spied a herd of deer and determined to feast on the fattest one. However, the presence of the Woodmen prevented this outrage. Since he
could easily deceive the Lion, over whom he had much power, he had
nothing to fear from that quarter. Accordingly he decided to poison
the stream from which the Deer drank. The last plot was successful. In
addition, he destroyed several other beasts of the Forest—the Unicorn,
the Crocodile, and the Basilisk.

Eventually the Bear tired of meat and decided to restrict his diet to
honey. In order to convince the husbandmen of the soil that the Bees
were expensive and unnecessary, he bribed the Fox to disguise himself
as a shepherd dog. The Fox, in turn, consulted the Chameleon. Pretending to be skilled physicians, the Fox and Chameleon wound their
way into the confidence of the husbandmen. The two deceivers
pointed out that the honey produced by the Bees was poisonous and
that several other countries—"Scotland, Denmarke, and some more
pure partes of the seauenteene Prouinces" of the Netherlands—had
removed the Bees (I, 225, 11–12). While the puzzled husbandmen listened to these lies, the Fox and the Chameleon were studying Galen
in order to find ways of replacing the old traditions and customs with
new, absurd restrictions of their own. One day, however, a Fly flew by
and reported their machinations to Linceus, who traced them, discovered their plots, arrested and imprisoned them, and brought them to

trial. In the meantime the Bear died. Rumor has it that the Fox and the Chameleon were hanged.

Pierce thanks the knight for the tale but requests him to return to his original subject, the identity of the Devil. The subsequent discourse is a close translation, with slight adaptations to Nashe's own plot, of a dialogue of Gregorius Pictorius on the nature of spirits. The Knight repeats his earlier statement that some people believe that the Devil and his companions are merely fictions representing man's ill feelings toward his fellowman. Plato, on the contrary, states that three kinds of devils exist. The first are those imperceptible spirits made of pure air. The second kind are those that rebelled with Lucifer and were cast into Hell. These, usually termed detractors and accusers, are the malignant spirits commonly identified with the Devil. The third kind Plato terms "Daemona" and are possessed by wise men.

Lucifer's followers, of which the Knight is one, go about tempting men to wish to be looked up to as gods. They also inspire revenge and violence. One of them mentioned in the Bible is the spirit of lying. The watery spirits of the West entice men to gluttony and lust. The southern spirits cultivate unlawful love and unnatural desires. Other airy spirits combine with the thunder and lightning to produce infectious vapors. The spirits of fire live "vnder the regions of the moon" (I, 231, 19–20) and must superintend their evil deeds from there. The spirits of earth live in the woods, where they mislead and frighten travelers. The underearth spirits which live in the ground and have control over precious metals cause earthquakes and at night move about as ghosts. The lying spirits invented cards, dice, and gunpowder. Finally there are the spies and talebearers who rejoice in darkness and feed upon dead bodies.

Pierce interrupts the Knight in order to inquire whether or not these spirits are visible. The Knight replies that they can assume any shape whatsoever but usually appear as men. He adds that all except those called angels are evil. Yet none of these evil spirits has the power to injure a person in the state of grace. God permits the Devil to torment a man with evil in his heart.

Pierce's next question is whether or not the Devil can tell the future. The Knight answers that because of not being inhibited by a body and as a result of long experience the evil spirit can "coniecture" but that only God has the power of "prescience" (I, 237, 20–22).

When asked how a person can protect himself from the Devil, the Knight lists devices approved by Christian scholars and classical authors such as calling upon Jesus, using candles, rehearsing the articles of faith, and also superstitious acts such as brandishing swords, carrying red coral, jingling keys, playing harps, clashing armor, wearing curiously engraved symbols. However, the Knight assures Pierce that the only sure protection comes through prayer and faith.

IV Conclusion

Pierce thanks him for all this valuable information and hands him the supplication. At their next meeting Pierce promises to have "certain letters to diuers Orators & Poets" (I, 239, 9–10) also to be delivered to the Devil. In other words, if this pamphlet is successful, Nashe will write one or more sequels.

He ends with an epistle to the reader, usually placed at the beginning but here attached to the conclusion, as a sort of apology for taking up the reader's time. He would have included a formal dedication but has no patron. Instead he expresses his admiration for "thrice noble Amyntas" (I, 243, 7), who McKerrow suggests is Ferdinando Stanley, the Earl of Derby, given the same pseudonym in Spenser's Colin Clout (IV, 150–51). Chiding Spenser for neglecting to mention Amyntas in the first edition of his Faerie Queene, Nashe expresses the hope that Amyntas's name will appear in the second edition. He then composes a sonnet to that effect. Finally, presenting his pamphlet for Amyntas's approval, he concludes "this endlesse argument of speech" (I, 245, 15).

V Critical Commentary

After Nashe had learned from Martin Marprelate the effectiveness of colloquial English in An Almond, he demonstrated his skill in Pierce Penilesse, which ran through at least five editions between 1592 and 1595. Since it does not resemble any of the conventional literary types, critics have not paid as much attention to it as to The Unfortunate Traveller, which at first glance seems related to the modern novel. Pierce Penilesse is clearly a new form closely related to what today we might classify as journalism—a fairly loosely constructed social commentary written to inform and to entertain the reader. Nashe's own description of his persona as eager for news suggests the relation between the pamphlet and the modern news feature or magazine article:

I bring Pierce Penilesse to question with the diuel, as a yoong nouice would talke with a great trauailer; who, carrieng an Englishmans appetite to *enquire of news,* will be sure to make what vse of him he maie, and not leaue anie thing vnaskt, that he can resolue him of. (I, 240, 20–25—Except for the proper name the italics are those of the author.)

Thus this pamphlet is a sort of prototype of the syndicated article in a twentieth-century newspaper.

McKerrow feels that its "utter want of unity and of definite plan" (V, 18), which he terms "one of its most noticeable characteristics," is the result of the fact that its composition "extended over a considerable period." He suspects that it was originally intended as "an attack upon the niggardliness of the wealthy and the slight support accorded to men of wit," but that from time to time the author inserted other "oddments," such as his satiric comments on Richard Harvey. While agreeing with McKerrow on the length of time spent in writing it and on the insertions, Hibbard questions whether Nashe really planned a unified composition (p. 61). Although *Pierce Penilesse* may seem to lack plan or order, Hibbard explains that its structure is "rhetorical, not logical" (p. 65). Since the printer in his prefatory note calls the reader's attention to its apparent disorder as one of its main attractions, Hibbard believes that Nashe deliberately aimed at an effect of "casual, off-hand spontaneity" (p. 62). Hence the charge that the pamphlet fails to possess unity is, in Hibbard's opinion, "clearly irrelevant."

Except for the allegory of the Bear and the Fox, the third section taken from Pictorius's discourse on demons lacks what Hibbard terms the "infectious gaiety" of the rest of the work (p. 66). Stanley Wells dismisses the "animal fable" as "satire to which we have lost the key."[1] Conceding that "almost certainly the bear, the fox, and the chameleon stand for public figures of Nashe's time," he calls this an example of satire "so lacking in particularity that it does not even strike us as satire at all." Previous efforts to identify these allegorical figures are to Wells unconvincing, although he does not explain why. Nevertheless Nashe's evident embarrassment at the impact of his allegory on his readers impels his biographer to examine every possible clue to its meaning. Apparently it led him into the snare that every satirist tries to avoid—the threat of a suit for libel.

Nashe himself gives us a few leads. In his protests of innocence in *Strange News* (I, 259, 27 ff.; 320, 35 ff.) and in *Lenten Stuffe* (III, 213, 32 ff.) he takes for granted that the intelligencers persecuting him have arrived at their interpretations of his allegorical animals by means of heraldry. Since the cognizance of Robert Dudley, Earl of Leicester, was the bear and the ragged staff, McKerrow, following Collier, identifies the Bear as Leicester, who had died in 1588 and therefore might safely be attacked (IV, 139). As for the other principal animals in the fable, McKerrow assumes that the Fox might be Cartwright or Martin and the old Chameleon either Martin or Penry (IV, 139–40). And I have elsewhere[2] presented further evidence for identifying the Fox as Cartwright and the Chameleon that could assume the shape of "an Ape [or martin] to make sport" (I, 224, 26) as Penry, whom Nashe in *An Almond* had declared to be Martin Marprelate. Then the Bees against whom the Bear plots with the Fox would be the bishops of the Church of England, to whom Martin in his pamphlets disrespectfully refers as the "Bb." Their "stately Hyues" and "pretious Honny-combes" (I, 224, 8–9) would be their palaces and their livings. The epithet given them by the Fox and the Chameleon, "idle Drones," echoes the standard Puritan criticism that the clergymen of the Established Church were too lazy to prepare original sermons but instead depended on homilies.

Accepting McKerrow's identification of the Bear with Leicester, then, the Bear's hostility toward the Bees reflects the earl's generally known sympathy with the Puritans. His alliance with the Fox, whom he bribed with the appointment to be "the King's Poulterer for euer," could allude to Leicester's appointment of Cartwright to be master of Warwick Hospital in his later years.

Hibbard accepts my identifications of the Fox as Cartwright and the Chameleon as Penry. Moreover he takes for granted that Nashe was the victim of "intelligencers" whose representations of the fable "to some great man or other" involved its inventor "in a lawsuit" (pp. 83–84). However, he doubts that Nashe would have risked offending Leicester's powerful family. Therefore instead of Leicester as the Bear he nominates King Philip of Spain. In support of his candidate he cites Nashe's comparison, also in *Pierce Penilesse*, of the Spanish king to a wolf. Hibbard believes that this identification would best fulfill Nashe's statement in *Strange Newes* that in the figure of the Bear he sought to describe "the right nature of a bloudthirsty tyrant."

The greatest weakness in Hibbard's interpretation is that he ignores Nashe's implication that the Fox was bribed by the Bear to turn the husbandmen of the soil, that is, the common people, against the Bees, or bishops, so that the Bear could enjoy their "stately Hyues" and their honey. If, then, the Fox is Cartwright as Hibbard grants, it is inconceivable that this arch-Puritan would ever become the tool of his Catholic Majesty, the King of Spain. Anyone familiar with the writings of either Cartwright of Penry is aware of their intense hatred for anything Catholic. It seems unlikely, too, that anyone in Protestant England, especially in the years immediately following the defeat of the Spanish Armada, would become involved in an English law court for satirizing a Spanish monarch.

To Nashe's numerous satiric puzzles in the preface to *Menaphon* he thus has added another even more tantalizing enigma. Unlike those, however, the allegory of the Bear and the Fox possessed enough "particularity"—to borrow Wells's term—to bring down the wrath of persons in high places and to keep him uneasy for the rest of his literary career.

CHAPTER 4

Experiments in Drama and Poetry

I Summer's Last Will and Testament

WILL Summer, named after one of Henry VIII's famous jesters (appearing in the Quarto sometimes as Summers—III, 233 n.), with his fool's coat half on and half off comes onto the stage and formally presents a fairly long prologue filled with classical allusions. This he immediately follows with a familiar chat with the audience in which he ridicules the length of the foregoing prologue and also its style, which he describes as written in "an old vayne of similitudes" (III, 234, 27). Next he announces the theme of the production, namely, the imminent death of summer. Declaring that he intends to serve as a chorus throughout, he gives a few words of advice to the actors, takes a seat, and orders the action to start.

Since Will has referred to the time of performance as "this latter end of summer" (III, 235, 81), the audience is not surprised at the entrance of sick, feeble, gray-haired Summer leaning on the shoulders of Autumn and Winter and attended by satyrs and nymphs sadly singing of the approaching end of "fayre Summer" (III, 236, 105). They are followed by the god of seasonal change Vertumnus, "that turnst the yere about" (III, 238, 153), who acts as a sort of clerk of the court. Will Summer's first critical comment on the quality of the singing indicates to the audience that he is to be the interlocutor, who will interpret the action on the stage. Summer announces that in preparation for his departure he is about to make his will. He orders Vertumnus to summon Ver, or Spring, in whose care he had originally placed the meadows, flowers, and other delights of nature.

Ver immediately enters with his attendants singing a song extolling the joys of springtime. After the song Ver dances about until interrupted by Summer, who asks him how he has employed his wealth. Ver replies by calling out the hobby-horse and the morris dancers in order to perform their May-day antics. When Autumn and Winter ridicule this manner of accounting, Ver brings in three clowns and three maids, singing and dancing. At this point Summer, accusing Ver of being a spendthrift, cuts short the merriment, whereupon Ver launches into a long speech filled with satiric allusions and classical quotations in praise of the spender, the happiest of men. With a stern reprimand Summer sentences Ver always to be accompanied by Lent.

Next Summer summons Solstitium, here representing the summer solstice, the longest day of the year, when the sun has no apparent northward or southward motion and stands at the northernmost point of the ecliptic. He appears as an old hermit carrying scales in his hand in order to assure the balance of the sun before it starts southward. In a speech which McKerrow believes must have been added at a later date for the queen's benefit, Summer congratulates Solstitium and praises even-handed justice. Since only a few "dayes eyes" (III, 246, 405), or daisies, had been entrusted to Solstitium, Summer merely reappoints him as steward until they both die.

After Solstitium departs with the shepherds, who ushered him in playing recorders, Summer calls on Sol. He makes a grand entrance in shining robes with a musical fanfare. To Summer's query as to his stewardship he answers that his splendid appearance should be return enough for Summer's gifts. Here Autumn indignantly interrupts with the accusation that Sol is hypocritical and lascivious. Winter more specifically attacks him for doing nothing but cultivating hogs and destroying shrubbery. The two accusers believe that for these reasons Sol should not be allowed to defend himself. He, in turn, denies any wrongdoing and in his own defense points at his patronage of music and poetry. To Summer's complaint that he indiscriminately produces droughts and floods he blames the moon instead. In disgust Summer sentences him to suffer many eclipses.

Following a comic anecdote interpolated by Will Summer, Orion is called in along with his huntingmen blowing their horns. Autumn blames unhealthful days upon him. But he dismisses the charge as sheer superstition and launches forth into a brilliant defense of the dog. Unmoved by his eloquence Summer demands payment of his tribute. Orion's argument for nonpayment is that during dogdays when he is on high, no physician will prescribe any remedy and hence no patient will be poisoned. Summer banishes him for another year. He and his comrades, blowing their horns, depart.

Harvest next is summoned. In response to Summer's queries he merely sings a song. For this impudence both Autumn and Winter reprimand him. Summer's main criticism of him is that he selfishly hoards the bounty of the earth for his own consumption. Harvest merrily evades this allegation. However, when Summer persists, Harvest denies that he is a miser and asserts that, on the contrary, he gives all his wealth away. Convinced of his honesty, Summer then inquires about this year's crop. Harvest assures him that everything has been good—hay, rye, oats, barley, peas. In spite of sour comments from Autumn and Winter, which Harvest bluntly parries, Summer congratulates and dismisses him. Singing a merry song, he leaves the stage.

After Will Summer pokes fun at Harvest's straw costume, Summer orders Bacchus to be called. Dressed in vine leaves with a garland of grapes on his head and riding on an ass, he enters along with his singing comrades. At once he begins to praise the virtues of wine. As soon as Summer can get a word in, he asks how the vintage has been this year. Ignoring him, Bacchus continues with his praise. When Winter repeats the question, Bacchus blames the poor harvest of grapes on the weather and on Sol. Autumn is skeptical. Bacchus evades his questions and asks Winter to drink with him. At Winter's refusal Bacchus tries Summer, who also turns him down. Nothing daunted, Bacchus invites Will Summer to be his drinking companion. Will, accepting, becomes the center of attention. When the drinking and singing is over, Bacchus dubs Will "Sir Robert Tospot." Finally Summer, calling for an end of the revelry, censures Bacchus for the ills that he brings upon mankind. The God of wine impudently replies with a mock curse, whereupon Summer orders him dismissed. With merry songs he and his companions depart.

While Will struggles to recover from his drinking party, Summer expresses his disillusionment with his servants. Both Autumn and Winter try to console him. Summer interrupts them with the announcement that he is making them his heirs. As he hands over his crown to Autumn, Winter objects on the ground that both spring and autumn are the favorite seasons for thriftless scholars, poets, philosophers, and a whole company of ragged knaves. Then Winter delivers a long speech condemning learning and praising ignorance, all written in Nashe's high style with many classical allusions and quotations. Will Summer is inspired to add in a colloquial vein his own low opinion of scholarship. Although Summer is unmoved by these arguments, he makes Winter Autumn's guardian.

Now it is Autumn's turn to object. He accuses Winter of performing cruel deeds with his weapons of snow and ice. Furthermore, Winter has two sons worse than himself, Christmas and Backwinter (a return of winter after its regular time). Winter denies everything. As far as the snow and ice are concerned, he maintains, he is preparing the soil by rotting Autumn's weeds and fruits and purifying it. Moreover, if his two sons have done anything wrong, he hopes that they will be brought in for questioning. Vertumnus goes out to call them. While he is out, Summer requests a sad lute song appropriate to his approaching end.

When Winter's two sons enter, Summer first asks Christmas why he does not come in with carols as in the old days. Christmas replies that times have changed: the hospitality of the past is now old-fashioned. Then he proceeds to preach a sermon against gluttony and miserliness in the spirit of Pierce Penilesse. Summer and Autumn both break in with denunciations of his insensitivity but to no avail. Aghast at his sentiments Summer points out that the nobility are expected to celebrate holidays and to win love through their generosity. When Backwinter comes up for his examination, he is rude and impudent. His only delight, he says, is in ice, snow, thunder, anything to injure the earth. Realizing that he has shocked Summer, he roars out his threat to be even worse than winter. Summer immediately orders him imprisoned in Winter's dark cell. Shouting imprecations, Backwinter is dragged off.

Summer now gives out his legacies: withered flowers and herbs, shady walks, pleasant open air, fragrant smells, and so on. To the queen he bequeaths all his "faire dayes remaining" (III, 291, 1843). Along with this bequest he asks Autumn to give his best fruits and Winter to be kind to her. Finally he is carried out by nymphs and satyrs singing a song resembling a litany. In the epilogue Will Summer and the little boy make repeated requests for applause as the play ends.

II   *Critical Commentary*

Nashe's main defense against Harvey's accusation that he imitated Greene was that he could match Greene in any literary exercise except that of plotting plays, in which Greene was "his crafts master" (III, 132, 23). A glance at the record of Nashe's dramatic production bears out this statement. Although his name has been associated with eight plays, two of which have been lost, only one of these can safely be attributed to him in its entirety, namely, *Summer's Last Will and Testament.*[1] And whether or not it can be called a play in the accepted sense is not clear. The interlocutor Will Summer seems to give Nashe's own estimate of it: " . . . 'tis no Play neyther, but a shewe" (III, 235, 75). Its plot is negligible: indeed, as the title indicates, it merely recounts an imaginary episode associated with the last hours of the main character Summer. Hibbard classifies it as an "occasional play," written for "particular actors and a particular audience . . . in a particular place" (p. 90).

In his opinion it demonstrates that "its author had abilities as a dramatic craftsman that his activities as a pamphleteer would hardly lead one to suspect" (p. 87). On the contrary, *Summer's Last Will and Testament* seems to be just the sort of play that a pamphleteer interested both in literary style and social satire would write and with it would exhaust his dramatic impulse. If, as Aristotle points out, the first three main elements of a play are plot, character, and dialogue, the first of these, the plot, has little or no development. All of the action occurs in one interval of time. Will Summer asks, "What can be made of Summers last will & Testament?" (III, 235, 77 ff.). His answer to his own question is a summary of what action there is: "Summer must come in sicke: he must call his officers to account, yeeld his throne to Autumne, make Winter his Executour, with tittle tattle Tom boy: God giue you good night in Watling street."

As for Nashe's characterization, his dramatis personae all are personifications of calendrical abstractions. Hibbard, however, commends his treatment of the seasons in that he gives "distinct attributes and a personality of his own" to each whereas they could have become "mere allegorical ghosts, distinguishable from one another only by their names and, perhaps, their costumes" (p. 93). I should like to add "particularly by their costumes." In a way this "shewe" resembles a typical Broadway musical extravaganza: thin plot, much singing and dancing, beautiful or eccentric costumes. If we compare Nashe's play involved with the final hours of a life with Eugene Ionesco's *Exit the King*, which is similarly involved, we understand why the former is only a "shewe" whereas the latter is a play. The audience viewing Ionesco's play quickly identifies with the King, who is a sort of Everyman slowly coming face to face with the inevitability of death.

Nashe's dramatic piece is a series of speeches expressing what we might expect the seasons to say if they could speak. What apparently is more important to him is that each speech gives him an opportunity to display his literary versatility or his social satire. Hibbard points out the transformation of Ver from a season, spring, to a familiar social type in Elizabethan London, the upstart from the country who sells his patrimony and comes to the city to spend it (p. 94). At the same time Ver delivers a "mock encomium" or satirical sermon, which is a skillful piece of sophistry in defense of improvidence. In it he employs all of the standard rhetorical devices—parison, repetition, rhetorical questions, and so on—that Nashe uses in such pamphlets as *Christ's Teares* and *Lenten Stuffe*. Similarly Orion, the dog star, presents a "long apologia, borrowed from Sextus Empiricus," in praise of the dog (p. 96).

Hibbard also calls attention to the "variations of style as well as attitude" (p. 96) by means of which Nashe attempts to individualize his personifications. For example, the holiday characters representing the May-day games, the hunters, Harvest, and Bacchus have the "most vitality and significance." Hibbard incidentally notes that Nashe maintains morality by having Summer somewhat unenthusiastically condemn these holiday figures (pp. 96–97). Furthermore Nashe's contrast of styles as described by David Kaula in his analysis of *The Unfortunate Traveller*—the artificial rhetorical style as opposed to the colloquial idiom[2]—comes into play here. For Ver's sermon, Sol's self-defense, and Orion's apologia Nashe demonstrates his skill in the formal style. Hibbard calls attention to his use of "down-to-earth prose" (p. 98), on the other hand, for Harvest representing the country bailiff. Just as Nashe employs the low style for Jack Wilton for the purpose of debunking or parodying the more elevated styles, so Will Summer speaks with a "lively colloquial idiom" (p. 103), representing "Tom Nashe, wit, buffoon, satirist, and literary critic" (p. 102).

In addition to such well-known rhetorical forms as the mock-encomium, the satirical oration in defense of the dog, the sermon on gluttony, *Summer's Last Will and Testament* contains seven songs varying in length from Bacchus's four lines (III, 264, 968–71) to the several stanzas of "Adieu, farewell earths blisse" (III, 282, 1574–1615). In them Nashe has a chance to show his skill at writing lyric poetry. Of course the songs of Ver and his troops, of Harvest, and of Bacchus are cheerful in keeping with the happiness of the singers themselves and the occasions being celebrated. Nevertheless Hibbard senses a general sadness throughout:

To Nashe and those for whom he wrote life itself appeared as a brief holiday from the terror of death. His play is pervaded by a sense of mutability, subdued to a pitch at which it does not conflict with the general lightness of tone, yet ever present as a kind of ground bass. (p. 90)

Nashe's first song, "Fayre Summer droops" (III, 236, 105–16), and "Adieu, farewell earths blisse" both mourn the approaching death of

Summer. The last song, "Autumne hath all the Summers fruitefull treasure" (III, 292, 1872–85), is sung as the funeral procession winds out with the body of Summer. Adding to the serious effect, each stanza of the last two poems has a repetitious ending like the response of a litany.

In "Adieu, farewell earths blisse" is one stanza containing an evocative line that has puzzled the critics. The entire stanza is as follows:

> Beauty is but a flowre,
> Which wrinckles will deuoure,
> Brightnesse falls from the ayre,
> Queenes haue died yong and faire,
> Dust hath closde *Helens* eye.
> I am sick, I must dye:
>   Lord, haue mercy on vs.

The third line, "Brightnesse falls from the ayre," is suggestive but not at all clear. McKerrow writes, "It is to be hoped that Nashe meant 'ayre,' but I cannot help strongly suspecting that the true reading is 'hayre,' which gives a more obvious, but far inferior, sense" (IV, 440). In other words, McKerrow believes that Nashe is merely describing the transitoriness of feminine beauty, a standard sonnet convention. Indeed, in the preceding lines he refers to "wrinckles"; therefore it would seem logical that he might next mention "hayre." Furthermore two lines afterward he mentions the "eye."

When carefully analyzed, McKerrow's emendation is almost distasteful. In the first place the verb *falls* is not appropriate for either *brightnesse* or *hayre*. If by "brightnesse" McKerrow is thinking of *luster* or *sheen*, then the appropriate verb would be *fades* (e.g., "silver threads among the gold"). Accordingly, if we are to treat "ayre" as a printer's misreading, we might as well emend "falls." If in McKerrow's emendation the verb "falls" is taken to refer to "hayre," then we have the unpleasant picture of baldness. This immediately would bring to mind another familiar association of ideas between baldness and venereal disease, which is an Elizabethan commonplace.

Fortunately most subsequent critics have inclined toward the present reading. William Empson selects the line as "an example of ambiguity by vagueness," which may suggest "a variety of things": the sun and moon passing under the earth, falling stars, flying creatures falling to the ground, hawks or lightning or meteorites flashing upon their prey.[3] Citing a passage from *Hamlet* in which Shakespeare contrasts "the air" with "the grave," Harry Morris concludes that "brightnesse" is a synonym for "beauty—the youth and fairness—of fabled queens" and that "ayre" means "the light of day, or even the dark of night."[4] In other words, Nashe here would imply that beauty is destined to be buried in the grave. A more specific definition of "brightnesse" appears in an erudite essay by Wesley Trimpi, who maintains that it means lightning or, metaphorically, the plague or any other unexpected disaster.[5] Citing many classical parallels, especially Seneca's *Quaestiones Naturales*, he then interprets the line within the context of Nashe's play. But although he quotes classical authorities to prove that "lightning falls most frequently in autumn,"[6] my own observation of this natural phenomenon is that in northern climates it is more typical of weather in midsummer than in autumn.

Finally, Walker Percy in his article "Metaphor as Mistake" writes that this line "may or may not have been a mistake.'"[7] If it is a mistake, the emended reading "haire" is "appropriate to the context, adequate poetically but less beautiful." If, however, Nashe intended it as it appears in print, Percy asks if it is not possible that the poet is referring "to that particular time and that particular phenomenon of clear summer evenings when the upper air holds the last trembling light of day: one final moment of a soft diffused brilliance, then everything *falls* into dusk?"

Likewise preferring to retain the present reading, I should wish even further to "particularize" Percy's interpretation. Since the general theme of this play is the change of seasons from summer to autumn, I suggest that Nashe may be referring to the shortening of the days toward the autumnal equinox, the *particular* occasion for its performance. Among country folk, always sensitive to seasonal change, one of the most frequent exclamations heard toward the ending of a late August or September afternoon is, "How short the days are getting!" The brightness of the long midsummer day is fast becoming a memory. All too early for them the amethyst shades of an autumnal evening are stretching toward the zenith from the East and are swiftly replacing the rosy twilight tints that prevailed earlier in the season. Just as in *Exit the King* theatrical time is synchronous with real time, so in Nashe's "shewe"—if this is the appropriate designation for this static performance—the action is confined to the last hours of summer immediately preceding the autumnal equinox. This interpretation would considerably strengthen Hibbard's contention that *Summer's Last Will and Testament* was written for "a particular time of a particular year" (p. 90). A concluding comment: the very fact that the critic seems impelled to repeat the word *particular* attests to the essentially realistic attitude of this playwright-journalist.

III   The Choise of Valentines

Nashe's only other venture into a genre that could not be classified as a pamphlet is *The Choise of Valentines,* extant only in manuscript until privately printed in 1899. It is a remarkably vivid piece of pornography, totally lacking in the subtlety of such erotic poems as Marlowe's *Hero and Leander* or Shakespeare's *Venus and Adonis.* Nashe makes no attempt to disguise his sexual references with classical analogies and legends. Instead, reporter that he essentially is, he recounts a visit to a London brothel. Anything remotely resembling such beautiful pictures of natural scenery as Shakespeare's description of the dawn, beginning "Lo, here the gentle lark, weary of rest," would be totally out of place in this detailed account of an act of sexual intercourse. A twentieth-century parallel might be a novel by a writer who, if we may judge from his own self-evaluation, seems more interested in being classified as a journalist than a novelist.[8] In *An American Dream* Norman Mailer interrupts an account of a murder to present the explicit details of illicit sexual intercourse.[9] His vivid reporting of sights, sounds, and smells is remarkably similar to that of his Elizabethan predecessor. Thus Nashe's two ventures into poetic literature, his "shewe" and his erotic poem, are negative evidence that his true genius lay in his ability to report and interpret the Elizabethan scene to his own contemporaries.

CHAPTER 5

The Terrors of the Night

I *Summary*

NASHE dedicates *The Terrors of the Night* to Miss Elizabeth Carey, the daughter of his host in the Isle of Wight, Sir George Carey. Following the dedicatory epistle is a second brief epistle to the reader complaining of the activity of spiteful critics. He opens the main text with the conventional apology that his pamphlet was "hastily vndertooke" merely to pass the time and to please some friends "heere in the Countrey," presumably at Conington (I, 345, 1–2).

Night is the "Diuells Blacke Booke" (I, 345, 12) containing all of the misdeeds of men. It is a dark dungeon where a man is forced to recall his own past faults. It is God's reminder that there is a Hell ruled over by the Prince of Darkness. The raven and the dove sent out from the Ark symbolize night and day, respectively. According to Scripture, the raven picks out men's eyes in the Valley of Death so that they cannot look to Heaven for aid. When men are thus blinded by darkness, the Devil offers them temptations.

The Devil seldom appears except at night. In pagan times people sacrificed to their deities after sunset. The English goblins and fairies, as well as those in classical times, traveled abroad only during the night. However, to sinful men the Devil can assume a fairly pleasing shape in the day but never at night, when he is most terrifying. He will attack only when a man is alone or physically weakened and ill. Then he comes as sin and the vengeance of God. He especially haunts children, fools, invalids, and madmen. Sometimes he appears as a relative to his unsuspecting victim. He frequents churchyards and graveyards in order to make people believe that the bodies and souls of the dead belong to him. In fact, he is constantly raking among the bones of the dead like a miser counting his riches. He can quickly alter his appearance.

To speak of the Devil as though he were unique is a mistake. Devils are multitudinous and omnipresent. Microscopic in size they dwell in

57

all of the elements—earth, air, fire, and water—and even cling to the human body. Furthermore, devils are only one classification among a multitude of spiritual beings. Everything either possesses, or is, a spirit—fire, lightning, gunpowder, worms, bubbles in streams, fleas, mustard, rings, even crumbs of bread. The spirits of fire, the purest and the most perfect, are happy but undependable. They inspire excellence in the people possessed by them: for example, Socrates and Mahomet. Since Reginald Scot in *The Discoverie of Witchcraft* has fully explained their names and governments, Nashe will add only that they are extracted by alchemy from metals and wines. They have nothing to do with sensual individuals but only with lovers of pure beauty. Although relatively good, these spirits are ambitious not for virtue itself but only for seeming virtuous.

The spirits of water are dull and malicious but ineffectual. They possess drunkards, misers, and women. They were the original inventors of beer. They cause all sorts of rheumatic ailments and chiefly afflict sailors and vintners, particularly those who dilute their wine. The spirits of earth live in misers, witches, and soldiers who love iron and gold, the excrements of the earth. These spirits abound everywhere but chiefly in the Indies. The spirits of air, all show and no substance, abide in boastful, cowardly carpet knights, politic statesmen who advance their own private interests under pretense of contributing to their country's good, faded old women who try to hide their deformities, and children infatuated with toys and dolls.

The spirits of earth and water, which induce melancholy, are more powerful at night than are those of fire and air. Sufferers from the melancholic humor have terrifying visions. Melancholy frequently precedes serious illness and causes all kinds of delusions, of which dreams are one manifestation. A dream is the remnant of a fancy of the preceding day and hence never duplicates itself. What was merely imagined during the day becomes a dream at night. Dreams are chaotic. Although they usually echo the daily experiences, they sometimes are induced by noises subconsciously heard, uncomfortable clothing, or indigestion. The dream itself, however, does not resemble the causative agent.

The melancholic humor produces not only dreams but "all terrours of the night whatsoeuer" (I, 357, 18–19). Of this humor there are two kinds, one affecting women and lasting only an hour, the other corrupting the blood and causing madness. Both are induced by excessive study and may be cured by moderate exercise.

Our senses are the gates through which our dreams pass. If we have feelings of guilt caused by our sins during our waking hours, especially the sins of treason and murder, we shall have terrible dreams. The guilty man tends to be a prey to superstition. Glowing ears, itching nose, smarting eyes control his destiny. The sounds of a raven or a cricket terrify him. He finds his fortune in spiders (dead or alive), in nosebleeds, and in spilled salt.

Perhaps because witches frequently are asked to interpret dreams, Nashe turns to the subject of witchcraft. Just as Proserpine, the first witch, dwelt half the year in Heaven and half in Hell, so witches ever since have mixed religion with diabolism. Certain countries find more significance in dreams than others. The Persian King Darius and Hannibal both foresaw their downfalls and deaths in dreams. In India women in their sleep are made pregnant by devils. In Iceland spirits in the likeness of dead relatives converse with the living. To the constable's nocturnal challenge other spirits like rogues reply that they are on their way to get warm at Mt. Hecla, which is assumed to be the mouth of Hell because of the dreadful sounds heard near it. Witches in Iceland traffic in familiar spirits, favorable winds, and storms. There they live on mountains of ice. They also have a bottomless lake which freezes any bird flying over it and which gives forth a sulphurous smell when the ice in spring breaks up with the sound of a thunderclap.

After this digression concerning Iceland Nashe mockingly comments on the triviality of his subject and his failure to find a patron. Resuming his discourse he impatiently discards some popular superstitions concerning dreams: for example, that a happy dream foreshadows misfortune and a sad dream good luck. Evil following mirth is really brought on by fear resulting from adherence to this superstition. In answer to critics citing the dreams of political disaster recorded in history Nashe terms them visions. But he immediately adds that many interpreters of these dreams or visions were traitors hired by an enemy to arouse fear. By "revealing" treasons in which they themselves had a part they were averting suspicion from themselves.

As if imparting a confidence, Nashe describes the evolution of any famous conjurer. He is a man of small education, perhaps a surgeon's or an apothecary's apprentice, who has spent his savings on loose living and is looking around for a profitable trade not involving much hard work. In addition to collecting a few cast-off boxes and knickknacks he will concoct some ointments and syrups and then will travel into the country where he will set up business among uneducated farmers. After building up a reputation through his eccentric speech and manners, he acquires a few old illegible manuscripts and surrounds himself with trinkets. In order to create an atmosphere of mystery he speaks in an ambiguous manner. Becoming more and more successful, he approaches London and finally enters the outskirts of the city. As his reputation spreads, he is introduced to court by some nobleman on condition that all profits to be made will be shared between them. Once in court, he speaks broken English and boasts of his success.

Eventually having used up all his tricks, he sets up a conjuring school. For this new enterprise he selects an associate hired to fraternize with thieves and cutpurses in order that his master will be able to tell his clients where stolen articles are hidden. Gradually he worms his way into the confidence of great noblemen. Malcontents plotting against the government come to him for advice. He plays off contrary factions, one against another. While pretending that his knowledge comes to him from a familiar spirit, he actually is using the information unwittingly given him by each group. Some less skillful conjurers, deceiving their clients with magical incantations, even pick their pockets.

Recently, however, the Devil has become a puritan and will not respond to anything resembling ceremony. Furthermore, he is trying to get as much work done as possible before the Judgment Day. Once upon a time he had a sense of humor and enjoyed playing tricks on people. Now he will not even give a man a dream about a hidden pot of gold, which, if only a dream, brings some happiness. Formerly he never dared approach a person in daylight, but now he is open and aboveboard in his dealings with men.

As if growing impatient with the subject, Nashe shrugs off the possibility of foretelling the future by dreams. He believes that physical conditions during sleep induce dreaming. Humorously recalling some old wives' tales about fortune-telling, he agrees with one of their theories about dreams, namely, that they largely depend upon what has been eaten at supper. Nashe compares the absurdity of using a dream to tell the future to that of reading it in the face or in the palm. He knows of a hundred examples of famous wise men—Socrates for one—whom physiognomists took for fools or criminals. He concludes that prophesying from dreams or physiognomy is a trick invented by someone pandering to popular taste. As proof he cites a number of historical examples in which dreams have proved false; however, he excepts heaven-sent dreams such as those of the saints and martyrs of the Primitive Church.

Since people have enough trouble in everyday living, they should not look for more in dreams but should let the terror experienced in them remain there. The relation between dreams and actuality is similar to that between a long sickness and death. The dream usually turns out to be worse than the reality. It is better to starve to death in a few days than to suffer a lingering illness over several years. An invalid is like a seasick traveler longing for a good voyage, such as Nashe himself had had when he visited the Isle of Wight, a blessed place both geographically and politically.

After a digression in praise of Sir George Carey and his family, Nashe repeats his conviction that "the feare of anie expected euill, is worse than the euill it selfe" (I, 376, 9–10) and returns to his discussion of dreams. When a man is lying in bed, he tends to think over his recent experiences. If he has been unfortunate, every ill seems worse than it really was. If he has been fortunate, he becomes overwhelmed with joy. Some people even have died of happiness—certainly an easy way to die, much like being bitten by an asp. The heart of a man who dies of grief, on the contrary, seems to be devoured piecemeal by vultures. From either excess, joy or grief, come our dreams, which are the exhalations of our always active brains.

Lest the reader infer that Nashe discredits all apparitions, he emphasizes that he is merely warning the overcredulous. As evidence that he keeps an open mind on the subject, he recounts a case that he had witnessed the preceding February while he was living in the country. A certain distinguished gentleman, falling ill, saw, or pretended to see, his chamber adorned with silken nets and silver hooks. He became terrified lest he be caught in the nets or mangled on the hooks. Then a company of sailors came in to carouse with him. When he refused to drink with them, they danced about and left him. Next entered some devils dressed like Turkish Janissaries, all bejeweled, carrying chests out of one of which they extracted a beautiful tent. After it was set up, Lucifer appeared and sent an ambassador to the sick man, promising him untold wealth. Expressing full faith in God's providence, the man refused. The vision at once vanished.

Afterward a troop of beautiful naked virgins came to tempt him. Walking up and down in order better to display their charms, they offered to seduce him. At his refusal they disappeared. Then a group of nuns entered and offered to pray for him. Hearing his story, they knelt and prayed for a half-hour. Just as he caught sight of a slender naked foot starting to steal betwixt the sheets to him, a messenger from a neighboring knight brought him a cordial which, when tasted, caused all the visions to vanish. But shortly after tasting it he went mad and two days later died.

Nashe concludes his story with the statement that "this incredible
Narration" (I, 382, 25) was his original inspiration for writing this pamphlet. In order further to convince his reader of his veracity, he
describes the marshy, misty environment of the gentleman's house,
which was well known to be haunted. The poor man's sickness had
been suspiciously abrupt in its inception and brief in its duration. His
sudden death further indicates a supernatural visitation. Nashe's last
effort to convince his reader is his comparison of the gentleman's vision
with that of a Mr. Allington years before, at the beginning of the present queen's reign.

Nashe tells another story of a prominent citizen whose coach was
followed by a couple of mysterious hogs that could not be chased away.
Arriving home, he had them locked up in the barn. Even though he
hid the key, in the morning the hogs had disappeared. Nashe points
out that widowers who broke their promises and neglected their children have been haunted by their dead wives. Other people have been
pursued wherever they rode by small animals conjured up by witches.
However, these animals, if defied, were put to flight.

At last Nashe has become tired of telling tales. As his good night to
his reader he offers a prescription for a quiet sleep. First, a man must
be moderate in drink and avoid gambling and loose women. If he is a
poor man's son, he should be respectful to his father. Those men who
are soldiers in name only should forsake their debauchery and get a
decent occupation. Those who prey on young gentlemen should make
restitution for their ill-gotten goods. Travelers interested only in the
vices and absurd mannerisms of foreign countries must reform. Subtle
poisoners, traitors, and judges and magistrates who misuse their high
offices and accept bribes—all these must expect unhappy nights. All
evil things happen at night—the Deluge, Christ's betrayal, the rape of
Lucrece; hence the name given them in Scripture, the "workes of dark-
nesse" (I, 386, 13). Even if we have no more religion than might be
derived from classical myths, the doleful choristers of the night—the
screech owls, the nightingales, the croaking frogs—might cause us to
refrain from sin. Nashe ends his pamphlet with the warning that the
person who does not do enough good during the day to offset the evils
of the night will be punished on the Day of Judgment.

II   *Critical Commentary*

Although McKerrow assures his reader that he has not attempted a
critical evaluation of Nashe's writings, he finds it difficult to maintain

this neutral position in discussing *The Terrors of the Night*. He begins as though he were going to allow for differences of opinion: "It is a slight production, which has been viewed very differently by different critics" (V, 23). Unable thus impersonally to continue, he immediately adds: "To me it seems to be a hasty piece of work, almost certainly composed for the most part of a mere stringing together of matter taken from elsewhere, and on the whole of very little importance either as regards Nashe's biography or the history of letters in his time." The meaning of the belittling phrase "a mere stringing together of matter taken from elsewhere" is partly clarified in his comment on the sources of the pamphlet: " . . . the bulk of *The Terrors of the Night* might well have been gathered by miscellaneous reading" (IV, 197). Yet he admits being unable to identify any of these sources. He tentatively suggests Reginald Scot's *Discoverie of Witchcraft*. Since Nashe in his pamphlet specifically directs his reader to that work in order to find the names of the spirits of fire, McKerrow's hesitation seems unnecessary.

Quite different from McKerrow's lack of enthusiasm is Hibbard's defense of the pamphlet. Willing to concede its slightness, he believes that in requiring "carefully considered conclusions and a reasoned argument" McKerrow is looking at it as if it were an article in the *Review of English Studies* (p. 118). The work, Hibbard explains, is "an attack on superstition and credulity" (p. 113). He is convinced that "the rambling, desultory, inconsequential fashion in which Nashe treats the various forms of credulity that he deals with conveys, far better than any carefully worked out discourse on them could, his mocking contempt for them" (p. 115). Moreover, Hibbard would not condemn its failure to provide us with biographical data. More important than these facts to him is what it reveals of Nashe's cast of mind and the age he was living in. Summarizing his appraisal of the pamphlet, he calls it "a piece of literary clowning" and adds the commendation, "Good clowning in writing, no less than in the theater or the circus, is neither a common nor a contemptible thing" (p. 118).

In analyzing its structure, Hibbard finds two "unifying factors": first, what he terms "the real unifying factor" (p. 112), namely, a "combination of over-wrought description" and "mocking skepticism"; second; " the only unifying factor," namely, the personality of the performer" (p. 117), in this instance Nashe himself. A similar alternation of description overwritten to the point of parody, or what David Kaula terms the rhetorical or high style, followed by a colloquial or low style, also appears in *The Unfortunate Traveller* and other pamphlets.[1] In both *The Terrors of the Night* and *The Unfortunate Traveller*, according to Hibbard, Nashe's personality provides the necessary unity, although in *The Unfortunate Traveller* it is thinly veiled under the persona of Jack Wilton (p. 178).

After thus disposing of McKerrow's main criticisms Hibbard places the pamphlet in what to me is the proper category for each of Nashe's prose writings, that is, journalism:

It is one of the first, if not the first, prose works in English that exists for no other end than to give the pleasure a discriminating reader can find in a difficulty overcome, the difficulty in this particular case being that of making something out of nothing by sheer literary artifice, by a display of stylistic ingenuity that carries with it the impress of a personality. (p. 118)

In short, what Nashe has written is a sort of "special feature" for the London reading public.

A second dispute with, contrary to McKerrow's estimate, considerable bearing on Nashe's biography has to do with the date of composition of *The Terrors of the Night*. In the dedicatory epistle Nashe tells Mistress Elizabeth Carey that she already knows why he happened to choose this subject. This statement, writes McKerrow, "strongly suggests" that Nashe composed this pamphlet while he was a guest of Sir George Carey during the winter of 1592–93 (IV, 197). In the text of the pamphlet, when Nashe begins his "strange tale" of the gentleman whose visions preceded his death, he writes, "It was my chance in Februarie last to be in the Countrey some threescore myle off from London" (I, 378, 12–13). Based on the assumption that Nashe was residing in the Isle of Wight in 1592–93, McKerrow dates the gentleman's death during February 1592 (IV, 197). Accordingly he assumes that Nashe composed his pamphlet before February 1593. He also takes for granted that Nashe was working on three other pamphlets during the same winter—*Strange Newes*, *Christ's Teares*, and *The Unfortunate Traveller*—which subsequently were entered in the Stationers' Register and published during 1593 (V, 22, 24). *The Terrors of the Night*, however, was entered twice, the first time on June 30, 1593, and the second on October 25, 1594—a most unusual procedure. The date of the earliest and only publication of this pamphlet is 1594.

A second reference to Nashe's visit to the Isle of Wight occurs in his second reply to Harvey, *Have with You*, in 1595, when he denies Harvey's accusation that Nashe had spoken "certaine words" against him "that Christmas" at a tavern in London (III, 95, 36–96, 1). In this denial Nashe states that he was in the Isle of Wight "then and a great while after." In order to date the publication of these important writings, it is necessary to determine to which Christmas Nashe is referring, 1592 or 1593. This statement seems to have shaken McKerrow's confidence in his earlier assumption that Nashe was in the Isle of Wight in the winter of 1592–93. Annotating Nashe's reference to "that Christmas," McKerrow writes as follows:

This must, I think, mean the Christmas of 1592, for we know that Harvey was then in London. . . . At the same time I do not see how we can definitely prove that it was not the following year [1593] that is referred to, for we have no direct evidence as to where either Nashe or Harvey were at that date. (IV, 349)

Furthermore, while still holding to the belief that *The Terrors of the Night* was composed during the winter of 1592–93, McKerrow is baffled by the double entry in the Stationers' Register (IV, 197). He is certain, however, that additions must have been made to it in 1594 just before it was published. In the first place Nashe refers to the edition of Camden's *Brittania* published in that year. McKerrow also believes that the complimentary passage dealing with the Carey family, along with the dedicatory Epistle to the daughter, must have been added at the same time.

Hibbard accepts all of McKerrow's conjectures and contributes a few of his own. For instance, he gives as a possible reason for Nashe's presence at Carisbrooke Castle the supposition that he may have been a tutor to Elizabeth Carey (p. 107). In order to interpret the double entry he postulates that Nashe may have called back the manuscript sent to the printer before the first entry for the purpose of inserting the dedication and the reference to the Isle of Wight (p. 109).

But the last, and the most convincing, word on the subject comes from Harlow, who, as was explained in the biographical sketch, gives substantial proof that Nashe did not spend the winter of 1592–93 in the Isle of Wight. In February 1593, on the contrary, he was the guest of Robert Cotton at Conington, where he wrote the first draft of *The Terrors of the Night*. He did not visit the Careys until the winter of 1593–94. Hence "that Christmas" mentioned in *Have with You* was actually the Christmas of 1593, when Nashe explained that he was not in London but in the Isle of Wight. Furthermore, his references to

Harvey's "incensing" the lord mayor against him probably refer to the trouble stirred up by his attack on the citizens of London in *Christ's Teares* published in 1593 rather than, as McKerrow from his erroneous dating infers, "some earlier affair" (IV, 349). *The Unfortunate Traveller*, then, was published in 1594.

Thus the investigation of this little pamphlet so lightly dismissed by McKerrow has not only provided the student of Nashe with a greater understanding of his biographical data but also has won some admirers for its own merits. In defense of *The Terrors of the Night* Hibbard enthusiastically writes, "Showmanship and style carry the day in what is, surely, one of the most sophisticated prose-works of the age" (p. 117).

CHAPTER 6

Christ's Teares Over Jerusalem

I *Introduction*

NASHE dedicates his serious pamphlet *Christ's Teares Over Jerusalem* to Lady Elizabeth Carey, the wife of Sir George Carey. He compares this dedication to the playing of sea porpoises before the "storme" of his "Teares" (II, 9, 10–11). Always alert for a pun, he apologizes for possible "Tares" among his "Teares" because of his inexperience in writing on a theological subject. He has long planned to sing Lady Elizabeth's praises but has heretofore lacked both the wit and the style. She already has been honored by such poets as Spenser. Although in comparison with their tributes Nashe's present writing is a mere trifle, he hopes before long to present her with "more polished labours" (II, 10, 28). Unlike other women she has shown her generosity to poets. Her holiness of life has inspired him to venture into this new field of divinity. If she will accept this treatise, he will before long write something else "beyond the common mediocritie" (II, 11, 23).

Next Nashe addresses an epistle to the reader which he opens with the announcement that he is abandoning satire. As a token of his change of heart and, incidentally, of style, he apologizes to "Maister Doctor *Haruey*," whom he has recently "rashly assailed" (II, 12, 13 ff.). In recognition of Harvey's "aboundant Schollership, courteous well gouerned behauiour, and ripe experienst iudgement," as well as his "milde gentle moderation," Nashe retracts his previous invective in *Strange Newes*. He also apologizes for "some spleanatiue vaines of wantonnesse," probably his unpublished poem *The Choise of Valentines*, and promises to amend his life. He concludes this prefatory matter with a list of errata containing his own "faultes" as well as those of the printer.

The epidemic of plague raging in London, 1592–94, has moved Nashe to compare it with the terrible hardships experienced by the Jews during the siege and destruction of Jerusalem. Hoping that he can persuade his fellow citizens to reform their ways, he asks Christ to

inspire him with the sacred tears that He wept over the Holy City
when He prophesied its downfall.

Jerusalem, "too-to much presuming of the promises of old" whereby
God has favored His Chosen People (II, 16, 22), had grown proud and
had ignored first the prophets sent by God and then His "only natural
Sonne" whom He sent as a carpenter's son (II, 18, 4–5). The Savior, a
humble man, ignored the proud and wealthy and associated with fishermen and sinners. The only outward signs of His divinity were the
miracles that He performed and the authority with which He
preached. But when, in spite of all that He did and said, their hearts
were not touched, He warned them of the dire woes that would befall
them. In the midst of His prophecies, as if regretting His bitterness, He
began to weep and exclaimed:

O Ierusalem, Ierusalem, which killest the Prophets, and stonest them that are
sent vnto thee: . . . How often would I haue gathered thy Chyldren together,
as the Henne gathereth her Chickins together vnder her wings, and ye would
not! . . . Therefore your habitation shall be left desolate. (II, 21, 16 ff.)

At this point Nashe changes from the third person to the first as though
he were Christ speaking "in a continued Oration thus pleading" with
the citizens of Jerusalem.

II   *The Oration*

In this hypothetical speech he has an opportunity to apply the principles of rhetoric that were a part of the standard preaching in the
churches of the day. He takes the scriptural passage word by word and
develops an elaborate exegesis, replete with alliteration, repetition, and
biblical allusions.

Comparing Jerusalem to the sinful cities of Sodom and Gomorrah,
the imaginary preacher threatens its people with famine, sword, and
pestilence. Although he is aware that his words are falling upon deaf
ears, he forbids Satan to harm the city. In return for their abuse he will
give them only blessings. They, however, have ears and hearts of stone
and will not listen. If among nations an injury to an ambassador is a
crime worthy of punishment, the Jews must expect that "the King of
all Kings" will certainly avenge the death of His ambassadors, namely,
the prophets and Christ (II, 24, 2–3). The angels and even the Devil
will remind Him of his duty. Every murderer must be punished. If

these people would kill the representative of a king, they would kill the king himself. In other words, if they would stone the prophets, they would stone Christ.

Then Nashe takes the several biblical references associated with the word *stone* and uses them as exhortations. The citizens of Jerusalem and their sons shall suffer. Anyone who destroys men's bodies, the temples of the Holy Ghost, as St. Paul describes them, defies God Himself. If, therefore, they kill one of His prophets, they commit an even more heinous sin, for which their habitation shall be destroyed and they shall be scattered throughout the world.

Taking the next sentence of the scriptural text, Nashe rings the changes on the word *gather* as on *stone* in the opening sentence. The preacher speaks of his compassion in *gathering* together the Israelites like lost sheep and deplores their hardness of heart in *gathering* against him as he weighs it against the many times when he has tried to *gather* them. Had they *gathered* together at his word, they could have possessed all the riches of Heaven. Now they are scattered as prey for the Devil. Instead they should *gather* to resist him by *gathering* alms for the poor. All worthwhile things are *gathering*: angels about the throne of God, grains of corn in bread, stones in building, men in a city, geese, bees, stars, the parts of a man, the waters in the sea, the earth, the trees in the forest, the parliament. The failure of the people of Jerusalem to *gather* into Christ's church will be held against them. Although Christ became man in order to defeat Hell, He found that He must defeat Jerusalem, which, even though He blessed it with His birth, He eventually had to curse. Unlike the angels, who praise and obey Him, these people would not listen. Therefore their enemies *gathered* about the city in order to attack them before the angels drove them into Hell.

All their suffering could have been avoided had they permitted Christ to *gather* or tame them as animals are tamed by man. (Here Nashe joins the word *tame* with *gather* and repeats them as synonyms.) But since they would not heed His warnings, they shall be given over to the Devil. The preacher now tries to explain that in hating one who desires their good they really hate themselves and therefore cannot love their neighbor as the divine law commands. Moreover, their enemies who destroy them will not be held responsible. Their blood will be on their own heads. After all his warnings they cannot be excused for ignorance. His tears, indeed, have wasted away his eyes so that he no longer has any left to wash a sinner clean. His hands are worn to the bone with beating his breast in prayer for them. Had he been in Heaven, he would have drowned all their trespasses as in the Deluge the sins of the world were drowned in the sea where they continue to cause turbulence. Another reason for the restlessness of the sea is that Christ cast out devils into a herd of swine, which then were drowned. Afterward these devils entered into sea monsters and now lie in wait for ships.

Sin finds rest only on earth and then always at night when God hides all other objects from man's sight so that he can look into himself and repent. In order to prevent repentance the Devil provides the sinner with eyes of despair or of false security in telling himself either that there is no God or if there is a God that He will not interfere. The man thus misled quotes Scripture in order to excuse his misdeeds. In fact, the Devil will imitate God in everything except humility. By pride, which breeds envy, the Devil maintains his kingdom. Pride can tolerate anything but virtue. The first act of a proud tyrant is to remove all virtuous men. Christ's only enemy was the pride that prevented Jerusalem from *gathering* itself under His wing. Because He came to call the meanest sinners, as well as the wealthiest, to repentance, He did not come in pomp. His only reason for leaving Heaven was His love for man.

Having exhausted the rhetorical possibilities of the first half of his text, Nashe turns to the second: "As a Henne gathereth her Chickins, so would I haue gathered thy chyldren." By His preaching Christ would have "clocked and called" His followers to Him (II, 43, 1). "What is more tender then a Henne ouer her Chickins?" asks Nashe, dwelling on this simile and continuing as the preacher. Although the people of Jerusalem have refused to listen to him, the time will come when they will regret their deafness. His voice has resounded so that all the streets and high places are filled with but one echo, "Thou wouldst not," which will be their damnation. This one phrase will become the indictment of Jerusalem. Just as the man seeing a salamander burning in a fire tried to save it by casting water on the flames and was stung, so the preacher has sought to snatch the people of Jerusalem from their destruction but they would not be saved.

Coming to the end of his scriptural text, "Therefore your habitation shall be left desolate," he prophesies the destruction of the city. Its palaces built on the sands of shallow conceits shall fall. The hostile ships anchoring in the harbor of Joppa will make it a "Marine-cittie" as big as Jerusalem (II, 48, 2). All the land thereabout will be laid waste. The only defenders remaining will be the enemies of the city. All religious ceremonies will be done away with. The priests will be slain at their altars. The Temple with its tabernacle will be made desolate. The sun and moon will be red as blood as a witness against the crimes of the people, who are Abraham's sons only in that whereas he would have sacrificed his own son they would sacrifice the Son of God. By sacrificing Him, however, they injure only themselves. To Him, on the contrary, they give salvation. Upon the cross He can spend none of His godhead reserved for the conquering of Hell, which, unlike Jerusalem, can be overcome. The Romans, being heathen and therefore inferior to the Devil, who at least knows and fears God, will conquer stubborn Jerusalem.

Although the exterior of the Temple is beautiful, inwardly it is rotten. Had Jerusalem listened to Christ, her Temple might have remained intact until Judgment Day. Praying first for the Temple and then for his murderers, the preacher again appeals to Jerusalem. Repeating his original text in its entirety and also his prayer for his executioners, he bids farewell to the city and reminds its citizens of the scriptural prophecies of his coming and his own futile appeals. Although he has incessantly entreated Jerusalem, she has not listened. Therefore she will be left to desolation. As the preacher foretells the terrible fate of the city, he plays on the word *desolation* as previously he played on *stone* and *gather*.

III *The Destruction of Jerusalem*

Concluding the oration, Nashe resumes his own personality and turns to consider how Christ's prophecies were fulfilled. Forty years after Christ's death the Jews began to tire of Roman rule. Eleazer, the son of Ananias, drove out the Romans and assumed control. This rebellion was accompanied by disturbances in the heavens and other evil portents. The Jewish people, however, remained obdurate.

Eventually the Romans under the Emperor Vespasian returned and began to devastate Palestine, particularly Jerusalem. They piled corpses even over the sepulcher of Christ. But before they had arrived, three factions had already been formed in the city—one under Eleazer, one under Jehochanan, one under Schimeon. The first two leaders were wicked enough, but the third was most evil. Schimeon reveled in all forms of sin so abominably that he was banished. Assembling all the dissatisfied elements from the city, with an army of twenty thousand he advanced upon Jerusalem, killing and destroying everything in his

path. Once within the city walls he joined with Eleazer and Jehochanan. After displacing the Sanhedrin, killing the High Priest, and
turning the Temple into an armory, the dissidents began to disagree
among themselves. Next came the plague. As the factions grew, the
slaughter became more terrible. Any person attempting to perform his
religious duties was put to torture and death. The religious utensils
were defiled. The Temple became a shambles. Then, fearing the
besieging Romans, the dissidents decided to set up another high priest
and mockingly installed a plowman.

As Christ had prophesied, the city was visited by fire, famine, pestilence, and death. The seditious Jews burned vast storehouses of food.
Wealthy men were murdered for their possessions. Anyone who
mourned their death was also killed. All the rivers, wells, and cisterns
were choked with corpses. Then the famine began. People became so
hungry that they ate anything that they could get their hands on—
moss, weeds, brush, vermin. Everyone hoarded what little food he had.
They stole from one another, even members of the same family. Miriam, a noble matron, killed and ate her only son, not through hatred
but through hunger. Nashe reproduces her soliloquy just before she
beheaded her son, in which she rationalizes her horrible deed.

Using the rhetorical device of repetition as in Christ's oration, Nashe
at the beginning combines two words, *fire* and *famine*. In her apologia
Miriam explains that she has no food for her son. She herself has to
choose between famine or murdering him for sustenance. She has
always hoped that in her old age he would be her comfort and that
finally he would bury her. Now she is sending him to intercede with
God for Jerusalem. Rather than let the Romans destroy him, she will
kill him and suffer the shame of her unnatural act. With eyes averted
she then cut off his head and cooked him. The rebel soldiers, smelling
the odor of baking, broke into her house and threatened her with death
for concealing food. Pointing at her dead son, she rebuked them and
placed the responsibility for the deed upon their heads. They were
overwhelmed with horror at her act and at the eloquence of her grief.

In addition to Miriam and her son more than 100,000 people died
in the city. Driven by the pangs of hunger, many citizens fled to the
enemy but were revolted by the sight of food and died. Some of them
swallowed their gold and jewels with the hope of reclaiming them
from their excrements. However, when the Roman mercenaries discovered the deception, they killed the refugees and ripped open their
corpses in order to get at the concealed treasure. When the siege was

over, Titus led 16,000 prisoners to Rome. Except for the Sanctuary, which the Roman leaders respected, the city was set on fire and burned down. Thus for stoning Christ and his prophets was Jerusalem made desolate. Nashe concludes with the statement that if he were to try to describe Hell, he would use the desolation of Jerusalem as his model.

IV *The Proud Citizens of London*

Turning to his own city which for its wickedness deserves as great a desolation as Jerusalem, Nashe prepares what he terms a "Looking-glasse" (II, 80, 18) wherein the citizens can see their vices. For his logical plan of presentation he returns to the Seven Deadly Sins, which had proved successful in *Pierce Penilesse*. In *Christ's Teares*, however, he selects only the first of the Sins, Pride, and subdivides it into its offspring: its "Sonnes"—Ambition, Vaine-glory, Atheisme, Discontent, Contention—and its "Daughters"—Disdaine, Gorgeous-attyre, and Delicacie (II, 81, 6 ff.).

The first son, Ambition, is a great courtier, walking on tiptoe, gaudily dressed, talking in terms of great wealth, hating every rival, eager for the plaudits of the crowd, jealous of his honor. Such a man as this was David when he numbered his people, or Herod when he spoke in angelic apparel, or Absalom, or Julius Caesar when he conquered the world. Yet, along with Alexander, all of these ambitious men have returned to dust, the inevitable end. Nashe cites similar examples of "swelling" ambition in London: the rich citizen over the courtier and vice versa; one company against another; indeed, the members within a company among themselves; youth against age; the wives of these men among themselves. In fact, ambition is the essence of sin, which is man "swelling or rebelling against God" (II, 84, 7). When the soul thus swells, both soul and body suffer. Therefore Christ came to teach us humility, the most difficult virtue. Instead of kings God chose fishermen, too low in the social scale to be tempted. At first, of course, the Devil looked for Christ's followers among the doctors, the high priests, or the elders—all of them already tainted with ambition. Realizing his error he stirred them up against Christ and then turned to carpenters and fishermen, all of whom except Judas ignored him. Nashe here inserts a warning to fishermen to beware of the Devil, who still suspects them and wishes to get even with them.

Every man who would avoid the sin of ambition must stay away from London and the court. Except for food and clothing everything that a man desires may be termed ambition. His Christian duty is to fight against it. Even Nashe's rhetorical displays in this pamphlet he regards as his own ambition to please his readers, which he will try to overcome. He reminds the citizens of London that they were made from dust like that in their streets. He recalls that the Jews in mourning put on sackcloth, ashes, and dust as a reminder of their humble origin. After St. Augustine had delivered an eloquent speech before the emperor and had won universal acclaim, he realized that this praise was nothing but air. As a result he became aware of the vanity of human knowledge and arrived at a state of "the true heauenlie content" (II, 89, 36). This reflection gives Nashe an opportunity to formulate a meditation or soliloquy comparing the unhappy scholar ambitious for fame with the contented beggar.

Although Christ calls us to His happiness, although we all are aware of death and burial around us, we convince ourselves that we shall live forever. Our struggles to gain higher positions are inspired by Lucifer, who, seeing men eager to gain wealth, is stimulated to capture their souls. Eventually, however, every man must die. Like the citizens of Jerusalem he will not know the time of his visitation. If he has not gathered himself under Christ's wing, he too will be left desolate.

A special type of ambition is avarice, the urge to accumulate wealth, which usually accompanies ambition. Riches unaccompanied by ambition are harmless. In London the usurers urge the spendthrifts to borrow money for pleasure. When the latter cannot repay, they are driven to desperate straits. The usurer at first by his thrift and sobriety builds up a good reputation. Then he begins to frequent the inns and taverns where he becomes acquainted with young spendthrifts. When these gallants suffer gambling losses and need money, he hastens to lend it to them with half the value of their jewels as collateral. Once having borrowed from the usurer, they are sure to come again. Then, however, he will probably not give them money but instead "some hundred poundes" worth of silks and velvets provided that they will make assurance before a judge (a sort of promissory note) (II, 94, 22–23). The third time the prodigal youths attempt to borrow, the usurer lends them "baser commodities"; and the fourth time, only "Lute strings and gray Paper." Finally he refuses them altogether and demands payment.

When the usurer has disposed of all of his worthless "pedlary" among unsuspecting young men and has collected a fortune in negotiable paper, he spreads the rumor that his kindness has driven him bankrupt. He employs an elderly relative to tell his sad story to his creditors, who are only too glad to accept a fraction of what is owed them. Then with everything settled he goes back into business. He cashes in the notes that he has collected and in three terms emerges a wealthy man. Nashe asseverates that as proof of this account of the rise of a usurer he has in his possession a "whole Booke of young Gentlemens cases" which might embarrass many a usurer in the city (II, 95, 19–20).

Aiding and abetting the usurers are the merchants who display their silks and velvets in order to attract unsuspecting gallants from the country, now either at court or attending the Inns of Court. Fathers who send their children to London to be educated in the ways of the world are placing them in danger of becoming proud. Had these children been properly trained, they never would be misled by usurers, who should be restrained by law. Whereas St. Augustine made it a matter of conscience that in youth he had led a group of boys to rob a neighbor's pear tree, these usurers think nothing of robbing a man of his whole estate. Nashe compares the usurer to a sheep, a bear, a fox, or a hog. Quoting appropriate scriptural passages, he urges all usurers to reform or forever to perish. By giving to the poor and turning to God, they may save their souls.

Here Nashe stresses the importance of good works. However, lest his reader may think him an advocate of Roman Catholicism, he is careful to insert this marginal note: "It is not my meaning in all this discourse of good deeds to seioyne any of them from Fayth" (II, 104). Nevertheless in his main text he asserts that the English tend to use the doctrine of salvation entirely through faith merely to satisfy themselves. Unlike the "Idolatrous Gentiles," who built temples to the gods for every victory, the English Protestants begrudge money for churches, alms-houses, and hospitals (II, 106, 29). Their clergymen give no alms; consequently the parishioners give none. Yet in the time of St. Augustine the poor customarily begged and received alms from their preachers and ministers.

The second son of Pride, Vaine-glorie, less significant than Ambition, represents all people who place excessive value on nonessentials such as foreign dress, unusual hair styles, perfumes, affected speech, swearing, boasting of vices, or quarreling, stabbing, and killing just to be considered fine gentlemen. Specifically included in this classification are Pausanias, who killed Philip of Macedon, and Herostratus, who burned the famous Temple of Diana, and more generally, Spaniards,

soldiers, poor poets, many excellent musicians, architects, social butter-
flies, ascetics, and persons who order monuments built in their own
honor.

Examining what Christ had termed vainglory in the Jews as the
cause of their "desolation," Nashe defines it as hypocrisy and asks
whether or not it exists in London. He finds it in the laws against the
common people, in persons who perform good works only in order to
be chronicled (like judges who seem righteous but who accept bribes),
in haughtiness, and so on. Nashe offers no specific examples of these
various misdemeanors but warns the people of London to avoid vainglory, not to boast of it. All sin is bestial and turns men into animals.
If England is to remain secure, her people must eschew ambition and
vainglory.

The third son of Pride is Atheism, which afflicts people whose good
fortune has made them forget God. In a paragraph reminiscent of
Donne's famous sermons on the same subject given many years later,
Nashe explains that either worldly success or contempt for divine
authority will make an atheist (II, 115, 1–11). But at the hour of death
both God and the Devil will appear to him as they appeared to Julian
the Apostate. Inwardly even those people denying the existence of the
Trinity really admit it. Most people who are atheists are thus misled
because they cannot perceive God through their senses. As a result they
deny that He made the firmament, that there is a Hell, that Adam was
the first man, and that Moses had divine assistance in performing his
miracles. Because some Protestant writers discredit the Apocrypha, the
unbelievers would discard the entire Bible.

Although admitting his own unworthiness, Nashe will attempt to
confute the atheists. Dividing them into two classes—inward and outward—he defines the former as those people who use religion as a
cloak for their own worldly designs. This type of atheist will assume
the appearance of piety and will quote Scripture in the performance
of evil deeds. He masquerades as a preacher of the gospel while at the
same time, under the pretense of suppressing Roman Catholicism, he
is really attacking the Established Church. (Nashe here evidently is
pointing at the Puritans.) The outward atheist establishes reason as his
god and questions all of God's teachings. If Aristotle despaired because
he could not understand the mysteries of the Nile, why, asks Nashe,
should the ordinary man expect to comprehend Heaven and God? If
even the angels do not know all of God's thoughts and plans, it is inconceivable for a sinner to know them. Although a king may be many

miles from his kingdom, he still remains king. How much more does God, who is omnipresent, retain His divinity! As a servant who prospers abandons his master, so do men corrupted by wealth and worldly success turn against God. The poor or miserable man never is an atheist. Moreover the atheist always dies an unhappy death.

Everything in nature—the night, air, fire, human breath, the planets, the sea, birds, animals, the human body—testifies to the existence of God. Nashe recommends Father Robert Parsons's *First Booke of the Christian Exercise appertayning to Resolution,* a Jesuitical tract, as a remarkable exposure of atheism. He adds that in England atheism is more dangerous and more widespread than sectarianism. Unlike the Italians, the English are too well fed to spend their time in confuting atheism. Cambridge and Oxford make too much of young men possessing piety but no wit. Nashe regrets that these universities expect their students to become austere overnight. The learned professors forget that "that religion which is soone rype, is soone rotten" (II, 123, 9–10).

The unwise selection and rapid advancement of inexperienced preachers have contributed to the spread of atheism. Consequently the ministry is full of "cow-baby-bawlers and heauy-gated lumberers," whose sermons are tautological, full of words but empty of thought (II, 123, 24). Nashe advises these preachers either to get some wit of their own or to cherish men of wit. They must learn to sweeten their sermons in order to attract their congregations to religion. Since the atheists whom they will encounter are men of great learning, the preachers themselves should be thoroughly conversant with the Church Fathers and the classics. Christ's command to forsake everything and follow Him is not directed against learning. Two of His greatest followers, Luke and Paul, were learned men. Just as God told Adam that he must earn his bread by the sweat of his brow, so the preacher desiring the "heauenly Bread" of theology in order to nourish his congregation must earn it by hard study (II, 125, 28). Since all of the human arts are the handmaidens to theology, the preacher must acquire them all.

He must learn to use natural similitudes in order to draw people to God. Yet today a preacher who does not make his sermon a "hotchpotch" of Scripture, frequently misapplied, is scorned (II, 127, 3). As a matter of fact, the scriptural reference should be used only as a final proof, a "last volley of the victorie" (II, 127, 33); otherwise it is comparable to taking the name of God in vain. Furthermore all writers, Christian and pagan, may bear witness to God. St. Paul never hesitated to quote the heathen poets. Even the Scripture uses metaphors and similitudes associated with everyday life. In an argument with an atheist, who scorns the Bible, commonplace reasons frequently are very effective. But though he may ignore the voice from the pulpit, on his deathbed he shall be rebuked by God. Nashe ends his condemnation of atheism with an appeal to the ecclesiastical authorities to "proclaime disputations, threaten punishments, bee vehement" in their sermons attacking this widespread evil. For as he eloquently expresses it, "Fall *England,* farewell peace, woe-worth our Weale and tranquillitie, if Religion bids vs farewell" (II, 129, 15–21).

The fourth son of Pride, Discontent, afflicts people who aspire to a social position above their class and means but are unable to achieve it. It is also caused by mental depression, excessive or improper diet, overstudy, family and business troubles. Its manifestations are "bannings, cursings, secrete murmurings, out-rage, murder, iniustice,"all of which provoke the judgment of God (II, 130, 9–10). It often leads to suicide. Because of discontent Jonah was swallowed by the whale and forced to live three days and nights in its belly. The discontented man usually is unsuccessful in business. The only form of discontent pleasing to God is that which a man feels about the vanities of the world and the prospering of the wicked. Few men in London feel discontented about the prevalence of sin. On the contrary they are filled with envy and dissension. Discontent leads to conspiracy, war, infidelity of wives, and heresy.

The fifth son of Pride, Contention, carries out the wishes of the other four sons. Lawyers, heretics, and the military-minded Swiss people thrive on it. From Cornelius Agrippa Nashe cites disputes over translations of unimportant words that have rent the early Christian Churches. Comparable to these in folly are the present-day disputes about liturgy, vestments, and preaching. These contentions cause unrest and division in religion.

Disdain, the eldest daughter of Pride, is far more heinous than ambition. It is particularly prevalent among fair women, who refuse to admit that any other woman can possess the quality of beauty upon which each prides herself. After citing such biblical examples as Rachel, Leah, Sarah, Hagar, and Joseph's brethren, Nashe turns to London, where the wealthy scorn the poor and the various classes and occupations scorn one another.

The second daughter of Pride, Gorgeous Attire, is a vice of both men and women. Each uses it in order to attract the opposite sex. With its aid all women since Eve have been both tempters and tempted. To this end they paint, wear magnificent hairdress, and decorate their persons. Nashe warns them that it is not their decorated exteriors that offend God but rather their proud souls. In order to counteract this pride he describes the eventual deterioration of their bodies in the grave. Having exchanged their silks and shining robes for the winding sheet, they will have to face God for judgment. He vividly describes their inevitable punishment in Hell, which is bound to be increased unless they stop tempting and corrupting men.

Women, indeed, are to blame for men's absurd fashions borrowed from other countries. The Englishman will spend all his money in order to give the appearance of wealth. Yet he too must eventually rot in the grave. With the exception of fishermen and farmers everyone lives beyond his means and social position. As a result the ancient nobility is almost displaced by upstarts who through this form of pride have entrapped and despoiled them. The only purpose of gay apparel is for rioting and revelry. In paying attention only to appearances people forget to nourish their souls. By concentrating on fine garments the wearer forgets to guard against sin. Man's attempt to improve on God's workmanship will bring down divine vengeance.

In Delicacie, the last daughter of Pride, are included Gluttony, Luxury, Sloth, and Security. This is the sin of the women of London, who pay too much attention to their diet, to their affected manner of speaking and walking, and to furnishing their houses. In their concern for these trivialities they neglect their souls. The saints and martyrs voluntarily avoided the delicacies of life and practiced mortification. Today in London, however, mortification is considered superstition. Not by prayer alone, but also by fasting and abstinence, will the soul be sanctified. Regarding the first subdivision of Delicacie, Gluttony, Nashe considers it a besetting sin of the English, who seek to turn every religious holiday into an occasion for feasting. Although Gluttony in itself is not too evil, it leads to other sins. However, having discussed this subject elsewhere (in *Pierce Penilesse*), he will not bore his reader with any further comment.

Lust, the second subdivision of Delicacy, was once hidden from public view. Now even the nobility openly practice it by daylight in the heart of the city. The suburbs, of course, are filled with houses of prostitution licensed through bribes paid to the magistrates. While pretending to be married gentlewomen, the prostitutes swear, rob their patrons, and neglect their religious duties. Indeed, they resemble the

Devil incarnate. They will sell their bodies for half a crown or a little more, sometimes less. If we condemn the Turks and Moors for selling Christian slaves, how much more should we blame these women who sell both body and soul? At twenty the natural bloom on their cheeks has been replaced by artificial coloring. By forty they are physically exhausted. The children whom they have borne will on the Judgment Day testify against them. Those women who have prevented birth shall be accused of murder.

If the Devil were to be asked what he saw at night in London, he would answer as follows: whoredom, drunkenness, pandering, robbery, revelry, cuckoldry, vanity, theft, murder, and conspiracy. Living in royal style, the prostitutes pretend to be Catholic so that they will not have to attend church, where they would be ridiculed. When arrested, they pose as martyrs.

Nashe explains at some length how the prostitute sets herself up in business. First, she bribes the justice or the alderman's deputy. Then she makes friends with her neighbors. She orders the construction of secret entrances and exits along with secret panels and sliding doors for hiding in case of a raid. She acquires a patron whom for payment she admits without fee. Under the pretense of being a fortune-teller, a physician, a conjurer, or a painter, the bawd will explain the presence of any questionable inmate as a young gentlewoman waiting to be placed with some lady of nobility or else a widow attending a lawsuit in London or even the wife's niece or cousin. In order to protect the customers of these houses Nashe recommends legalized prostitution. Finally, weary of the subject, he urges the prostitutes to repent and quotes several passages from the Bible and the classics condemning adultery and fornication.

The third subdivision of Delicacy is Sloth. The individual practicing this vice is slow in good works, in attending church, in business affairs, in avoiding sin, and in defending any good cause. Although Nashe concedes that some slowness is a virtue, such as slowness to anger, to judgment, and to revenge, he excepts the sloth of magistrates who let a case hang so long in court that a man is ruined or who accept bribes. Other examples of sloth are soldiers who, returning from the wars, refuse to work, ministers who will never preach, lawyers working only for bribes, and people listening to flatterers.

Already the Lord has begun to make plague-stricken London desolate. Nashe exhorts the citizens to reform their ways. He first blames the usurers and engrossers of corn who have hoarded money and grain until the air is infected with the stench. Next he calls to account the adulterers who have brought grief to the land. Then he censures extortioners, proud men, hypocrites, and murderers. "Post ouer [attribute] the Plague to what naturall cause you will," he declares, "I positiuelie affirme it is for sinne" (II, 158, 21–22). London is the "seeded Garden of sinne," in which the most honest people are either lawyers or usurers (II, 158, 28). Most of the prominent citizens have attained their eminence through deceit or the robbery of orphans. Therefore the Lord, knowing their hidden wickedness, might as well kill with the plague as these sinners kill with oppression.

In spite of the evils of the city the virtue of the queen is unimpeachable. Although God delays His punishment for her sake, all citizens should begin to practice penance. Some cruel and uncharitable people have thought to purge their homes by casting out their infected servants to starve and die in the fields. Unlike other countries England has no hospitals for the exposed, the infected, and the dangerously ill. Now that this country is Protestant, charity is at its lowest ebb. No one gives alms to the poor. No pensions are provided for wounded veterans or poor scholars. College livings are not increased but diminished. Only gold and silver are in demand. The memory of the charitable man will live on. The sole salvation for the wealthy misers of London is almsgiving. In order to emphasize the efficacy of prayer in this dire emergency Nashe cites the example of Gregory Nasianzene (corrected by McKerrow to Gregorius Magnus—IV, 246), who during an outbreak of the plague in Rome assembled all of the clergy and the citizens to public prayer. As a result the plague ended after four days.

Unlike the Romans, the English either continue in rioting and recklessness or else despair of God's providence. But Nashe asserts that long life is not always a blessing. Christ Himself died young. The death of a good man by the plague is not necessarily a punishment but rather an indication of divine love. Like an earthly father God desires to correct us so that we may enjoy life everlasting. Therefore it is better for London to suffer and be loved than to go to eternal damnation.

At this point Nashe attempts to sketch what eternal punishment will be like. To the average person it means merely a conglomeration of fire and brimstone. In order to clarify the concept, Nashe uses various images to explain the meaning of the word *eternal*. He expresses amazement that even though birds and animals avoid snares men rush into unbaited ones. Fearful of breaking man-made laws, which offer no reward but only a penalty, we remain indifferent to God's laws, which present great rewards along with great penalties. If God withholds his punishment for a time, it is only to increase its ultimate effect.

In order to remind himself of the omnipresence of God, a man should imagine that he sees Him everywhere in nature—in the planets, in the seasons, in the storms. Since we do not commit many of our sins in the presence of other people, with God always with us we should not commit them at all. Because London will not look for God and thinks that He does not see her sins, He has smitten her with the plague. Some victims, indeed, have noticed on themselves the print of a hand or have felt a blow as if from an invisible hand. People like to attribute the plague to fortune, to hot weather, to the planets, to all sorts of superstitious manifestations, most of them false. Yet the mere fact that we have revolted from God is a sufficient cause of our imminent ruin. We have already been warned by the comet, the earthquake, and the famine. The sword will be next. Certainly, if the Lord left the city of His Chosen People desolate, He will punish London. Nashe exhorts the citizens to join him in praying for mercy.

V   *The Second Epistle to the Reader*

Nashe opens his second epistle to the reader on a note of exasperation, the cause for which at once becomes evident in his repudiation of his earlier offer of peace to Harvey. Religion or conscience had originally driven him to apologize. In spite of his willingness to seek peace as a fitting preparation for writing on his "holy subiect" (II, 180, 11), Harvey has published "sixe and thirtie sheets of mustard-pot paper" attacking both him and his friends (II, 180, 23–24). Since Harvey has deceived him by his pretenses of friendship, Nashe will return to battle and never listen to another overture of peace.

Next he assures his reader that his reference to the University of Wittenberg in *The Unfortunate Traveller* is not a satire on any English university (in other words, on Cambridge). Indeed, he expresses his deep regard for Cambridge and for everyone matriculating there except the Harvey brothers. Then he defends what some critics of *Christ's Teares* have called his "puft-vp stile . . . full of prophane eloquence," his "boystrous compound wordes," and his "Italionate verbes" ending with *ize* (II, 183, 23–26). His style, he asserts, is no more "puft vp" than that of any other man writing with spirit. Moreover, even the Fathers of the Church condescended to quote from the heathen writers. As far as compounding words is concerned, he does it "to make the royaller shew" with what "worthlesse shreds of small English" he possesses in his vocabulary (II, 184, 16–17). He ends his verbs with *ize* in order to impress his reader with their "boystrous" sound. Finally he invites his critics to rail upon him and thereby to advertise his pamphlets.

VI *Critical Commentary*

Christ's Teares, written in the late spring or early summer of 1593, falls into two distinct sections: first, the events, real and imaginary, having to do with the destruction of Jerusalem by the Roman armies in A.D. 70 and second, a description of the sins of London in the manner of *Pierce Penilesse*. The first section likewise falls into three parts: first, an indictment of the citizens of Jerusalem for ignoring God's warnings; second, an imaginary oration by Christ to these citizens; third, the story of the siege and fall of the city, largely taken from Peter Morwyn's translation of the *History of the Latter Times of the Jews' Commonweal* by Joseph Ben Gorion. Both McKerrow (IV, 213) and Hibbard (pp. 124–25) believe that a sermon by the popular preacher John Stockwood (1584) probably was Nashe's primary inspiration in composing this pamphlet: *A very fruitfull and necessarye Sermon of the moste lamentable destruction of Ierusalem, and the heauy iudgementes of God, executed vppon that people for their sinne and disobedience: published at this time to the wakening and stirring vp of all such as bee lulled a sleepe in the cradle of securitie or carelesnesse, that they maye at length repente them of their harde hartednes, and contempt of God his word, least they taste of the like plagues for their rebellion and vnrepentance, not knowing with the wilfull inhabitants of Ierusalem, the daye of their visitation.*

Although Hibbard concedes that *Christ's Teares* is "the longest and most serious," "the most carefully planned and orderly" (p. 122), of all of Nashe's writings, he finds few other redeeming qualities in it. While praising the caricature of the contemporary preacher in his pulpit, the satirical description of the merchants' wives dressed in the height of fashion, and the imaginary account of the process of bankruptcy (p. 143), he dubs it "the worst thing Nashe ever wrote" (p. 122), possessing "all the fascination of the positively and thoroughly bad," also a "monument of bad taste, literary tactlessness, and unremitting over-elaboration for which it is not easy to find a parallel" (p. 123).

Perhaps some of Hibbard's uneasiness about *Christ's Teares* stems from the same source troubling the critics of *The Unfortunate Traveller*, namely, the difficulty of finding an appropriate literary classification for it. Hibbard himself notes that it is "different in kind from Nashe's other works" (p. 123) and follows the mirror convention, a "well established literary mode" in which history is used for moral and didactic purposes (p. 124). He also quotes E. D. Mackerness, who places it within a subdivision of this mode, "the literature of warning" (p. 124).

Hibbard also finds in *Christ's Teares* other categories for particular sections. For example, while terming Christ's oration "really an elaborate sermon" (p. 130) like any given by an Elizabethan preacher, he identifies Christ with the tragic hero in the Senecan tradition like Hieronimo or Titus Andronicus (p. 134). In fact, according to Hibbard, Nashe "clearly thought of the first part of *Christ's Teares*, including the account of the fall of Jerusalem as well as Christ's sermon, as a kind of prose tragedy, the sermon being a tragical prologue to the tragical fact of the city's destruction" (p. 133). He maintains that Nashe "seems to have conceived of tragedy as violent and sensational action tricked out in extravagantly passionate speech" and accordingly fills Christ's mouth with "high astounding terms" (p. 134).

As for the second part of *Christ's Teares*, the attack on the sins of London, Hibbard classifies it as belonging to the literature of complaint, a medieval genre which John Peter divides into four categories:[1] first, attacks on professional and business classes; second, attacks on less definite classes such as atheists, backbiters, and misers; third, attacks on specific abuses like swearing or the use of cosmetics; fourth, general themes such as the fear of death, dissolution, and decay, which colors the author's whole attitude (pp. 141–42).

As usual, Hibbard hesitates to state flatly that Nashe here is working with an entirely new form, the pamphlet. Yet this admission would account for many of the excesses and lapses of taste that Hibbard deplores. Moreover, the two forms that he mentions, the mirror convention and the complaint, were primarily didactic, whereas *Christ's Teares*, in his opinion, is not. In fact, in analyzing Nashe's imaginary oration he writes, "Essentially a clown and an exhibitionist, he could not turn preacher merely by removing his red nose" (p. 127). Hibbard sums up his criticism of this pamphlet with the comment, "Entertainment, not instruction," was Nashe's "real vocation" (p. 139).

Rather than condemning this pamphlet as a literary monstrosity, then, the student of Nashe might do well to analyze its stylistic elements, which give a better understanding of his writing as a whole. Reinhard H. Friederich, in discussing "verbal tensions" in *The Unfor-*

tunate Traveller, notes that Nashe employs "a good deal of imagery" depending on verbal instead of visual movement so that "the literary experience comes before the visual one."[2] Similarly, in *Christ's Teares* Hibbard calls attention to "the great gulf between the words and the facts, between the horror he [Nashe] tries to convey and the impression of callous sadism that he creates" (p. 140). Specifically referring to Christ's oration, Hibbard explains that unlike the great preachers who tried to extract every possible significance in a word, Nashe pumps significance into the words from the scriptural passage that the orator had taken as his text (e.g., *stone, gather,* and so on) so that "words beget words in an incessant, bubbling stream" (p. 130).

Instead of trying to force this pamphlet into a conventional literary mode, Hibbard is on the right track in accepting C. S. Lewis's analogy between the construction of the oration and the process of musical composition (p. 131). However, since a "keyword" is hardly comparable to a *leitmotif* (Lewis's comparison),[3] which is an extended musical phrase, Hibbard's parallel with a theme and variations is more apt (pp. 131 ff.). Here, again like Friederich, Hibbard argues that the evolution of the passage is determined by *verbal* association instead of by any development of sense or argument. Nevertheless, while recognizing Nashe's "enterprise," "ingenuity," and "artifice" in using this musical approach, Hibbard considers it totally ineffective (p. 133).

McKerrow and Hibbard disagree on the significance of this pamphlet in its own time. McKerrow remarks that it "does not seem to have attracted any great amount of notice at the time of its publication" (IV, 213). Hibbard, on the contrary, wryly comments: ". . . far from attracting little attention when it first came out, it attracted altogether too much for its author's comfort and safety" (p. 122). He also notes that it was "the only major work by Nashe that was republished in the seventeenth century" (p. 123). For the reissue in 1594 with a new epistle to the reader Hibbard gives two reasons: first, its place in the Harvey-Nashe controversy and, second, the attack on the citizens and merchants of London considerably modified in the second issue. Moreover Hibbard also believes that Nashe's "hundred vnfortunate farewels to fantasticall Satirisme" (II, 12, 4–5) in his first epistle may have been an attempt to mollify certain people offended by his allegory of the Bear and the Fox in *Pierce Penilesse* (p. 126). The apparent occasion for the second edition was the outbreak of the plague in 1613. Evidently the publisher thought Nashe's pamphlet appropriate to the time.

From the furor caused by Nashe's attempt at a theological treatise
it is evident that he could not restrain the pen dipped in "*Aquafortis*,
& Gunpowder" as he had expressed it in *Pierce Penilesse*. His satirical
comments in *Christ's Teares* brought down upon his head the wrath
of the Lord Mayor and aldermen of London, in order to escape which
he took refuge with the Careys on the Isle of Wight.

CHAPTER 7

The Unfortunate Traveller

I *The Jests of Jack Wilton*

NASHE dedicates *The Unfortunate Traveller or the Life of Jack Wilton* to the right honorable Lord Henry Wriothesley, Earl of Southampton and third Baron of Titchfield, to whom Shakespeare dedicated his *Venus and Adonis* and *The Rape of Lucrece*. Following this dedication and a list of errata for the benefit of his "Gentlemen Readers," he addresses an induction to "the dapper Mounsier Pages of the Court," in which he tells them that his persona Jack Wilton, also "a gentleman and a page" (II, 207, 30), commends the pamphlet to them with the hope that they will cherish and honor the chronicle itself. If, however, they find it necessary to use the sheets as "wast paper," they have his approval.

The narrative opens in 1513 in France, where the armies of Henry VIII are besieging the cities of Tournai and Turwin (Térouanne). Jack Wilton has left the English court and is merrily living by his wits in the army camps on the Continent. In this opening section Jack recounts a series of tricks played on his unsuspecting companions. His first victim is a nobleman whose only contribution to the war effort is selling cider and cheese to the soldiers. Under pretense of deep admiration and affection for this man, Jack warns him of imminent danger threatening his enterprise. After pretending to hesitate Jack confides that someone has "buzzed in the Kings head" that this drunken lord is sending provisions to the enemy (II, 214, 1). When asked whether or not the King believes this information, Jack says that the King always has considered the lord "a myser and a snudge" and has vowed to give Turwin "one hot breakfast onely with the bungs" of his cider barrels (II, 215, 12–13). Jack advises him to distribute among the soldiers "such victualls or prouision" as he possesses. As a result the whole army has all the cider it can drink. The lord, in turn, goes to the King and offers to give up his lands in return for "some reasonable pension to liue" (II, 216, 18). Although weary of war, he protests that he will stand by his King as long as any enemy threatens. Amazed at this change, the King makes inquiry and discovers the hoax, whereupon he orders Jack "pitifully whipt." The lord, however, persists in begging the King to accept his offer, and the King jestingly agrees.

Jack's next victim is "an ugly mechanicall Captain," whom he for a time supports by cheating at dice (II, 217, 17). In order to be rid of this parasite, Jack eventually urges him to become a spy in the King's service. When the Captain yields to Jack's persuasion, Jack furnishes him with money. But as soon as the supposed spy departs, Jack goes to the English marshall general and tells him that the Captain has deserted. The Captain, in the meantime, goes to the French camp and, "rayling egregiously against the King of *England*," offers his services (II, 222, 35–223, 1). The French King immediately becomes suspicious and orders him searched and questioned before a courtier pretending to be the King while the real King listens to the examination. The Englishman's lies are so patent that the French King interrupts and orders him tortured into a confession. The Captain admits that he has been persuaded by Jack to kill the French King and to return to the English camp. When after further torture he holds to his story, he is whipped out of camp and sent home with a defiant message, which subsequently is returned in kind.

On another occasion Jack presents himself disguised as a woman to "another Switzer Captaine that was farre gone for want of the wench" (II, 225, 11–12). After being wined, dined, and paid "the earnest-penie of impietie," the tormentor excuses himself and departs. Next he frights with a false alarm a company of clerks who have been profiteering at the expense of the soldiers. When these cowards flee, they leave behind their clerical paraphernalia and whatever money is in their desks as spoils for the mischievous page.

After the siege Jack returns to his occupation as page at Windsor and Hampton Court, where he continues his tricks with his fellow pages. When the "sweating sicknes" begins to rage in England, he flees overseas with the intention of joining the Swiss army or the French, whichever he finds the stronger, in their conquest of Milan. As he comes on the scene, a great battle is being fought with terrible slaughter on either side. The French, assisted by the Venetians, emerge victorious and are given Milan as "a pledge of reconciliation" (II, 232, 2).

II   *Jack's Continental Tour*

This episode ushers in the second section of Nashe's narrative, which takes the form of a sort of continental travelogue. From Milan Jack travels to Münster, where John of Leyden and his Anabaptist followers are withstanding a siege by the Emperor and the Duke of Saxony. Had not famine weakened the Münsterians they might have held out against this vastly superior force. After a year, however, they are forced to issue forth with any kind of weapon at hand and take to the field, where they kneel down and pray for victory. (Here Nashe inserts a digression against "sects and schismes" evidently directed at the Puritans in England—II, 237, 9 ff.). Returning to John of Leyden, he, as Jack, remarks that if the Anabaptists were not immediately to receive an answer to their prayer they would curse God. However, at the appearance of a rainbow they believe that God has sent them assurance of victory. Accordingly they rush into battle and are horribly massacred. John of Leyden is hanged for his part in this insurrection. Nashe ends the story with a warning to all Anabaptists and Puritans.

(In this account it should be noted that Nashe is not concerned with historical time. The battle of Milan occurred in 1515, the Anabaptist uprising in 1534. Thus in traveling from Milan to Münster Jack covers nineteen years. Furthermore Nashe has confused the Münster affair with the battle of Frankenhausen, fought in 1525 between the Anabaptists under Thomas Muntzer and the Elector of Saxony. McKerrow suggests the possibility that if Nashe did not purposely combine the two accounts he may have been writing from memory and hence may have confused the man Muntzer with the town Münster—IV, 268.)

Since no more wars are being fought in Christendom, Jack decides to return to England. At Middleborough, however, he meets Henry Howard, the Earl of Surrey, his late master, whom he is delighted to see again. At the Earl's invitation Jack decides to accompany him on his travels. When Jack inquires why the Earl has left England, the latter explains that he is in love with Geraldine, a lady-in-waiting to the dowager Queen Katherine, whom he has met at Hampton Court. Surrey describes the remarkable beauty of his beloved with all of the exaggerated terms of the typical sonneteer. He explains that he has asked her permission to travel a year or two in Italy, her native country. Giving her consent, she has asked him when he reaches Florence, the city of her birth, to defend by open challenge her beauty against all comers.

With Venice as their first goal they stop off at Rotterdam, where they meet Erasmus and Sir Thomas More, with both of whom they have pleasant conference. Erasmus tells them of his plans to write *In Praise of Folly* (actually published in 1509, eight years before Surrey was born). More discusses his projected *Utopia* (the first Latin edition of which was published in 1516).

From Rotterdam the Earl and Jack travel to Wittenberg, where they participate in the welcome given by town and gown to the Duke of Saxony, the "chiefe Patrone of their Vniuersitie" (II, 246, 14). After the Duke is greeted by the heads of the University in full academic regalia, the University Orator gives a "very learned or rather ruthfull oration" (II, 246, 22–23) filled with Ciceronian rhetoric, after which the "iunior graduats" (II, 247, 5) overwhelm the Duke with salutations. The townsfolk are represented by "a bursten belly inkhorne orator called *Vanderhulke* " (II, 247, 26), possessing a lugubrious appearance and an equally absurd manner of speaking. After this speaker has delivered his mock-oration, which Jack reports in full, the Duke is invited to witness an academic comedy almost as ridiculous as the two orations.

Next day the travelers attend a disputation between Luther and Carolostadius, which Jack dismisses as more full of sound and fury than good logic. He is especially amused by the absurd mannerisms of the less important participants in the disputation, all of whom adhere to the principles of Ciceronian rhetoric. At this point Nashe digresses in order to deplore the tendency in England, as well as in Germany, to equate eloquence with Cicero's oratory. Returning to the academic festivities, Jack spots the scholar Cornelius Agrippa, said to be the "greatest coniurer in christendome" (II, 252, 7). For the amusement of the audience the magician summons up the spirits of Ovid and Plautus. Then at the request of Erasmus in the audience he presents the spirit of Cicero, who impressively delivers one of his great speeches. At this point Agrippa, bored with the crowds, decides to cut short his stay in Wittenberg and to return to the Emperor's court. The two Englishmen accompany him.

On the way the pair hit upon the plan of exchanging identities: Jack is to masquerade as Surrey; the latter, assuming the name of Brunquell, will become Jack's servant. While at court, they hear of many more of Agrippa's magic feats. In order to please Surrey, Jack requests the magician to show the "liuely image" of Surrey's beloved Geraldine (II, 254, 6). The sight of the beautiful lady inspires the Earl to compose an "extemporal dity" in her praise and recalls to his mind his original intention to visit her native country (II, 254, 13). Without more ado the travelers, retaining their disguises, depart for Italy, the setting for the third and final section of *The Unfortunate Traveller*.

III   *Jack's Adventures in Italy*

Arriving in Venice, they meet a famous panderer who invites them to the home of the courtesan Tabitha. Nothing in her house would indicate the profession of its owner. After giving them both a magnificent welcome, during which she observes that Jack appears extremely wealthy, she tries to persuade the Earl, still disguised as the servant, to murder his supposed master. Surrey agrees to shoot Jack at the first opportunity. When Tabitha and her pretended accomplice enter Jack's room, he tells them that in a dream he had been forewarned of their plot. As his supposed servant feigns terror and drops his gun, Jack pounces on him. Seemingly overcome with remorse, Surrey confesses and accuses Tabitha and her panderer. In order to avoid being arrested she gives Jack a large amount of gold, which he turns over to another courtesan. Unfortunately for him, however, this woman is a confederate of Tabitha and knows that the gold coins are counterfeit. As a result she has both Englishmen turned over to the master of the mint. This official is inclined to befriend them until some other Englishmen, hearing that an English Earl has been arrested for counterfeiting, come to visit and recognize the real Earl of Surrey. Fearing that a conspiracy against the state is intended, the master of the mint has both culprits thrown into prison. The treacherous Tabitha now plots with her panderer to pretend to interpret in defense of the two prisoners but actually to misinterpret by mistranslating and thus to convict them.

While in prison, Jack meets Diamante, the victim of her husband's jealous suspicions. A would-be borrower whom her husband has turned down for a loan has spread the rumor that she has been unfaithful. Jack swears that until he came along she has lived chastely. Surrey, of course, is no threat to her virtue. His love for Geraldine gives him a chivalrous regard for all women, the typical attitude of the Elizabethan writer of sonnets. In fact, he composes a sonnet in praise of Diamante's beauty on the spot. As might be expected from Nashe the satirist, its true author, this sonnet is filled with innuendos making it more or less a parody of Petrarchan conventions. Further contributing to the anti-Petrarchan spirit of this episode, Jack adds that while his master "beate the bush and kepte a coyle and a pratling," he himself "caught the birde" (II, 263, 16–17).

After a brief interval Mr. John Russell, an English diplomat visiting Venice, persuades the noted author Pietro Aretino to plead for his fellow countrymen. Thanks to Aretino's efforts Tabitha and her panderer are tried, found guilty, and executed. (At this point Nashe again steps into the narrative in order to praise Aretino for his relentless scourging of abuses, particularly in the political sphere.)

Shortly after Jack is liberated, Diamante becomes pregnant. About the same time, either because of jealousy or the famine, her husband, Castaldo, dies. Jack again appeals to Aretino for legal assistance, as a consequence of which Diamante inherits all of her husband's possessions. Sharing her fortune with Jack, she agrees to tour Italy with him. Under her influence Jack deserts the Earl but retains the title and the state that had been thrust upon him. The Earl himself continues on to Florence, his original destination. On the way, however, he hears of another person with his name traveling with much pomp and ceremony. Surrey eventually overtakes Jack at Florence and surprises him sitting in his "pontificalibus" with his courtesan at supper, "lyke *Anthonie* and *Cleopatra* when they quaft standing boules of Wine spiced with pearle together" (II, 267, 21–23). Although Jack is much embarrassed, Surrey thinks it all a big joke. In apologizing Jack assures him that, because of Diamante's largesse, the Earl's good name has not in any way been demeaned. Surrey accepts this apology with one reservation, namely, that Jack will not continue traveling with his courtesan. Rather than leave the Earl again, Jack agrees to give up Diamante and return to his original state of "poore Jack Wilton," Surrey's servant (II, 269, 30).

Next day the pair visit Geraldine's birthplace, where the Earl becomes so inspired that he writes a sonnet and "many other poems and epigrams" in the very room where his beloved was born (II, 270, 33). Then he proceeds to publish "a proud challenge in the Duke of Florence court against all commers (whether Christians, Turkes, Iewes, or Saracens) in defense of his *Geraldines* beauty" (II, 271, 8–10). For the tournament Surrey is dressed in armor decorated with lilies and roses on a base of nettles and weeds, all of which are watered by streams issuing from his helmet. His horse is made to resemble an ostrich. On his shield is Geraldine's picture on the outside and "a naked sword tyed in a true love knot" with "the mot *Militat omnis amans*" signifying that "in a true love knot his sword was tied to defend and maintaine the features of his mistres" (II, 273, 19–22).

Next to Surrey in the lists is the Black Knight, dressed in order to terrify his opponent with a headpiece like an oven emitting sulphur and smoke. Then follows the Knight of the Owl, with an ivy-covered tree on his armor, his helmet shaped like an owl, and a bee in sheep's wool on his shield. On a horse harnessed with leaden chains rides a knight in rust-colored armor with a helmet resembling flowers growing in a narrow pot and on his shield several worms covered by a block. The fifth is the Forsaken Knight, wearing a helmet crowned with cypress and willow garlands, his armor covered by a soiled yellow wedding garment. Following him comes the Knight of the Storms, with a helmet resembling a moon and with armor fashioned in waves representing moonshine on the water. The seventh knight is dressed to imitate a mountain. The armor of the eighth is ornamented with a hawthorne bush at the base of which are toads and grasshoppers. On his shield is the picture of death relieving the wants of unfortunate children. Finally comes the Infant Knight, whose armor depicts a helpless baby set adrift on the sea. On his shield appears a goat destroying a young tree. On the shields and sometimes elsewhere on the trappings of all of the knights are appropriate impresas. Jack ends his account of the contestants with the descriptions of numerous other shields.

Having emphasized the bizarre appearance of the contestants, he comments with tongue in cheek on the absurdity of their behavior in the lists. Since only the Earl of Surrey follows the rules of the tournament and unseats all whom he encounters, he is proclaimed master of the field and his Geraldine "the exceptionless fayrest of women" (II, 278, 33). Although the Duke of Florence wines him and dines him in order to induce him to remain in Italy, the Earl is called back to England by the King.

After Surrey's departure Jack and Diamante set out for Rome, where they lodge with an acquaintance of Diamante's late husband, who shows them about the city. The first sight that interests Jack is the sign of an exterminator of lice and scorpions. Next he mentions "the church of the seuen *Sibels*," the house of Pontius Pilate "as one goes to St. Paules church not farre from the iemmes *Piazza*," and a prison where a man was kept alive by sucking his daughter's breasts (II, 280, 11–25). In addition to innumerable tombs of martyrs and relics brought from Jerusalem, he sees the ruins of Pompey's theater, Gregory VI's tomb, Priscilla's grate, and the remains of the ancient Roman forum.

In Rome, where short hair is the fashion for men, Jack's long English haircut attracts the attention of the street urchins. He is also arrested for carrying a rapier but is pardoned when he pays his fine and identifies himself as a stranger in the city. The law against weapons is intended to curb outlaws who occasionally slip into the city, commit murder, and flee.

Next the Roman gardens attract his fancy. He describes the extensive use of musical instruments in landscape gardening, where wind instruments are inserted in the waterpipes. In a merchant's "summer banketting house" (II, 282, 21) Jack beholds a crystal vault with sun, moon, and stars which move as in the sky accompanied by music suggesting the fabled music of the spheres. The floor is painted with flowers. In the trees surrounding the house silver pipes are attached to the boughs so that the birds sitting on them appear to be singing. Under the trees all species of animals are lying down amicably together, the ferocious mingling with the meek, as in the Golden Age.

After a word of praise for Roman charity, especially as shown in their hospitals, Jack recounts the horrors of the great plague of 1522, during which Esdras of Granada,"a notable Bandetto, authorised by the pope because he had assisted him in some murthers" (II, 287, 5–6), and Bartol, "a desperate Italian," plan by night to break into rich men's houses infected by the disease. If only women are found alive, the villains intend to ravish them and steal their gold. For fear of contamination no one will respond to the women's cries for help. While Jack and his courtesan are staying at the home of a "noble & chast matrone" Heraclide, attended by only one servant, the two criminals break in (II, 287, 19). Esdras runs to attack Heraclide, mourning for her unconscious or—as she believes—dead husband. Bartol, in turn, attacks Jack and his companion. When Jack snatches up an unloaded pistol in self-defense, Bartol threatens to stab Diamante. In spite of Jack's efforts to bribe Bartol, the villain ravishes the courtesan and locks Jack in his room, where through a crack in the floor he can behold Esdras murdering Heraclide's servant and attempting to seduce her.

The noble matron first begs for death and then swoons. Upon recovering consciousness, she threatens her assailant with death from catching the plague. He replies that the dice have too often run in his favor to permit him to fear so small a danger as sickness. Since he already has made whores of his mother and sister, he sees no reason why he should not do likewise with her. After threatening her with his sword and dragging her up and down by her hair, he forces her to yield to his lust with her husband's inert body as a pillow. Finished he takes her possessions and departs. First lamenting her ravishment, she stabs herself and falls on her husband's body. The shock of her fall causes him to regain consciousness. He rises, lights a candle, and beholds his wife and servant lying dead. Then he goes searching for the murderer. Finding only Jack locked in his chamber, the enraged husband assumes him to be the culprit. As a result Jack is again cast into prison. With the rope around his neck he makes a full confession. A "banisht English Earle," who happens to be among the onlookers, requests that the execution be stayed. In Jack's defense the Earl tells that he saw Bartol covered with blood carried into a "Barbars shop," where he had recounted the events at the home of Heraclide (II, 296, 6 ff.). He also tells that Esdras afterward had robbed him of Diamante and had beaten him. The Earl's testimony is sufficient to restore Jack to freedom. When he attempts to express his gratitude for his delivery, the Earl gives him a long, tedious lecture on the evils of traveling in foreign countries, which he concludes by bewailing his own exile from England.

Happy to get away from his verbose benefactor, Jack goes looking for his courtesan. In order to shelter himself from a rainstorm he is hugging the wall when he falls through the cellar door of the house belonging to Zadoch the Jew. Looking upward he beholds his courtesan kissing an apprentice. He is about to punish her when they both are apprehended by the Jew himself. According to Roman law, if a felon breaks into a house or robs a man on the highway, he becomes the property of the person who catches him, either to serve him or be hanged. Zadoch decides to sell Jack to his friend Zacharie, the Pope's personal physician, for dissection. The doctor carefully examines Jack and locks him up in a dark chamber to await the day set for the anatomy lecture. There, living in fear and trembling, he is purged and starved by his captor.

Fortunately for Jack, as he was being taken by Zadoch to Zacharie, he had been seen by Juliana, the wife of the Marquis of Mantua and the Pope's concubine. Much impressed by his handsome appearance, she attempts to buy him from Zacharie. At the Jew's rude refusal she arranges for him to minister to the Pope, who has fallen ill. Into the medicine prescribed by the doctor she pours a strong poison, which instantly kills the Pope's taster. Informed that Zacharie is the physician, the Pope condemns him to death along with all the other Jews in Rome. In order to cover up her treachery, Juliana requests that the sentence be changed to banishment and that all of Zacharie's goods be forfeited to her. Then she sends her servants to bring Jack, completely unaware of his destination, to her chamber. At first she pretends to be enraged.

At this point Jack digresses in order to explain that Diamante after being seized by Zadoch had been imprisoned in his house where under pretense of forcing her to tell how much money she had received from his apprentice he has daily stripped and scourged her. After Zacharie's goods have been confiscated, he runs to Zadoch in order to inform him of the misfortune that has befallen him and the rest of the Roman Jews. Zadoch becomes furious and threatens all kinds of revenge against the Pope. But Zacharie points out that their real enemy is Juliana and suggests that they send Diamante, ostensibly as a peace offering to Juliana but actually as a poisoner. Accordingly, outfitted in great splendor, the courtesan is presented by Zadoch to Juliana, who, instantly captivated by her beauty, promises to appeal to the Pope for the Jews. As soon as Zadoch's back is turned, however, Juliana gets from Diamante her whole story. Diamante also warns Juliana that her life is threatened. Juliana takes the poison given her by Diamante and puts it on a shelf in her closet. Then she absents herself from her lustful pleasures with Jack long enough to see that Zadoch and Zacharie are involved in treacherous acts against the Pope. Zadoch is captured and tortured to death, but Zacharie escapes.

In the meantime Diamante becomes lady-in-waiting to Juliana and personal caretaker of Jack. Although delighted to see his former companion, he is gradually becoming exhausted by Juliana's sexual demands upon him. Finally, on St. Peter's Day, while Juliana, arrayed as an angel, is attending the papal festivities, Diamante and Jack pack up her jewels, plate, and money, put them into a boat, and set sail on the Tiber. Juliana's discovery of their escape upsets her so that she calls for a glass of wine. Her maid mistakenly brings her the poison given her by Diamante. Finding Juliana unconscious, the unsuspecting girl pries open her mistress's mouth and administers the poison. Jack reports that he has heard that the Pope has sentenced the maid to drink the rest of the poison as punishment for the death of her mistress.

Jack and Diamante continue on to Bologna, where they behold the execution of Cutwolfe, the brother of Bartol, the former confederate of Esdras. Before Cutwolfe is executed on the wheel of torture, he is permitted an oration. He confesses that he has slain Esdras for killing Bartol in a quarrel over a courtesan. He describes how he had trailed the Spaniard all over the Continent and had finally cornered him in Bologna. With the gun at his breast, Esdras had made an eloquent appeal for mercy, but Cutwolfe had remained unmoved. Finally, when Esdras had promised to commit heinous crimes, even to forswear all hope of salvation, Cutwolfe had hit upon a "notable newe Italionisme" including the soul as well as the body of his victim (II, 325, 20). He would ask him to renounce and curse God, to sign over his soul to the Devil, and to pray to God never to pardon him. As soon as Esdras had agreed to these terms, Cutwolfe had ordered him to open his mouth and had shot him in the throat so that Esdras could "neuer speake after, or repent him" (II, 326, 23).

As the horrified beholders call for Cutwolfe's death, the executioner needs little further persuasion but goes to work with artistic ingenuity. So shocked is Jack at the sight of the tortures inflicted on the criminal that he marries his courtesan, leaves Italy, and within forty days arrives at the English camp in France where Henry VIII is meeting the Emperor and the French King.

IV *Critical Commentary*

In the opening lines of the dedication of *The Unfortunate Traveller* Nashe refers to this pamphlet as a "phantasticall Treatise" which he hopes will provide his reader with "some reasonable conueyance of historie, & varietie of mirth" (II, 201, 17–18). He also acknowledges that he has written it in "a cleane different vaine" from his other compositions. Had he been a bit more explicit as to what this "vaine" was, he might have forestalled a great many pages of scholarly conjecture.

Since *The Unfortunate Traveller* is a narrative written in the first person like the modern autobiographical novel, many critics have tried to find a place for it in the evolution of the novel. In summarizing Nashe's sources, McKerrow somewhat skeptically mentions E. E. Jusserand's classification of this narrative with the Spanish picaresque romance *Lazarillo de Tormes*. McKerrow himself disagrees on the ground that the hero of the picaresque tale is a rogue, interesting only because of his knavery, whereas Jack Wilton is not a rogue at all, Indeed, McKerrow adds, had Jack been intended to be a "vulgar rogue and trickster," he would hardly have been shown as a friend of the Earl of Surrey (V, 23).

Yet those scholars favoring Jusserand's analysis qualify the term *picaresque* in various ways. Declaring that McKerrow has misunderstood "the real quality of a *picaro*," Fredson T. Bowers argues that Jack satisfies the requirements for an English version of that type.[1] He explains that "writers in the sixteenth and seventeenth centuries in England seldom regarded the Spanish picaresque novel as more than a collection of knavish jests."[2] As far as Jack's association with Surrey is concerned,

Bowers insists that the Earl is portrayed as "a gulled and ridiculous figure" whom Jack despises.[3] Accordingly Bowers concludes that "in *The Unfortunate Traveller*, even in a partly imperfect shape, Nashe produced the first English picaresque novel."[4] Similarly Arnold Kettle calls *The Unfortunate Traveller* "perhaps the most remarkable picaresque story in our language."[5] Like Bowers he maintains that Jack has "almost all the characteristics of the outcast rogue."[6] Although Kettle recognizes that Nashe was essentially a journalist and a pamphleteer, he still considers *The Unfortunate Traveller* a novel.[7] And Lionel Stevenson states that Nashe is writing "in the vein of the picaresque novel."[8] Stevenson explains that the Elizabethan journalist was "exploiting the picaresque novel as an antidote to sentimental romanticism."

Ernest A. Baker, on the contrary, maintains that "the one thing Nashe did not do was to imitate the Spanish rogue-story."[9] Moreover, this historian of the novel considers it "going too far" to call *The Unfortunate Traveller* "the first of the anti-romances." He prefers to define Nashe's realism as "an effort to present the romance of actuality." Yet Nashe's fondness for realism apparent in his allusions to historical events and personages has impelled a few scholars to term *The Unfortunate Traveller* the first historical novel. Nashe's disregard for chronological sequence is no obstacle to the reader familiar with *Kenilworth*, in which Sir Walter Scott introduces Shakespeare as a mature playwright, the well-known author of *A Midsummer Night's Dream*, when at the time of the Queen's visit to Kenilworth Castle he was only eleven years old. H. F. B. Brett-Smith in the introduction to his edition of the narrative is doubtful "whether or no" Nashe "was our first true picaresque writer," but he categorically declares that Nashe "certainly founded our historical novel."[10] Stevenson likewise agrees that *The Unfortunate Traveller* "can be classified as the first historical novel."[11] Even Hibbard begins his analysis with the statement, "It looks as though Nashe had stumbled on the historical novel long before anyone else" (p. 145).

Still other critics deny that *The Unfortunate Traveller* is a novel at all. Walter Allen, for example, declares that in the sense of that term as we use it today it does not qualify.[12] John Berryman in his edition of the tale holds a similar viewpoint.[13] As for its being "our first historical novel," Walter R. Davis states that "it certainly is not."[14] Altogether denying that it has any pretensions to realism and discounting as nonsense the suggestion that Jack Wilton is comparable to a character in a modern novel, Hibbard places himself on the negative side with the following statement:

At the back of all this theorizing lies the tacit assumption that in some way or other *The Unfortunate Traveller* is a novel, but, since Nashe shows no interest either in the telling of a coherent tale, or in the depiction of a consistent character, still less in the development of that character in response to events within a society that has some relation to actuality, it is hard to see how the assumption can be justified. (pp. 177–78)

Considering these manifest differences of opinion among scholars trying to stretch *The Unfortunate Traveller* on the procrustean bed of the novel, it is refreshing to find others willing to look at Nashe's tale as a unique art form.

The new approaches are mainly stylistic. Davis notes that the work is divided into three clearly defined parts within what he aptly calls "the travelogue frame."[15] Furthermore he admits that it has no clear beginning, middle, and end and adds that Nashe could have gone on to relate several more adventures without disturbing the form that he has adopted.[16]

Other scholars seeking to establish among the three parts that unity to which the reader of the novel is accustomed offer a variety of solutions. The most popular of these is to regard Jack as the connecting link. In spite of the fact that Richard H. Lanham on almost every page of his article calls *The Unfortunate Traveller* a novel, he remains uneasy about its form. Doubting that it is a "picaresque novel," a "satire," or a "random collection of jests and stylistic parodies," he terms it "a certain kind of fiction, one that poses a minor dilemma for critical theory."[17] Commenting that Nashe seems to draw "no fine line between himself and his fictional spokesman,"[18] Jack's (and hence Nashe's) personality becomes "the central form" of the novel.[19] Lanham suggests that its literary form may somehow be related to Nashe's own neurotic psychology and that, indeed, it may be a reflection of the author's subconscious mind which expresses itself in a "consistent pattern of anti-social violence."[20] Thus *The Unfortunate Traveller* emerges as "a fictional autobiography."[21] With this classification Davis seems to concur.[22]

Similarly Margaret Schlauch believes that the only unity in Nashe's narrative is "that supplied by the person of the fictional narrator."[23] Hibbard recognizes that it lacks the unity required in the true novel but points out that like *Pierce Penilesse* and *The Terrors of the Night* it is held together by "the personality of the author" (p. 178).

Alexander Leggatt, however, refuses to identify Jack as the hero of the typical novel. To him Jack is "not a coherent character but a series of effects":[24] the practical joker, the preacher, the thief, the penitent. Leggatt considers it out of place to speak of Jack as a "developing character" because Nashe gives no explanation why Jack's character changes.[25] According to Leggatt, Nashe obtains a sort of coherence by using devices which later novelists were to employ more purposefully, namely, interrelated strands of action, a coherent pattern of images associated with the frailty of the flesh, and a development in the central figure which in a way corresponds to the now familiar theme of the education of the hero. Stanley Wells fails to find any organizing principle whatsoever in the narrative: "It has no organizing principle; it is not a unified work of art."[26] He believes, however, that it provides the variety of mirth that Nashe promises his reader.

Although still convinced that the tale should be classified as a novel, or at least as a precursor of that form, Schlauch analyzes Nashe's dependence on the "hoary tricks of the rhetoricians," as for example in Heraclide's "inflated speech."[27] Using a similar approach Sister Marina Gibbons discovers a rhetorical pattern in Nashe's polemic throughout his pamphlet. His "frequent use of the oration" in recounting Jack's adventures is in her opinion sufficient proof of his "polemic bent": Jack's praise of the winekeeper in order to dispose him to accept advice, his use of persuasion in order to rid himself of the parasitic captain, the dilation on the Anabaptists, the ridiculous oration of Vanderhulke, Heraclide's appeal, Cutwolfe's defense, and so on.[28]

Agnes M. C. Latham concentrates on Nashe's satire. She finds it difficult to deny that *The Unfortunate Traveller* is "an early, perhaps an accidental, example of a historical novel."[29] But whatever he may have started out to write, he ended with "a spirited parody of popular literary themes and styles of the day."[30] Rather than a realist, he was "an artist in caricature."[31] Latham also seems inclined toward recognizing Nashe as a journalist rather than a novelist. But to her the word *journalist* is distasteful in that it "suggests among other things that he met and pandered to the public taste, however depraved that might be."[32] Consequently, although she enumerates all the topics included in the narrative that might satisfy the public taste for horrors, she excuses the author on the ground that these were so comprehensive that they must have been intended as burlesque. Her ultimate conclusion is that Nashe "is less the popular journalist playing to the crowd than the exuberant wit parodying stock commonplaces of Elizabethan journalism."[33]

Perhaps the most stimulating approaches to the study of Nashe's pamphlet and of his style in general come from those critics who have abandoned any attempt to classify *The Unfortunate Traveller* as a particular literary type and have turned to a minute examination of its rhetorical makeup. David Kaula, for example, believes that its originality must not be attributed to the fact that it has been termed the "first realistic novel in English," or that it resembles the picaresque novel.[34] He considers, indeed, that its reliance upon exaggeration and the macabre tends to lessen its verisimilitude. In his opinion the "chief distinction" of the narrative lies rather in the author's peculiar "stylistic dexterity." He notes that the tale is developed through a series of contrasts. He finds a pattern in its frequent images of physical violence offset by "certain allusions to the contrary, paradisiac condition."[35]

In his analysis of style, Kaula's chief contribution is to point out the alternation between passages of "ornamental rhetoric" and the "low," or colloquial, passages.[36] The "more elaborate rhetorical mode" develops the illusion being satirized, and the low style conveys "the elemental response to reality."[37] Within both modes Kaula indicates the rhythmical variations that make Nashe's descriptions effective.[38] As an example of the two styles Kaula cites the oration and execution of Cutwolfe. He feels that the "concentrated dramatic form and hyperbolic style" of the oration expresses "the same indomitable will which drove Cutwolfe to achieve his fantastic Italianate revenge and prompts him now to claim that through revenge man most nearly approaches the divine."[39] Contrasted with this rhetorical display is the description in Jack's "most colloquial manner" of the "efficient, workaday dismembering of [Cutwolfe's] body by the dexterous executioner." Kaula's view that Nashe deliberately sets out to "parody" or "debunk" literary and rhetorical modes[40] resembles Latham's earlier stated thesis, which has been somewhat qualified by Hibbard in his assertion that Nashe was an "improviser" rather than a purposeful reformer (pp. 146–47).

Another interesting stylistic analysis of *The Unfortunate Traveller* is that of Reinhard H. Friederich. Refusing to regard a majority of the passages and speeches in the narrative as "obvious parodies,"[41] he finds "apparently sincere lachrymose bombast" in *Christ's Teares* and "malicious satire, parody, and invective" in *Pierce Penilesse* and *Have with You* but none of these in *The Unfortunate Traveller*.[42] In Nashe's

choice of imagery, Friederich notes, the literary experience precedes
the visual one.[43] As Friederich expresses it, "particular schemes of
thought, or topoi, influence longer passages." The choice of words prepares the reader for a situation and also for the intended satire, if any.
Accepting Kaula's distinction between the elegiac or tragic high style
and the low style, Friederich remarks that Nashe uses "an extravagantly overdrawn style" for the orator in contrast to the speaker's
[Jack's] normally low style.[44] For example, Heraclide's plea containing
familiar rhetorical figures is convincing. As she proceeds, however, her
speeches become filled with even more elaborate rhetoric which Nashe
by no means intends as parody.

Friederich is convinced that what baffles the students of Nashe is
that since the ordinary reader of prose fiction "tends to base his first
judgment on contents rather than on form, he gets increasingly frustrated when the form bends contents and characters in a direction of
its own."[45] The exasperating ambiguity of Cutwolfe's oration, also
noted by Gibbons,[46] is disconcerting because it is not what the reader
would expect in a typical speech before an execution. In other words,
the avenger is "unsympathetic in literary terms."[47] Friederich concludes that Nashe may not "achieve the serious playfulness of the great
Baroque masters" but that his writings reveal "some of the excitements
and disturbances inherent in the work of art as a self-conscious *artistic*
problem."[48] In short, Friederich seems to have freed himself from the
tyranny of adherence to literary types and is willing to look at *The
Unfortunate Traveller* as an artistic masterpiece in its own right rather
than as a failure as a novel.

Although Hibbard does not actually provide a new category for
Nashe's tale, he leads his reader to it when he calls Jack's father Pierce
Penilesse (p. 149). He notes that in the midst of Jack's jests "the pamphleteer takes over from the story teller" (p. 151). The second part of
the narrative, indeed, Hibbard terms "undiluted pamphleteering" (p.
154). In other words, like the writer of an article in a modern Sunday
Times "Travel Section," Nashe is exploiting the associations that certain towns had for him and his readers. Hibbard also discards Latham's
theory that the Heraclide-Esdras episode is intended as parody since
Nashe is just as "excessive" in *Christ's Teares*, in which he obviously
is completely sincere (pp. 147, 169).

Entirely disagreeing with those critics who find expert characterization in Jack Wilton, Hibbard declares that Jack is not a realized human
being because of too many inconsistencies in the narration. As Hibbard

expresses it, "the evolution of the book was determined by two factors which apply to most of Nashe's other writings and which have no necessary connection with the novel at all: first, the need of the pamphleteer-journalist to get something down on paper, and secondly, the overpowering urge that this particular pamphleteer-journalist had to show his paces in as many kinds of writing as possible" (p. 178).

Hibbard's conclusion thus frees the critic from the dilemma of the traditional literary classification—a novel or not a novel. The student of Nashe, then, may evaluate *The Unfortunate Traveller* as a variant of the pamphlet or, if he must adhere to conventional forms, the sort of novel that a journalist might write.

CHAPTER 8

Nashe and Harvey

I   The Significance of the Quarrel

NASHE'S "quarrel with the Harvey family," as McKerrow terms it, was in his opinion "by far the most important event of Nashe's life as a man of letters" (V, 65). Yet Nashe's editor confesses bewilderment as to why the spectacle of two men abusing each other in print should attract the interest of Elizabethan writers and readers. Moreover, he feels uncertain of the true attitudes of the two contestants:

We cannot say for certain what was the first cause of the ill feeling , nor why the dispute was so long drawn out and so acrimonious, nor yet can we be sure how far it was inspired by actual enmity between the principals and how far by considerations of policy: how much was due to the desire of self-defense, and how much to that of self-advertisement. (V,66)

In keeping with our portrait of Nashe as an ambitious young journalist it would appear that among his motives for attacking Harvey both "policy" and "self-advertisement" played a much larger part than "enmity" or "self-defense." And a review of the main facts in the controversy will reveal that Harvey was almost equally ambitious to gain fame as what today would be termed a news correspondent.

II   The Background of the Controversy

Like most other "wars," this one was not a spontaneous phenomenon but may be traced back to incidents which at the time of their occurrence did not foreshadow the conflict to come. In 1580 a volume of letters between Gabriel Harvey and Edmund Spenser was published, supposedly by a "Wellwiller of the two Authors" who had received them from a "faithfull friende" who, in turn, had been given Spenser's permission to copy them.[1] In this volume, entitled *Three Proper and wittie Familiar Letters: lately passed betweene two Vniuersitie men touching the Earthquake in Aprill last, and our English refourmed Versifying,* is an essay entitled "Master H's short, but sharpe, and learned Iudgement of Earthquakes," which is so verbose and so pedantic that Harvey probably could never have found a printer for it alone and therefore had apparently passed it off as part of a letter to Spenser.

But the main subject of the Harvey-Spenser correspondence is the state of "English versifying," the discussion of which is begun in the first of the three letters by Spenser himself. After Harvey in the second letter delivers his "goodly discourse" on earthquakes, he devotes his third letter to the future of English prosody and to his theories concerning it. Assuming the position of mentor, Harvey presents his arguments for the use of the hexameter, in which the poet would concentrate on the proper use of long and short vowels and a uniform orthography. He supports his theories with numerous examples of his own composing and with comments on Spenser's similar experiments in the *Shepheardes Calendar*.

From Spenser's brief opening letter and Harvey's lengthy reply it is evident that the two men delighted in discussing poetic theory and in exchanging samples of their own compositions. They apparently also enjoyed playing jokes on their readers with false dedicatory letters and poems supposedly written by friends which would serve to advertise their writings. Wellwiller's fulsome praise of Harvey's two long letters with merely a condescending glance at Spenser's modest contribution suggests Harvey's own hand:

The first for a good familiar and sensible Letter [Spenser's], sure liketh me verye well, and gyueth some hope of good mettall in the Author, in whome I knowe myselfe to be verye good partes otherwise. But shewe me, or *Immerito* [Spenser], two Englyshe Letters in Printe, in all pointes equall to the other twoo [Harvey's], both for the matter it selfe, and also for the manner of handling, and saye, wee neuer sawe good Englishe Letter in our liues.[2]

This exaggerated outburst gives Wellwiller the opportunity to advertise Harvey's other literary achievements:

And yet I am credibly certified by the foresaide faithfull and honest friende, that himselfe hathe written manye of the same stampe bothe to Courtiers and others, and some of them discoursing vppon matter of great waight and importance, wherein he is said, to be fully as sufficient and hable, as in these schollerly pointes of Learning. The whiche Letters and Discourses I would very gladly see in Writing, but more gladly in Printe, if it might be obtayned.

Then, as if unable to restrain his admiration for Harvey, Wellwiller repeats his praise of the latter two letters:

And at this time to speake my conscience in a worde of *these two following,* I esteem them for twoo of the rarest, and finest Treaties, as wel for ingenious deuising, as also for significant vttering, & cleanly conueying of his matter, that euer I read in this Tongue: and I hartily thanke God for bestowing vppon vs some such proper and hable men with their penne, as I hartily thanke the Author himselfe, for vsing his pleasaunte, and witty Talente, with so muche discretion, and/with so little harme, contrarye to the veine of moste, whych haue thys singular conceyted grace in writing.

Furthermore, although Spenser's letter opens with the fairly conventional "To my long approued and singular good Frende, Master G. H.," Harvey's two letters are given flamboyant titles: the first, "A Pleasant and Pitthy Familiar discourse, of the Earthquake in Aprill last," and the second, "A Gallant familiar Letter, containing an Answere to that of M. *Immerito,* with sundry proper examples, and some Precepts of our Englissh reformed Versifying."

Harvey's high opinion of his own literary talents, which appears in all of his writings, is reflected in this exaggerated praise of these two very ordinary and comparatively dull letters. It does not seem too far-fetched, then, to accept Nashe's opinion that Harvey wrote his own dedicatory letter and published *Three Proper and wittie Familiar Letters* himself. Commenting on this alleged literary deception Nashe writes as follows:

Signior Immeritò (so called because *he was and is his friend* vndeseruedly) was counterfeitly brought in to play a part in that his Enterlude of Epistles that was hist at, thinking his very name (as the name of *Ned Allen* on the common stage) was able to make an ill matter good.
    I durst on my credit vndertake, *Spencer* was no way priuie to the committing of them to the print. Committing I may well call it, for in my opinion *G. H.* should not haue reapt so much discredite by beeing/committed to Newgate, as by committing that misbeleeuing prose to the Presse. . . .
    . . . but for an Author to renounce his Christendome to write in his owne commendation, to refuse the name which his Godfathers and Godmothers gaue him in his baptisme, and call himselfe *a welwiller to both the writers,* when hee is the onely writer himselfe; with what face doe you thinke hee can aunswere it at the day of iudgement? (I, 295, 35 ff.)

Then, after quoting Wellwiller's two laudatory passages, Nashe asserts, "You must conceit, hee was in his chamber-fellowe *wel-willers* cloke

when he spake this: the white-liuerd slaue was modest, and had not the
hart to say so much in his owne person, but he must put on the vizard
of an undiscreete friend."

Similarly E. K.'s dedicatory letter in the *Shepheardes Calendar*,
beginning "To the most excellent and learned both Orator and Poete,
Mayster Gabriell Haruey," and ending with a postscript advertising
Harvey's "so many excellent English poemes,"[3] would suggest that
Harvey once again is assuming that pseudonym "to write in his own
commendation," as Nashe expresses it. This identification is hinted at
in *Three Proper and wittie Familiar Letters*, in which the two writers
exchange confidences ostensibly intelligible to each other but meaning-
less to the reader who lacks the key to the secret. Spenser, for example,
tells Harvey that in a "Glosse (running continually in maner of a
Paraphrase)" to his *Dreames* he has included "many things wittily dis-
coursed of E. K."[4] In the second volume of letters published the same
year, *Two other very commendable Letters of the same mens writing: both touching the foresaid Artificiall Versifying, and certain
other Particulars*, Spenser again makes a vague, somewhat ambiguous
reference to E. K.: "Maister E. K. hartily desireth to be commended
vnto your Worshippe: of whome what accompte he maketh, your selfe
shall hereafter perceiue, by hys paynefull and dutifull Verses of your
selfe."[5] Since Spenser nowhere else in his letters resorts to abbreviations
or to any other ambiguity of personal reference, this pointless secrecy
regarding the identity of E. K. suggests a playfulness parallelled by
Harvey's allusion to the *Shepheardes Calendar* in *Three Proper and
wittie Familiar Letters*, where he refers to Cuddie, one of the pastoral
characters in that poem, as *"alias* you know who."[6]

These harmless deceptions ordinarily might have passed with the
two volumes of Harvey-Spenser letters into well-deserved oblivion but
for an ill-advised attempt at satire by Harvey himself. Among his
examples of the English hexameter he includes a satirical poem
describing the Italianate Englishman, whom Roger Ascham a few
years before in his *Scholemaster* had condemned as the devil incarnate[7]—in other words, a popular Elizabethan type suitable for caricature. For some reason or other—Chauncey Sanders attributes it to
Harvey's unpopularity among his fellow students at Cambridge[8]—
John Lyly called the attention of his patron, the Earl of Oxford, to
Harvey's poem and induced the earl to believe that it satirized him.
Almost ten years later, without admitting that he himself was the
informer, Lyly, in *Pappe with a Hatchet* (1589), refers to Harvey as
a writer who "writing a familiar Epistle about the naturall causes of an

Earthquake, fell into the bowells of libelling, which made his eares quake for feare of clipping."[9] In the deleted section of Greene's *Quippe for an Vpstart Courtier* (1592), possibly written by Nashe, Harvey is said to have been "orderly clapt in the Fleet" for being "the first that invented Englishe Hexameter" and for composing "other familiar letters and proper treatises."

In *Foure Letters and Certaine Sonnets* Harvey in his own defense admits that he was accused of libel but denies that he ever was imprisoned:

. . . an other company of speciall good fellowes, (whereof he was none of the meanest that brauely threatned to coniure-vpp one, which should massacre Martins wit, or should bee lambackd himself with ten years prouision [Lyly in *Pappe with a Hatchet*] would needs forsooth verye courtly perswade the Earle of Oxforde, that some thing in those letters, and namely, the Mirrour of Tuscanismo, was palpably intended against him; whose noble Lordeship I protest I neuer meante to dishonour with the least preiudicial word of my Tongue, or pen. . . . But the noble Earle, not disposed to trouble his Iouiall mind with such Saturnine paltery still continued, like his magnificent selfe: and that Fleeting also proued, like the other, a silly bullbeare, a sorry puffe of winde, a thing of nothing.[10]

And in his second reply to Nashe, *Pierce's Supererogation*, Harvey specifically names Lyly as his accuser:

Papp-hatchet, desirous for his benefit, to currie fauour with/a noble Earle, and in defecte of other meanes of Commendation, labouring to insinuate himselfe by smooth glosing, & counterfait suggestions (it is a Courtly feate, to snatch the least occasionet of aduantage, with a nimble dexteritie); some years since prouoked me, to make the best of it, inconsideratly: to speake like a frend, vnfrendly; to say, as it was, intolerably; without priuate cause, or any reason in the world: (for in truth I looued him, in hope praysed him; many wayes fauored him, and neuer any way offended him). . . .[11]

Yet doubt is cast on Harvey's denial of even a brief imprisonment in the Fleet because of references in his earlier discussion of "those infortunate Letters" not only to his "publike displeasure" but also to his "inestimable, and infinite displeasure" experienced in connection with the alleged libelling.[12] Whatever the truth of the matter may have been, this early literary indiscretion provided Nashe with ammunition in his first signed attack on Gabriel Harvey in *Strange Newes*.

The next incidents contributing to the creation of ill will between Nashe and the Harveys were Richard Harvey's sneering comments: first, a fairly general attack on Lyly and the other anti-Martinists in *Plaine Percevall;* and second, a bitterly personal criticism of Nashe in the *Lamb of God.* McKerrow surmises that Lyly's reference in *Pappe with a Hatchet* to the charge of libeling the Earl of Oxford which resulted from the publication of Harvey's *Three Proper and wittie Familiar Letters* might have induced Richard to write *Plaine Percevall* (V, 75). McKerrow points out that according to its title page it was intended to "botch vp a Reconciliation between Mar-ton and Mar-tother" but that it actually spent most of its criticism on the anti-Martinists, specifically mentioning "the Cooke Ruffian, that drest a dish for Martins diet," namely, Lyly.

Richard's second pamphlet, the *Lamb of God,* was entered in the Stationers' Register on October 23, 1589, about the time of the publication of his first pamphlet (V, 172). However, it was composed after the appearance of Greene's *Menaphon* with Nashe's preface containing his list of the names of contemporary writers who graced the English literary scene, including Gabriel Harvey (III, 320, 28). In *Strange Newes* Nashe ridicules the *Lamb of God* as "a learned booke, a labourd booke" made up of the sermons that Richard had preached "three yere before he put it in print" (I, 270, 27). To this dull pamphlet he had attached an epistle "To the fauourable or indifferent *Reader,*" in which he rebuked Nashe by name for presuming to set himself up as a critic even though brother Gabriel was included among the foremost writers of the day:

I was loth to enter this discourse, but vppon request where I might be commaunded: I prouoke not any but *Martin* who prouoketh all men: I was desired to giue like iudgement of certaine other, but it becummeth me not to play that part in Diuinitie, that one *Thomas Nash* hath lately done in humanitie, who taketh vppon him in ciuill learning, as *Martin* doth in religion, peremptorily censuring his betters at pleasure, Poets, Orators, Polihistors, Lawyers, and whome not? and making as much and as little of euery man as himselfe listeth. Many a man talketh of *Robin Hood,* that neuer shot in his bowe; and that is the rash presumption of this age, that euery man of whatsoeuer qualitie and perfection, is with euery man of whatsoeuer mediocrity, but as euery man pleaseth in the aboundance of his owne swelling sense. Iwis this *Thomas Nash,* one whome I neuer heard of before (for I cannot imagin him to be *Thomas Nash* our Butler of *Pembrooke Hall,* albeit peraduenture not much better learned) sheweth himselfe none of the meetest men, to censure Sir *Thomas Moore*, Sir *Iohn Cheeke*, Doctor *Watson*, Doctor *Haddon*, Maister *Ascham*, Doctor *Car*, my brother Doctor *Haruey*, and such like; yet the iolly man will needes be playing the douty *Martin* in his kinde, and limit euery mans commendation according to his fancy, profound no doubt and exceeding learned, as the world nowe goeth in such worthy workes. (V, 179–80)

Then he urges Nashe and other young upstarts like him to practice humility as they acquire knowledge:

Good my maisters, either study more, or presume lesse: excellent learning and perfit iudgement is not so easily gotten, either in diuinity or in humanity: you may soone be of resolute opinion in both, but resolute iudgement either in the one or in the other is not euery mans gift, I speake not without consideration, howbeit, if I erre more or lesse either in this or any other point, as I and my betters are subiect to error, I am ready to submit my opinion to euery sounder reason, and will neuer stand in contention with any better iudgement. Yet let not *Martin*, or *Nash*, or any such famous obscure man, or any other piperly makeplay or makebate, presume ouermuch of my patience as of simplicitie, but of choice. As I am easily ruled by reason, so no feirce or prowde passion can ouerrule me; no carping Censour, or vayne Paphatchet, or madbraine Scoggin or gay companion, any thing moue me; no man reddyer to yeeld to a good argument euen against my selfe, but light words and toyes I can as lightly contemne.

But the very fact that Nashe in his preface to *Menaphon* includes Gabriel Harvey among the foremost English writers of the day would indicate that before Richard's insulting attack he himself had felt no ill will toward the Harvey family.

For two years Richard's pretense that he at first had mistaken the author of the preface to *Menaphon* for "our butler of *Pembrooke Hall*" went without comment from Nashe. McKerrow expresses amazement that the writers criticized in Richard's epistle should have delayed to reply until the publication of the *Quippe* under the name of Robert Greene (V, 77 n.). But McKerrow seems to overlook the fact that only three writers are mentioned: two by pseudonym, Martin and Paphatchet, and one by his real name, Nashe. Lyly may have felt that his remark in *Pappe with a Hatchet* about the alleged libeling was sufficient attention to the Harveys. Nashe, who was the real butt of Richard's bitter pen, would be the logical man to reply.

As a possible explanation for Nashe's delay, McKerrow suggests that he may have been waiting for Greene (V, 78). But during the period

1590–92 Nashe was working on his first important pamphlet, *Pierce Penilesse*, the composition of which in McKerrow's opinion "extended over a considerable period" (V, 18). This task doubtless meant more to him than a reply to the Vicar's sour comments on his lack of proper reverence for the great writers of his time. If the deleted attack on the Harveys in the *Quippe* was Nashe's doing, as has been suggested,[13] then Nashe, with good reason, as McKerrow believes, would regard it as his "direct reply to the *Lamb of God* (v, 77 n.).

This first attempt at retaliation on Nashe's part, however, was frustrated by Greene's fatal illness, as a result of which the passage attacking the Harveys was deleted soon after printing had begun. At the time two different reasons were advanced for this deletion. Harvey states that Greene, fearful of being charged with libel, had offered ten or twenty shillings to the printer to suppress the offending passage. Nashe, on the contrary, holds that it was deleted at the request of Greene's physician out of deference for the medical profession, one of whose members, John Harvey, was ridiculed in it. A third reason why Greene may have felt free to excise it is that he probably did not write it.

III   Harvey's Reaction to the Quippe

Before Greene was able to have the passage attacking the Harveys removed from every copy of the *Quippe*, some copies were published. One of these fell into the hands of Gabriel Harvey, who at the end of August 1592 had come to London on business. Incensed by this personal attack on his family and himself, he inquired for the whereabouts of Greene, under whose name the *Quippe* had been published. He learned that Greene was lying dangerously ill at a shoemaker's house near Dowgate. Before Harvey had decided how to proceed against him, Greene, whom he had never met, passed away. Like a typical journalist Harvey immediately rushed to the scene of the action in order to get all the details of Greene's final illness and death, reportedly caused by "a surfett of pickle herringe and rennish wine."[14]

He visited the shoemaker's house where Greene had spent his final hours and talked with the man's wife, Greene's "hostisse *Isam*." With all the flair of a veteran newsman Harvey reports what she had to tell him of Greene's dying moments:

He neuer enuyed me so much, as I pittied him from my hart: especially when his hostisse *Isam* with teares in her eies, & sighes from a deeper fountaine,

(for she loued him derely) tould me of his lamentable begging of a penny
pott of Malmesy: and, sir reuerence how lowsy he, and the mother of Infortunatus [Greene's illegitimate son] were (I would her Surgeon found her no
worse, then lowsy:) and how he was faine poor soule, to borrow her husbandes
shirte, whiles his owne was a washing: and how his dublet, and hose, and
sword were sold for three shillinges: and beside the charges of his winding
sheete, which was foure shillinges; and the charges of hys buriall/yesterday
[September 4], in the New-churchyard neere Bedlam, which was six shillinges, and four pence: how deeply hee was indebted to her poore husbande;
as appeered by hys own bonde of tenne poundes: which the good woman
kindly shewed me: and beseeched me to read the writting beneath: which
was a letter to his abandoned wife, in the behalfe of his gentle host: not so
short as persuasible in the beginning, and pittiful in the ending.

> *Doll, I charge thee by the loue of our youth, & by my soules rest, that*
> *thou wilte see this man paide: for if hee, and his wife had not succoured*
> *me, I had died in the streetes.*
>   Robert Greene[15]

Harvey concludes his vivid account of Greene's final moments with the
description of Mistress Isam's touching tribute to the writer:
". . . whome his sweete hostisse, for a tender farewell, crowned with a
Garland of Bayes." But Harvey could not resist adding the spiteful
comment: " . . . to shew, that a tenth Muse honoured him more being
deade, than all the nine honoured him aliue."[16]

This report of Greene's pathetic departure from the world is dated
September 5. On the basis of Nashe's distinction in *Have with You to
Saffron-Walden* between Harvey's "first butter-fly Pamphlet against
Greene" (III, 130, 35) and "hys Booke he writ against *Greene*" and
himself (III, 131, 1–2) McKerrow theorizes that the second letter in
substance appeared in print before the publication of *Foure Letters* as
we now have it (IV, 153). In this preliminary publication Harvey, without mentioning Nashe by name, implies that Nashe had deserted his
friend before his death:

Alas, euen his fellow-writer, a proper yong man if aduised in time, that was
a principall guest at that fatall banquet of pickle herring, (I spare his name,
and in some respectes wish him well) came neuer more at him: but either
would not, or happily could not, performe the duty of an affectionate, and
faithfull frend.[17]

But little did Harvey realize how this supercilious accusation would
gall Nashe into action.

IV   *Nashe's First Acknowledged Reply to Richard Harvey*

Even though Nashe had succeeded in getting his attack on the Harveys in only a few copies of the *Quippe*, he was determined that some sort of reply should be published. Accordingly, in his illustrations of the deadly sin of wrath in *Pierce Penilesse*, almost finished by the summer of 1592—McKerrow dates its publication about September 1 of that year—Nashe interpolated an attack on Richard Harvey as a sample of his new "railing" or "martinizing" style.

This passage, which McKerrow terms an "afterthought" (V, 78), is a digression from Nashe's main theme, which is to present "news from Hell" citing examples of each of the Seven Deadly Sins in contemporary London. He does not refer to Richard by name but identifies him only as an anti-Aristotelian, the author of "an absurd *Astrologicall Discourse* of the terrible Coniunction of *Saturne* and *Iupiter*" (I, 196, 17–18), a vicar, the author of a "Sheepish discourse of the Lambe of God and his enemies," and the son of a ropemaker (I, 198, 7 ff.). Although he accuses Richard of publishing one of his almanacs—probably the *Astrologicall Addition* to the *Astrologicall Discourse*—under his brother's (i.e., John's) name, he does not mention Gabriel, whose literary talents he had already complimented in his preface to *Menaphon*. His reply to the unnamed vicar, he maintains, was written on the spur of the moment. But if he were given time, he adds, he would compose a masterpiece of railing that would astonish the world. Now, pressed for time, he is writing, as he puts it, "*Quicquid in buccam venerit*, as fast as my hand can trot" (I, 195, 19–20).

Concluding this example of his railing style, he proudly addresses his reader:

Redeo ad vos mei Auditores, haue I not an indifferent prittye vayne in Spurgalling an Asse? if you knew how extemporall it were at this instant, and with what hast it is writ, you would say so. (I, 199, 4–7)

His real purpose in attacking Richard Harvey comes out in his next sentence, in which he explains that he is merely giving the reader the pleasure of sampling his invectives:

But I would not haue you thinke that all this that is set downe heere is in good earnest, for then you goe by S. *Gyles*, the wrong way to *Westminster*: but onely to shewe howe for a neede I could rayle, if I were throughly fyred. (I, 199, 7–11)

This explanation he immediately backs up with a series of questions designed to emphasize that his railing is inspired by a spirit of fun rather than of anger:

So ho, *Honiger Hammon*, where are you all this while, I cannot be acquainted with you? Tell me, what do you thinke of the case? am I subiect to the sinne of Wrath I write against, or no, in whetting my penne on this blocke? I know you would faine haue it so, but it shall not choose but be otherwise for this once. (I, 199, 11–16)

Incidentally, in this explanation that his attack on Richard is not personal but just a means of "whetting" his "penne," he invents the epithet *Honiger Hammon*. This unusual name, McKerrow notes, is "the first of a very large number of fancy names which Nashe gives to the Harveys" (IV, 124). And like most of the epithets to follow, McKerrow finds it impossible to gloss.

V *Harvey's Reply to* Pierce Penilesse

Between September 5, 1590, when the second letter was written, and September 8 and 9, as the third letter is dated, Harvey read *Pierce Penilesse*. The first section of the third letter he devotes to a general defense of himself with particular attention to his alleged indiscretion in publishing his correspondence with Spenser in 1580. Then he takes up what he naturally assumes were Greene's—not Nashe's—charges in the *Quippe* regarding his invention of the English hexameter, his imprisonment in the Fleet, and his two brothers' shortcomings. The main part of this letter, however, is devoted to a reply to Nashe's attack on Richard and John in *Pierce Penilesse*.

It is introduced with a series of obvious puns typical of Harvey's heavy-handed humor:

. . . and who can tell, what dowty yoonker may next gnash with his teeth?. . . Flourishing M. *Greene* is most-wofully faded, and whilest I am bemoaning his ouer-pitteous decay; & discoursing the vsual successe of such ranke wittes, Loe all on the suddaine, his sworne brother, M. *Pierce Pennilesse*, (still more paltery, but what remedy? we are already ouer shoes, and must now go through) Loe his inwardest companion, that tasted of the fatall herringe, cruelly pinched with want, vexed with discredite, tormented with other mens felicitie, and ouer-whelmed with his own misery; in a rauing, and franticke moode, most desperately exhibiteth his supplication to the Diuell.[18]

In this section Harvey's lack of humor is particularly evident. Taking Nashe's complaints of poverty and misfortune at face value, he alternately scolds him and sympathizes with him.

First he scoffs at Nashe as a mere imitator of "the stile, and tenour of Tarletons president, his famous play of the seauen Deadly sinnes." Then he adds insult to injury by repeating his brother's original association of Nashe with "the maister butler of Pembroke Hal."[19] After repeating many of Nashe's railing phrases,[20] Harvey without warning completely reverses himself and suggests a reconciliation:

I hope this winde hath not shaken any suche corne, but fellow-schollers, (as Doctor Caius would say), and now forsooth fellow-writers, may bee made friendes with a cup of white wine, and some little familiar conference, in calme and ciuile termes. I offer them my hande: and request their: which I will accept thanckfully: & kiss louinglye. . . .[21]

He even goes so far as to return Nashe's compliment given him in the preface to *Menaphon* shortly before Richard had launched his attack. Even though he has just ridiculed Nashe's style, he proceeds to list him among the greatest writers of the age:

Good sweete Oratour, be a deuine Poet indeede: and vse heauenly Eloquence indeede: and employ thy golden talent with amounting vsance indeede: and with heroical Cantoes honour right Vertue, & braue valour indeede: as noble Sir Philip Sidney and gentle Maister Spencer haue done, with immortal Fame: and I will bestow more complements of rare amplifications vpon thee, then euer any bestowed vppon them: or this Tounge euer affoorded. . . . Such liuely springes of streaming Eloquence: & such right-Olympicall hilles of amountinge witte: I cordially recommend to the deere Louers of the Muses: and namely, to the professed Sonnes of the-same: *Edmond Spencer, Richard Stanihurst, Abraham France, Thomas Watson, Samuell Daniell, Thomas Nash,* and the rest, whome I affectionately thancke for their studious endeuours, commendably employed in enriching, & polishing their natiue tongue, neuer so furnished, or embellished as/of late.[22]

Apparently he hoped that with these flattering comparisons he might mollify Nashe into silence.

Failing to recognize the ability of his opponent, however, he unconsciously was providing him with ammunition for future attacks. For instance, with reference to the allusions in the *Quippe* to his father as a ropemaker, Harvey writes:

Euery man is to answere for hys own defaultes: my trespasse is not my fathers, nor my fathers mine: A Gibeline may haue a Guelph to his sonne, as Barthol saith: & hath neuer a Saint had a Reprobate to his father?[23]

Such comments as these, typical of Harvey's ineptness in sparring with a nimble-witted satirist like Nashe, were soon to be turned against the writer.

VI   *Nashe's First Direct Attack on Harvey*

Had Harvey not attacked Nashe in the third letter, the relatively mild treatment of his brother in *Pierce Penilesse* might have ended the matter. Moreover, Nashe himself in *Strange Newes* asserts that until the publication of *Foure Letters* he had never spoken or written anything derogatory of its author (I, 268, 34–269, 2). Of course, the attack in the *Quippe* had been published under Greene's name. And in addition to the compliment paid Harvey in the preface to *Mena-phon*, Nashe in *Strange Newes* confesses that while a student at Cambridge "and but a childe" he was a mildly enthusiastic admirer of the distinguished scholar, not knowing that he was the brother of Richard, whom he had "alwaies grudgd at for writing against *Aristotle*" (I, 269, 16 ff.).

Ignoring the ambiguity of Harvey's criticism, alternately scornful and cajoling, Nashe in *Strange Newes* impresses the reader with the zest with which he enters the lists. As McKerrow describes it, "it is difficult to resist the idea that its purpose was rather to bring the writer and his wit into notice than to clear him of the aspersions cast upon him" (V, 88). His main interest seems to be to entertain his reader with his railing style. Here at last was his opportunity to carry out his promise made in *Pierce Penilesse* that if anyone were to criticize him again as Richard Harvey had criticized him, he would "raile on him soundly . . . in some elaborate, pollished Poem" to be left to posterity as a "liuing Image to all ages" of "beggerly parsimony and ignoble illiber-altie" (I, 195, 13 ff.). The first of these "Poems" is *Strange Newes*.

CHAPTER 9

Nashe's First Reply to Harvey

I   *Its Dedication*

THE complete title of Nashe's first reply to Harvey's *Foure Letters* is *Strange Newes of the Intercepting Certaine Letters, and a Conuoy of Verses, as they were going Priuilie to victuall the Low Countries*. The scatological puns doubtless were inspired by two lines from an abusive sonnet directed against Greene, supposedly written by Harvey's friend Christopher Bird, in the first letter of Harvey's pamphlet:

> Sir reuerence, A scuruy Master of Art [Greene]
> Aunsweared inough with a Doctors fart.[1]

With such inept and tasteless passages as this Harvey was unwittingly opening himself up to ridicule.

In Nashe's dedicatory essay addressed to "Maister Apis lapis" in the midst of praising the pleasures of wine, concerning which the dedicatee apparently was a connoisseur, Nashe abruptly introduces the subject of his pamphlet, namely, the Harvey family. Whimsically paraphrasing Bird's description of the elder Harvey as "a right honest man of good reckoninge" who "hath mainetained foure sonnes in *Cambridge*,"[2] Nashe simply writes, "An honest man of Saffron Walden kept three sonnes at the Vniuersitie together a long time" (I, 256, 7–8), and immediately returns to his dedication. A few lines further on he quotes from Bird's distasteful sonnet the phrase which could logically be construed to describe Harvey's answer to Greene:

> There is a *Doctor* and his *Fart* that haue kept a foule stinking stirre in Paules Churchyard . . . this dodipoule, this didopper, this professed poetical braggart, hath raild vpon me, without wit or art, in certaine foure penniworth of Letters and three farthing-worth of sonnets. (I, 256, 33 ff.)

117

For the next few lines he continues with his dedication. Then he ties the two opening statements of theme together with a jibe at another of Harvey's humorless lapses, his defense of his father's trade and of himself as his father's son:

A fellow that I am to talke with by and by [Harvey], being told that his Father was a Rope-maker, excused the matter after this sort; *And hath neuer saint had reprobate to his father?* They are his owne wordes, hee cannot goe from them. You see heere hee makes a *Reprobate* and a *Ropemaker, voces conuertibiles*. (I, 257, 22–27)

Nashe concludes his dedication with a request for a drink for good luck in his forthcoming contest.

II *Nashe's Letter to the Gentlemen Readers*

The dedication is followed by a letter to the Gentlemen Readers, in which Nashe complains that certain passages in *Pierce Penilesse* have been willfully misinterpreted. This is his first reference to his ill-fated political-religious allegory of the Bear and the Fox (I, 259, 27 ff.). He warns his readers that he is satirizing vices and not individuals. His own fear of misinterpretation recalls to his mind Harvey's difficulties twelve years before when he was accused of libel because of his satiric portrait of the Italianate Englishman in *Three Proper and wittie Familiar Letters*. And turning to Harvey's most recent pamphlet of letters, Nashe with seeming exasperation exclaims, " . . . still he must be running on the *letter*, and abusing the Queenes English without pittie or mercie" (I, 261, 17–18). Then he designates Richard Harvey's *Lamb of God* as the beginning of his dispute with the Harveys. Crying "Saint Fame for mee," he plunges into his confutation.

III *Nashe's Comments on Harvey's Prefatory Material*

In his opening sentence Nashe again laughs at Harvey for adopting the medium of the letter in order to attack Greene and calls him a "Fawneguest Messenger twixt Maister *Bird* and Maister *Demetrius*." Selecting a phrase from Harvey's title page, "some matters of note,"

Nashe puns on the word *note* and incidentally condemns Harvey as a
poor poet and a "mountebancke of strange wordes" (I, 261, 21):

I agree with thee there are in it *some matters of Note*, for there are a great
many barefoote rimes in it, that goe as iumpe as a Fiddle with euery ballet-
makers note: and if according to their manner, you had tun'd them ouer the
head, it had beene nere the worse, for by that meanes you might haue had
your name chaunted in euery corner of the streete, then the which there can
be nothing more *melodiouslie addoulce* to your *deuine Entelechy*. O they
would haue trowld off brauely to the tune of *O man in Desperation*, and,
like *Marenzos* Madrigals, the mournefull note naturally haue affected the
miserable Dittie.
    Doe you know your owne misbegotten bodgery *Entelechy* and *addoulce?*
With these two Hermophrodite phrases, being halfe Latin and halfe English,
hast thou puld out the very guts of the inkehorne. (I, 265,10–24)

Still punning on Harvey's title page, Nashe writes that if the "curteous
mindes," to which Harvey directs his letters, are away from home, let
them be delivered to "*Megge Curtis* in Shoreditch to stop mustard pots
with." Nashe likewise laughs at Harvey's table of contents.

    With Harvey's heavy, opaque opening sentence in his dedicatory
letter—

May I craue pardon at this instant, as well for enditinge, that is vnwoorthy to
be published, as for publishing, that was vnworthy to be endited: I wil hereafter take precise order, either neuer to importune you more, or to sollicite
you for more especiall cause[3]

—Nashe has a field day:

The learned Orator in this Epistle *taketh precise order* he will not be too
eloquent, and yet it shall be (L,) *as well for enditing vnworthie to be published, as for publishing vnworthy to be endited*. (I, 267, 9–12)

Where Harvey writes, " . . . albeit against those, whose owne Pamflets
are readier to condemne them, then my Letters forwarde to accuse
them,"[4] Nashe deliberately reverses the balanced phrases:

Hee forebeares to speake much in this place of the one or the other, *because
his letters are more forward to accuse them than their owne books to condemne them.* (I, 267, 22–24)

As the excuse for this reversal, he repeats Harvey's slighting remarks on both Greene and himself: Greene is "pitifully blasted and faded," and Pierce Penilesse, or Nashe, is "the Deuils Orator by profession, and his Dames Poet by practice."

Nashe maintains that Pierce Penilesse has no more right to be called the "Deuils Orator" for making a supplication to the Devil than Harvey has to be honored with the title "Rhethoritian" for using the phrase "G. Harueii Rhetor" (which Nashe parodies as *Gabrielis Scuruei Rhetor*) on the title page of his oration on Cicero published in 1577. Nashe spitefully suggests that Harvey himself might well have earned the title "Deuils Orator" when he failed to win the oratorship of the university and consequently stooped to slander Dr. Perne, as well as Greene and other deceased persons (I, 268, 8 ff.).

The title "Dames Poet" much mystifies Nashe. But he presumes that Harvey invented it because "*Pierce* his father," that is, Nashe, was "*Dame Laws*. Poet, and writte many goodly stories of her in *An Almond for a Parrat*." Thus he implicitly accepts the authorship of that anti-Martinist pamphlet.

Harvey's expressed desire to withdraw from the controversy at this point Nashe recognizes for the rhetorical device that it quite obviously is: " . . . *id est*, when hee hath come behind a man and broke his head"—an allusion to the vicious attacks on both Nashe and Green in the main section of Harvey's pamphlet. In reply to his opponent's mutterings of "defamation and iust commendation," Nashe merely notes Harvey's evident embarrassment at being reminded of his father's occupation: " . . . what a hell it is for him, that hath built his heauen in vaine-glory, to bee puld by the sleeue and bidde *Respice funem* [Remember the rope], looke backe to his Fathers house." Moreover, he adds, those people who know Harvey's pharisaical nature will not believe that he is being slandered.

At this point Nashe denies that he had ever in all his life "in the least worde or tittle" spoken or written in a derogatory way about Harvey until his brother Richard without any provocation had compared him to Martin and had taken from him "all estimation of Art or witte" (I, 269, 1 ff.). And he asks, " . . . haue I not cause to bestirre mee?" Harvey, on the other hand, has published more than 200 lies about him. Had they been witty or merry lies, Nashe adds, he would not have cared. But they were palpable, damned, monstrous lies, "as big as one of the Guardes chynes of beefe." Actually, he points out, when he was in Cambridge, he was "indifferently perswaded" of Harvey himself, for he assumed from that scholar's apparel and manner of walking that he was a "fine fellow." Nashe never dreamed, however, that he was the brother of "*Io. Paean,*" that is, Richard, who had written *Ephemeron sive Paean* (IV, 121). Little did Nashe then think that this apparently distinguished individual was one of the "Hs of Hempe Hall"—another jest on the elder Harvey's trade. Hence, by coming to Richard's aid, Gabriel had completely destroyed the earlier good impression that he had made on Nashe.

Next Nashe refers to the short insertion about the Harveys in the *Quippe.* If Harvey complains that this reference to the family was abusive, Nashe asks which, Greene or himself, is guilty or are they both guilty? If the elder Harvey was abused by Greene and not by Nashe, then his son Gabriel should have attacked only Greene. If both are guilty, Nashe will answer for both. Or if he alone is guilty, he will answer for himself. With these ambiguous comments he conceals any part that he may have had in this pamphlet.

Furthermore he challenges Harvey to point out an instance in *Pierce Penilesse* wherein he "had so much as halfe a sillables relation" to him or "offred one iot of indignitie" to his father (I, 270, 1–2) . The only allusion to the elder Harvey was the reference to Richard as "the sonne of a Ropemaker." Surely, continues Nashe, Gabriel is not a "good sonne" if he is ashamed of his father's occupation, nor will he ever thrive if he despises the trade to which he himself is beholding. If his father had had "no traffike with the hangman," his learned son could never have had any shoes. If Nashe had had a ropemaker for a father, he adds with tongue in cheek, and somebody had accused him of it, he would have "writ in praise of Ropemakers & prou'd it by sound sillogistry to be one of the 7. liberal sciences." And the reader, by this time cognizant of Nashe's wit, knows that he is telling the truth.

The reasons for Nashe's falling-out with the Harveys, he asserts, were, first, Richard's "blundring" interference between the Martinists and the anti-Martinists in *Plaine Percevall* and, second, his attack on Nashe, Lyly, and other writers in the *Lamb of God.* The suspicion that Gabriel may have been involved in this attack prompted the insertion of "some seauen or eight lines" concerning the three Harvey brothers in the *Quippe* (I, 271, 15–25). Nashe interrupts this explanation with a rebuke to his opponent for abusing a dead man. Then he continues to comment on Richard's lack of literary ability in the *Lamb of God,* particularly his outlandish vocabulary and his affected citation of authorities. Here Nashe specifically selects certain passages which he interprets as indicating Richard's lecherous nature, earlier hinted at in the offending passage in the *Quippe*. Although Richard may be writing in metaphors, Nashe presumes that if in a theological treatise or in the pulpit he discusses the opening of the senses by "carnal mixture," which Nashe defines as "the very act of lecherie," he may privately practice what he preaches (I, 273, 16–17).

IV *Nashe's Refutation of Harvey's First Letter*

Returning to *Foure Letters* Nashe points out that the first letter from Bird when compared with Harvey's own writing turns out to be a letter written by Harvey himself with Bird's name affixed. Actually, Nashe continues, no matter who wrote it, it is merely a certificate of good character, which he himself would not accept as genuine unless the town seal were impressed on it. The statement in it that the *Quippe* is "one of the most licentious, and intollerable Inuectiues"[5] because it abuses the elder Harvey utterly baffles Nashe. How, he asks, is the old man abused merely by a reference to his craft? The remainder of the letter Nashe laughs to scorn. And in the sonnet at the end of it, also supposedly by Bird, Nashe recognizes Harvey's style, especially in the line referring to poetry "with shortest vowels, and with longest mutes."[6] Harvey's unusual use of the word *mute* in his discussions of metrics Nashe promises to point out as he goes along.

V *Nashe's Refutation of Harvey's Second Letter*

At Harvey's formality in writing Bird that "in the absence of M. *Demetrius*" he had found Mistress Demetrius "very courteous,"[7] Nashe pretends to be scandalized. He urges his opponent to keep such favors as this to himself: "A woman is well holpen vp that does you any curtesie in the absence of her husband, when you cannot keepe it to yourselfe, but you must blab it in print" (I, 276, 9–11). Recalling, however, that he had heard Mistress Demetrius to be a modest, sober woman, he desists from playing any further on Harvey's awkward admission. Nevertheless he takes this occasion to warn not only Bird and Demetrius, whom he has never seen, but all noblemen that they hesitate before showing Harvey any kindness. If they grant him a favor, he will exaggerate it and publish it to all the world.

He illustrates his point with the story of Queen Elizabeth's visit to Audley End in July 1578, when Harvey was selected to make a Latin oration. The queen, who always patronizes scholars, complimented him by saying that he looked like an Italian and by permitting him to kiss her royal hand. Nashe records Harvey's reaction to these kindnesses as follows:

Herevppon hee goes home to his studie, all intraunced, and writes a whole volume of Verses; first, *De vultu Itali*, of the countenance of the Italian, and then *De osculo manus*, of his kissing the Queenes hande. Which two Latin Poems he publisht in a booke of his cald *Aedes Valdinenses*, proclaiming thereby (as it were to England, Fraunce, Italie, and Spaine) what fauour hee was in with her Maiestie. (I, 277,7–14)

After a few derogatory comments on Harvey's examples of hexameters in his letter to Spenser from *Three Proper and wittie Familiar Letters* Nashe writes, "Come thy waies downe from thy *Doctourship*" and relearn the elements of poetry.

Then pausing, he suddenly remembers that Harvey never did take his doctorate at Cambridge. In fact, when the University Court at Cambridge told him to "performe all the Schollerlike ceremonies and disputative right appertaining" to the degree, he refused and transferred to Oxford. Therefore, since he did not actually earn his degree at the former university, Nashe does not consider it valid. He compares Harvey to a runaway apprentice who, after serving his apprenticeship in London, runs off to Ipswich to have his freedom confirmed, which would not be a legitimate freedom since he has not served his apprenticeship there. Accordingly, in Nashe's eyes, he still is "a plaine moth-eaten Maister of Art" (I, 278, 3–4).

Thus placing Harvey at a disadvantage regarding his title, Nashe attacks him for lying about Greene. Contrary to Harvey's allegation, Greene surfeited not of pickled herring but rather of fear of Harvey's pamphlet. Moreover, Greene did not "in his extreamest want," as Harvey puts it,[8] offer the printer twenty shillings to delete the passage in the *Quippe*. On the contrary, because one of the Harvey brothers, John, was a medical doctor, Greene's physician persuaded him "either to mittigate it, or leaue it out" (I, 279, 33–34).

After scoffing at Harvey for troubling to criticize inconsequential ballad-makers, Nashe reprimands him for reviving the memory of Spenser's embarrassment when his satiric poem *Mother Hubbard's Tale* was called into question. Harvey's real reason for bringing up Spenser's name, Nashe avers, is that he wants everyone to know that he is a friend of the distinguished poet. Furthermore, Nashe suggests that while condemning other people for using bold invectives and presumptuous satire, Harvey should remember his own bold invectives in *Three Proper and wittie Familiar Letters* and his bitter remarks there concerning Dr. Perne.

Nashe points out Harvey's inconsistency in now terming such satirists as Lucian and Aretino "a venemous and viperous brood of railers" whereas in his letters to Spenser he had praised them (I, 283, 23 ff.). Here Nashe digresses to defend all satirists on the ground that they use their words of reproof, their harsh style, in attacking the abuses of their times. Suddenly cutting short his defense with "*Sancta Maria, ora pro nobis*, how hath my pen lost it selfe in a croude of Poets" (I, 286, 26–27), he presents his principal defense of Greene as a good man and a prolific writer, who certainly was not the poverty-stricken creature described in the second letter. Coming to Harvey's reference to Greene's "fellow writer, that proper yoong man," Nashe, instead of thanking his opponent for the compliment, scoffs at his hexameters on Greene (I, 288, 19 ff.).

Turning next to Harvey's promise to Bird that he would soon have news for him, Nashe, always suspicious of Gabriel's veracity, writes: ". . . hee will . . . shape you a messe of newes out of the second course of his conceit, as his brother is said out of the fabulous abundance of his braine to haue inuented the newes out of *Calabria*" (I, 289, 14–18). Here Nashe is insinuating that an astrological pamphlet, supposedly setting forth the opinions of the astrologer John Doleta, was really written either by Richard Harvey, who wrote pamphlets on astrology, or else by his brother John, who wrote almanacs.

Any news that Gabriel discovered, Nashe insists, would prove as spurious as the recent pamphlet purporting to be a genuine dialogue by Cicero, which instead was compiled by the Cambridge scholar. This pamphlet was supposed to have been found in a wall where it had lain hidden for over a thousand years. Nashe proceeds to invent an absurd story about Harvey's alleged discovery, how the pamphlet had been revealed to him by the "Eccho at Barnewell wall," who implored him to "reade it, new print it, dedicate it *from thy gallery at Trinitie Hall* to whom thou wilt" (I, 290, 24–26). The dedicatory phrase here chosen by Nashe is Harvey's own pompous conclusion to the second volume of his letters to Spenser.[9] Nashe ends this imaginary account with ". . . hadst not thou stept forth to vnder-prop the ruinous wall of thy brothers reputation, I had neuer medled with thee; if thou hadst not leand too much to an olde wall, when thou pluckst *Tullie* out of a wall, the damnation of this Iest had bin yet vnbegotten" (I, 291, 10–14).

Along with the news of the "French occurrences," Harvey had promised Bird news of "the braue Earle of Essex, woorthy Sir Iohn Norrice, and their valiant knightes."[10] Nashe expresses the hope that the reputations of these men will not have to suffer at Harvey's hands. Only an expert writer should record their deeds of valor. Here Nashe breaks off with the jest that such sober thoughts as these will make him grow a beard, which he abhors.

VI *Nashe's Refutation of Harvey's Third Letter*

Going to the third letter, Nashe calls attention to the fact that Harvey is trying to give the impression that everyone is urging him to come to the defense of his father. This obvious pretense is further evidence of his overwhelming conceit, which in the past had prevented him from becoming orator at Cambridge. In other words, Harvey himself, not Dr. Perne as he complains, was responsible for his own frustration. In addition to reminding Harvey of his discomfiture at the loss of this honor, Nashe accuses him of using Spenser's name in order to peddle his two volumes of letters. Nashe also unequivocally declares that Harvey wrote the foreword to his *Three Proper and wittie Familiar Letters* under the name of Wellwiller. After berating him for this petty deceit, Nashe reminds him that he was referred to the Fleet until he submitted an apology for his slanders in these letters.

Here Nashe again digresses in order to scoff at each of the Harvey brothers for never writing anything without including one or the other or both of the other two brothers. Upon returning to his rebuttal, he takes up the reference in the *Quippe* to Gabriel as the inventor of the English hexameter, which seems to have offended him. Why, asks Nashe, should this title be considered an insult? Nevertheless he admits that the hexameter is ill suited to the English language:

The Hexamiter verse I graunt to be a Gentleman of an auncient house (so is many an english begger), yet this Clyme of ours hee cannot thriue in; our speech is too craggy for him to set his plough in: hee goes twitching and hopping in our language like a man running vpon quagmiers, vp the hill in one Syllable, and down the dale in another, retaining no part of that stately smooth gate, which he vaunts himselfe with amongst the Greeks and Latins. (I, 298, 33 ff.)

Nashe's opinion of the awkwardness of the hexameter in English prosody rather than Harvey's was destined to prevail.

Resuming his refutation of Harvey's attack on Greene, he indulges in a little billingsgate and repeats his accusation that Harvey was imprisoned in the Fleet. As evidence he cites the hexameter verses written by a certain "Maister Butler of Cambridge," who learned of the imprisonment from friends "newlie come from London" (I, 300, 12 ff.).

Continuing with the third letter, Nashe threatens another attack from Lyly, whom Harvey in this letter accuses of prejudicing the Earl of Oxford after the publication of the letter to Spenser. Nashe adds that even though he himself is not as talented as Lyly, he now has to rein in his style lest it cause "a generall hicket throughout England" (I, 301, 7–8). Since he is on the subject of the Marprelate controversy at the moment, this phrase appropriately echoes his warning on the title page of An Almond: "Therefore beware (gentle Reader) you catch not the hicket with laughing" (III, 339).

Except for a word or two concerning Harvey's deceased brother John, Nashe states that he will leave him for Greene to "cope" with in the next world. Harvey's boast that John was " a proper toward man, and as skilfull a Phisition for his age" as ever came to Norfolk, [11] Nashe scornfully parodies as "a proper toward man at a medecine for the toothake, & one of the skilfullest Phisitions, in casting the heauens water, that euer came there" (I, 301, 19–21). The phrase "in casting the heauens water" alludes to Nashe's conviction, already mentioned, that John wrote the Astrologicall Addition to Richard's Astrologicall Discourse. Now, sighs Nashe, John has gone to heaven to write more treatises on astrology.

At last Nashe arrives at his own defense. As he had promised in Pierce Penilesse, he begins by railing. He calls Harvey an "indigested Chaos of Doctourship, and greedy pothunter after applause," an "apparent Publican and sinner," a "selfe-loue surfetted sot," a "broken-winded galdbacke Iade" (I, 302, 2–4). And he asks the world to judge wherein he has "trespassed" in Pierce Penilesse that Harvey should accuse him of "gnashing" his teeth and should class him with traitors like Anthony Babington, who plotted against the queen and was executed for treason. Nashe also resents Harvey's reference to him as *"Greenes inwardest companion pinched with want"* (I, 303, 5 ff.). He denies, first, that he was Greene's companion "any more than for a carowse or two" and, second, that he was ever "pincht with any vngentleman-like want" when he wrote *Pierce Penilesse*. Then, as if reconsidering, he adds that though at times he may have been poor, as who has not, he never was "vext with discredit" as Harvey certainly was after the publication of his "familiar epistles." In fact Harvey himself in his first "tome of Epistles" had complained against adversity.[12]

In reply to Harvey's observation that in writing *Pierce Penilesse* Nashe had drawn much of his material from Tarlton's "play of the seauen deadly sinnes," Nashe remarks that Harvey had done a little borrowing of his own in using "aboue twenty phrases and epithites" invented by Nashe (I, 304, 24–25). Anyway, asks Nashe, was sin "so vtterly abolished" with Tarlton's play that no other writer may use the same subject? Write of what he will, in what language he will, Nashe tells Harvey, he will confute it. In rebuttal he discloses his "Methode" of composing *Pierce Penilesse* (I, 306, 1 ff.). After his explanation he condemns Harvey's criticism as utterly ineffectual and compares it to "light crawling" over his text "like a Cankerworme" (I, 307, 29–30). Nevertheless, in the next edition of his pamphlet he plans to delete many of the marginal notes about which Harvey has complained. In their defense, however, he states that he originally inserted them in order to show that writers before him had lamented their misfortunes; in other words, his own complaint was merely a convention and not a fact as Harvey interprets it.

To Harvey's argument that his brother's *Astrologicall Discourse* was heavenly because it was concerned with the stars whereas Nashe's pamphlet was a "notorious diabolicall discourse," Nashe replies that in his criticism of Richard's writing he was only echoing the "infinite scorne" of the entire nation (I, 308, 7). Furthermore the fact that his own pamphlet "intreats of the diuerse natures and properties of Diuels and spirits" does not make it a "diabolicall Discourse."

Regarding Harvey's charge that Nashe had been in trouble with Thomas Churchyard, Nashe asserts that Harvey is just trying to stir up trouble about an old quarrel, in which Churchyard had been unintentionally injured. As for having been confined to debtor's prison— another of Harvey's accusations—Nashe confesses that he and many other gentlemen have been there. Indeed, he adds, "a Gentleman is neuer throughly entred into credit till he hath been there" (I, 310, 6–

7). He concludes this section of his rebuttal with the statement that he has enough "christian veritie," "common sense," and "humilitie" for both Gabriel and Richard to compensate for the "Modestie" which the former says he lacks.[13]

And now that Richard's name has again cropped up, Nashe proceeds to recapitulate all of his previous criticism of that clergyman: that he had his "Batchlours hood" turned over his ears for abusing Aristotle, which he notices has not been denied, that he was a "bawd" to the stars in pretending to know all their secrets, that the planets had proved honester than he, and that his *Astrologicall Discourse* had made him a laughingstock in the city and at the university (I, 311, 1 ff.). As further evidence that Richard's supercilious remarks still rankle, Nashe maintains that his own ancestry is as good as that of the Harveys. He goes on to defend Thomas Nash, the master butler of Pembroke Hall, with whom Richard with malice aforethought had confused him. The butler's beard, asserts Nashe, is better than Gabriel's "prety polwigge sparrows tayle peak" (I, 312, 10). Nashe then apologizes to the butler for having to use his name and also compliments him.

At this point he repeats his assertion that Richard Harvey's *Lamb of God* is "monstrous and absurd," made up as it is of the froth of the folly of the schoolmen. As for Richard's having read the philosophy lecture at Cambridge, as Gabriel boasts, Nashe declares that so many other men have read it so much better that no one would even consider him. After citing examples of these other readers, Nashe jeers at Richard and his "twise sodden sawdust diuinitie" displayed in his theological treatise (I, 315, 3).

Returning to Gabriel, Nashe accepts the title of "a perse a" given him in *Foure Letters* because it had once before been given to a man whom Harvey had slandered, namely, the Italianate Gentleman in *Three Proper and wittie Familiar Letters*. Then as though he were Harvey, he cries, "Hold you your peace Nashe: that was before you were Idoneus auditor ciuilis scientiae" (I, 315, 18–19)—an allusion to Harvey's sneer at Nashe's youth and inexperience.[14] Speaking as himself, Nashe replies, "It may bee so, for thou wert a Libeller before I was borne." He ends his discussion of Richard with the comment that he had many a time been bored by the clergyman's lectures.

Countering Harvey's criticism that he depended upon poetical anthologies rather than on original sources, Nashe asserts that he has read more poets than his opponent. He then makes up a list of what he terms Harvey's "inkehornismes" (I, 316, 2 ff.). Although Harvey might allege Chaucer as authority for these terms, Nashe considers them barbarous. McKerrow, however, notes that many of them are accepted today (IV, 188). Nashe sums up his estimate of Harvey as a writer in the following vivid passage:

. . .the short shredder out of sandy sentences without lime . . . all lime and no sande; all matter and no circumstance . . . the galimafrier of all stiles in one standish, as imitating euerie one, & hauing no seperate forme of writing of thy owne; and to conclude, the onely feather-driuer of phrases, and putter of a good word to it when thou hast once got it, that is betwixt this and the Alpes. (I, 317, 24 ff.)

Beseeching John Stowe the historian to remember Harvey in his *Chronicles*, Nashe suddenly recalls that the other night he had found a reference to Richard's *Astrologicall Discourse* in Raphael Holinshed's *Chronicles*, in which that historian had deplored the devastating effect of Richard's "coosening prognostication" on the "common sort of people."

Replying to Harvey's censure of his "Prefaces, Rimes, and the very Timpanye of his Tarltonizing wit,"[15] Nashe asserts that the only "rimes" that he has ever composed are those in *Pierce Penilesse* (I, 318, 19 ff.). He will admit to having written two prefaces, which he asks Harvey to note contain no solecism or any "mishapen English word." Furthermore he protests that he has never borrowed from Greene or Tarlton and defies Harvey to compare his style with Greene's. In fact, he adds, both Greene and Tarlton "haue beene contented" to let his "simple iudgement ouerrule them in some matters of wit" (I, 319, 13–14). He then gives the stylistic evidence for his assertion that Harvey himself wrote the sonnet affixed to his first letter, to which Bird's name is signed. If Harvey now considers Nashe a professional in the art of railing, he has as yet seen nothing of what Nashe can do. Moreover, he intends to rail until Harvey begs to be hanged.

For a moment Nashe pauses to complain that Harvey is trying to persuade some prominent men that Nashe has satirized them in his *Pierce Penilesse*. Again he denies this charge and repeats that he only has glanced at vice generally, particularly in his "tale of the Beare and the Foxe" (I, 320, 35 ff.). In accepting Harvey's challenge that he produce his "thundring tearmes, steept in *Aqua fortis* and gunpowder," he tells Harvey that he will respond if Harvey will first show him the hand and seal of the university that he is a doctor "sealed and deliuered

in the presence of a whole Commencement" (I, 321, 32–34). He again
interrupts himself with the apology that his argument with Harvey is
ruining his style. Then he denies Harvey's assumption that he is poverty-stricken just because he stated that he, a scholar, is not as well
rewarded for his work as is a common laborer. To Harvey's smug boast
that Spenser had once complimented his hexameter verses, Nashe
maintains that Spenser was just being kind to him whereas he himself
is continually bringing in Spenser's name to enhance "euerie pybald
thing" that he writes (I, 323, 35).

If Harvey accuses Nashe of railing and scolding, Nashe wonders
what his opponent would term his own invective against Greene, in
which he mentions Greene's "lowsiness, his surfeting, his beggerie, and
the mother of *Infortunatus* infirmities" (I, 324, 20–23). Nashe, on the
contrary, insists that in his satire he is following the witty, humane
precedent of "*Tully, Ouid,* all the olde Poets, *Agrippa, Aretine,* and
the rest." With great pride in his satirical style Nashe then cites his
farewell to Richard Harvey in *Pierce Penilesse,* in which he leaves him
to be the scorn of poets and writers in London and to go hang himself
in the string of his own sance-bell. These witty words, he believes, are
sufficient answer to brother Gabriel's disapproval of his style.

Finally, concerning Harvey's complete reversal of attitude at the
end of the third letter in placing Nashe among the dear lovers and
professed sons of the Muses, Nashe asserts that he scorns any overtures
of peace and refuses to be impressed by the flattery of a man who in
the same letter has insulted him.

VII Nashe's Commentary on the Fourth Letter
and Harvey's Verses

The reason why Nashe skims over the fourth letter is that he regards
it for the most part as an old composition that Harvey has revamped
for the occasion. Even though in his third letter he has just called for
a reconciliation "with a cup of white wine, and some little familiar
conference," in his fourth letter he states that the "new-new writers,"
a category which would include Nashe, are "wonderfully beholdinge
to the Asse."[16] With this assertion he launches forth into a confused
discussion of the ass, which he concludes by calling "the one," presumably Greene, a "right Asse in print" and "the other," presumably
Nashe, a "right Calfe in print." Somewhat mystified, Nashe demands
to know how Harvey defines the word *asse.* After all, Cornelius

Agrippa called all philosophers, orators, and poets asses. At the same time Nashe notes that Harvey mentions no authors except those who might be quoted by any "Grammer Scholler" (I, 328, 35). If perchance Harvey is calling Greene an ass, Nashe wants him to know that though Greene may have published too frequently he delighted many readers.

Nashe then indignantly denies Harvey's insinuation regarding his allegedly licentious writing and immoral life. If his opponent persists in calling him "a base shifting companion," Nashe wishes to remind him of the way he used to cheat the bakers in Cambridge in "shifting" for his Friday-night suppers (I, 329, 27 ff.). As for Greene, Nashe will leave further defense of his behavior to other people who knew him better than Nashe did. Nevertheless he himself never saw any "base shifting or abhominable villanie" in Greene as Harvey implies. Nashe also denies Harvey's charges that he has spoiled his adherents, preyed on those who favored him, and dishonored his patrons.

Returning to Harvey's text, Nashe tries to puzzle out an allusion therein to "the Secretaries of Art, and Nature," who "wonderfully bestead the Commonwealth with many puissant engins."[17] After a futile attempt to make sense out of this passage, Nashe again laughs at his opponent for not possessing a "perfected degree" (I, 332, 9). He restates his opinion that the fourth letter is a warmed-over essay dating back perhaps to the time of the Marprelate controversy. In fact, Harvey's use of the Puritanical phrase "dumbe dogge," frequently applied to the Episcopalian clergyman, and also his lack of the proper reverence for Archbishop Whitgift in comparing him to Cartwright, suggest that he himself might have been a Martinist.

Arriving at the verses concluding *Foure Letters* Nashe at first states that he will examine only the sonnet signed by Spenser. Then he changes his mind because he suspects that Harvey himself composed it and then attributed it to Spenser, whose name "is able to sanctifie any thing" (I, 327, 2–3).

Nashe ends his first reply to Gabriel Harvey with a prayer for his opponent, "Lord, if it be thy will, let him be an Asse stille," and finally a sonnet proclaiming that as long as he himself is able to write he will fight against "waspes and droanes" (I, 333, 16 ff.).

CHAPTER 10

Nashe's Second Reply to Harvey

I *Harvey's Reply to* Strange Newes

THE composition of Harvey's reply to *Strange Newes*, namely, *Pierce's Supererogation*, McKerrow dates as some time between February and July 1593, and its publication about the middle of October of the same year (V, 95 ff.). During the summer of 1593, before the publication of Harvey's second pamphlet, a lull occurred in the Nashe-Harvey pamphlet war. As has been explained,[1] McKerrow speculates that acquaintances on either side were attempting to bring about a reconciliation. Whether or not Harvey willfully ignored Nashe's public apology in his epistle to the reader prefixed to the first issue of *Christ's Teares* is a matter of opinion.

Pierce's Supererogation consists of three main parts: first, the author's reply to Nashe's attack in *Strange Newes*; second, a long commentary on Lyly's insinuation of libeling in *Pappe with a Hatchet* made several years before; third, a criticism of Nashe's literary style. In the first section Harvey begins with an apology for wasting time in controversy when he might be writing about political and military affairs, the lives of great men, and the sciences. In censuring Nashe he summons all of his classical authorities to his aid. He even resorts to his old trick of attributing his own criticism of his opponent to an anonymous friend. Just as Nashe had attributed to Harvey himself Wellwiller's foreword to *Three Proper and wittie Familiar Letters* (I, 296, 16–20) and also the first letter and sonnet supposedly written by Christopher Bird in *Foure Letters* (I, 273, 26–30), so McKerrow believes that, "in the wording at least," this criticism from the anonymous friend "is evidently Harvey's own" (V, 91). The rest of the first section alternates between ridicule of Nashe and defense of himself.

The second section of Harvey's pamphlet, entitled "An Aduertisement for Papp-Hatchett and Martin Mar-prelate" and dated November 3, 1589, is an old reply to Lyly that Harvey asserts he never intended to publish until Nashe attacked him.[2] Since the Marprelate controversy had become history and the chief suspect in it, John Penry, had been arrested and hanged—at least by the date of publication assigned to the pamphlet by McKerrow—this section was stale news.

The third section is an attempt on Harvey's part to out-Nashe Nashe. Punning on the similarity in pronunciation between *Nashe* and *an ass*, Harvey presents a long pedantic essay in praise of all the famous asses in history. With reference to literary style he concentrates on Nashe's "absurde, and ridiculous wordes" and "Inkhornish phrases."[3] Since Nashe, using similar terminology, had already questioned Harvey's vocabulary, this approach seems decidedly unoriginal. Harvey's attention then momentarily is deflected toward Andrew Perne, whom he had previously attacked in his *Three Proper and wittie Familiar Letters* and in *Foure Letters.* Since Dr. Perne had died in 1589 before either of Harvey's last two pamphlets were published, this belated censure seems both tasteless and pointless. The section concludes with a eulogy in honor of the "Gentlewoman" who is going to come to Harvey's assistance against Nashe.[4] Apparently he is here merely personifying his own literary wit.

In the second pamphlet bound with *Pierce's Supererogation* and entitled *A New Letter of Notable Contents* Harvey after a few preliminary comments on politics and contemporary literature questions Nashe's good will in seeking reconciliation. He then devotes a few more pages to his "Gentlewoman," who is preparing to aid him.[5] In addition to giving a sort of preview of what her plan of attack will be, he makes several slighting remarks about Nashe's moral character, all of which, along with the entire pamphlet, have been interpreted by some scholars as a challenge to Nashe, providing we assume that Harvey had originally intended its publication.

At the appearance of Harvey's two-part pamphlet Nashe expresses in an epistle to the reader prefixed to the second issue of *Christ's Teares* his indignation for what he considers Harvey's treachery in brushing aside his apology. Nashe also scoffs at the much-heralded support from Harvey's "Gentlewoman," which in his opinion was just another name for his opponent's "vaineglorie." And he promises at a future date "to stretch him forth limbe by limbe on the racke" (II, 180, 30 ff.).

II   *The Organization of Nashe's Second Reply to Harvey*

The rollicking tone of the long satirical title of Nashe's second reply to Harvey foreshadows the liveliness of its content: *Haue with you to*

Saffron-walden or, Gabriell Harueys Hunt is vp, Containing a full Answere to the eldest sonne of the Halter-maker. Or, Nashe his Confutation of the sinfull Doctor. The Mott or Posie, in stead of Omne tulit punctum: Pacis fiducia nunquan, As much to say, as I sayd I would speake with him. Although this pamphlet is Nashe's answer to Harvey's rambling attack in *Pierce's Supererogation,* it is not organized like his earlier reply, in which he generally follows Harvey's text in *Foure Letters* section by section, quoted more or less as in the original and then answered, with pertinent passages inserted here and there from Harvey's earlier two volumes of letters. Instead, in *Have with You* he makes fun of his opponent's personal appearance and behavior. Only in the latter part of his pamphlet does he attempt to reply to specific charges made in *Pierce's Supererogation.* McKerrow attributes this change in organization to the fact that Nashe had not worked at the pamphlet for any extended period but had kept it by him for several months and had from time to time returned to it (V, 106).

III   *Nashe's Dedicatory Epistle*

Like Nashe's earlier controversial pamphlet, *Have with You* opens with a satirical dedication, this time to Richard Lichfield, the barber of Trinity College, "the most Orthodoxall [one of Harvey's unusual words in *Pierce's Supererogation*[6]] and reuerent Corrector of staring haires" (III, 5, 1–2). At the offset Nashe distinguishes "Dicke of Lichfield" from all other Dicks in "a huge dicker of Dickes in a heape altogether" (III, 6, 2 ff.). Then he asks the barber to help him trim Harvey. As a reward Lichfield may receive "manie gracious gallant complements" and a few English hexameters (III, 7, 2–7). Furthermore the haircutting profession is indebted to Harvey for spending "twice double his Patrimonie" in "carefull cherishing & preseruing his pickerdeuant." Moreover Gabriel's "deuine vicarly brother," "Astrologicall Richard," a few years ago "compyled *a profound Abridgement vpon beards*" (an allusion to an anonymous book *A Defence of short haire,* of which Richard may or may not have been the author), which "copiously dilated of the true discipline of peakes, & no less frutelessly determined betwixt the Swallowes taile cut & the round beard like a rubbing bush (III, 7, 22–28; IV, 305).

After a few more disparaging remarks directed at "Astrologicall Dick" Nashe beseeches Diamond Dick, the barber, to aid him in fighting his enemies. After all, the barber, a "Commaunder and a Souldier," with his "*Palermo* rasour" and his "sharpe pointed launce," has attacked many a man (III, 9, 17 ff.). Having delivered his plea for aid replete with the customary invectives, he composes an equally irreverent "grace" for the barber to read "in behalfe of the Harueys" (III, 11, 32 ff.).

Next he urges the barber to "commence"for his doctorate, for he would be as much a credit to the title as the Harveys and many other men who bear it (III, 13, 22 ff.). As proof of Nashe's professed desire to further Lichfield's progress in languages, he submits the pains that he has taken "to nit and louze ouer the Doctours Booke," which many a London cook has already used for cooking paper under pastries and basting paper on meats, in order to cull out some of the author's elegant phrases. These Nashe works into an imaginary conversation that the barber might have with any customer. Nashe recommends that Lichfield study "Gabrielisme," which will teach him not to "come forth with a rich spirit and an admirable capacitie, but *an enthusiasticall spirit & a nimble entelechy*" *(III, 17, 1 ff.)*.

IV   *The Epistle to All Christian Readers*

In the second epistle, "To all Christian Readers, to whom these Presents shall come," Nashe expresses his boredom with the quarrel, which he compares to a factional struggle which Harvey began and now does not know how to end. He in turn admits no hatred for the Harveys. All that he hopes to do is to prove to his friends his ability to meet their challenge. Nevertheless he warns his reader that he is about to raise against his opponent "a tempest of thunder and lightning worse than the stormes in the West *Indies* cald the *Furicanoes*" (III, 20, 4 ff.). Although now he is employing a "sober mortified style," in his main text he will demonstrate his eloquence.

Apparently conscious of the looseness of his earlier controversial pamphlets, he announces that this one is to be framed "in the nature of a Dialogue" with four "Interlocuters": Senior Importuno, whom he calls "the Opponent," Grand Consiliadore, the "chiefe Censor or Moderator," Domino Bentivole, who will support Importuno, and Don Carneades de boone Compagniola, who will deliver the sentence (III, 20, 32 ff.). Always the realist, Nashe assures the reader that these personages, unlike those in the dialogue in More's *Utopia,* represent his own good friends. Importuno, a "Gentleman of good qualitie," has urged him on in the controversy. Grand Consiliadore has furnished good advice and, like Importuno, has helped him map out his strategy. The last two are companions in whose conversation he particularly delights. He himself under the name of Respondent will "clap vp a *Colloquium*" that will bring Harvey to his knees (III, 23, 10–11).

V   *Nashe's Explanation for His Delayed Reply*

The dialogue opens with complaints from Nashe's friends that he has delayed so long that people will think that he lacks the ability to answer Harvey, or that perhaps he had hired someone to write the earlier reply, or that he either is dead or forbidden to write, or that having recently published "a treatise in Diuinitie" [*Christ's Teares*], it is against his conscience to reply. At any rate, until he replies, he stands a "disgraced and condemned man" (III, 26, 29 ff.).

Nashe in his own defense replies that he needs more time in which "to get perfect intelligence of his [Harvey's] life and conuersation, one true point whereof, well set downe, wil more excruciate & commacerate him" than railing (III, 29, 7 ff.). If only Nashe were free from financial worry, he would at once answer Harvey's last replies, which he terms "rags of treatises" against both Lyly and himself, which the author has been collecting ever since since Lyly accused him of libel. If only someone were to provide Nashe with meat and drink, he would produce his usual "suddaine extemporall answeres." He somewhat bitterly comments on the people egging Harvey and him to quarrel and even expresses the hope that the whole affair soon will be ended. For the time being he offers the excuse of poverty: "I am faine to let my Plow stand still in the midst of a furrow, and follow some of these newfangled *Galiardos* and *Senior Fantasticos*, to whose amorous *Villanellas* and *Quipassas* I prostitute my pen in hope of gaine" (III, 31, 1–5). From his choice of words in this passage he may also be offering an excuse for turning his hand to the genre of erotic poetry in *The Choise of Valentines*.

VI   *Preliminary Remarks on Harvey's Pamphlets*

Nevertheless Nashe does not want Harvey to think that his "indigent confession" means that he is calling for a truce. But he has been waiting for some company—doubtless Lyly (IV, 317)—to join him. Now, however, he must go ahead alone. Before turning to his refutation, he

reminds his friends of his epistle to Dick Lichfield, some parts of which
he has already read to them. Then he pretends to greet the carrier
heavily laden with more letters yet from the Doctor. The exhausted
man urges Nashe to destroy the letters. After paying him, Nashe begins
reading. Finding nothing in them but "dogs-tripes, swines liuers, oxe
galls, and sheepes gutts," he is disgusted (III, 34, 16 ff). It would be
impossible to take "an inuentorie suruay of anie one of them," they are
so long and tedious. Nashe terms Harvey "the onely pure Orator in
senseles riddles . . . that euer this our litle shred or seperate angle of the
world suckled vp." Just as Harvey in his earlier pamphlets has used the
names of Sidney, Spenser, and "other men of highest credit" in order
to make them sell, so here he uses *Pierce* in his title.

Next Nashe ridicules the huge size of *Pierce's Supererogation*. Seiz-
ing upon a misnumbering of pages, in which pages 200 to 220 are
numbered 100 to 120 and the remaining pages unnumbered, Nashe
accuses Harvey of being embarrassed by the length of his pamphlet.
Nashe himself weighed only the epistle to the printer and found that
it counterbalanced a cade of Herring and three Holland cheeses. In
fact, he had to remove his chamber door in order to admit the volume.
He even thought of calling the cooper and having it hooped up. He
later heard that it was being used in athletic contests by the Queen's
Guard instead of "the sledge or the hammer" (III, 36, 19–20). It is so
full of barren sand that it might well be compared to the continent of
Africa in size as well as in content. "Sixe and thirtie sheets it compre-
hendeth," cries Nashe, all written in Harvey's customary long-winded
style: he never greets a man without making a speech "as long as a
proclamation" or drinks to him without reading "a Lecture of three
howers long *De Arte Bibendi*" (III, 36, 34 ff.). The "certaine rare
Mathematicall Experimentes," which Harvey vows "to discouer and
search foorth,"[7] can doubtless be compared to the achievements of
"Doctour Ty," who chained a flea and trained it to do tricks.

At this point Nashe inserts a picture of Harvey "as hee is readie to
let fly vpon Aiax" or, as Nashe also expresses it, "with his gowne cast
off, vntrussing" as a result of his dismay upon hearing of the preparation of Nashe's second reply (III, 38, 16 ff.). An excellent likeness,
Nashe declares it. He concludes his self-satisfied description of the picture with threats to destroy his opponent with the fire of his wit.
Whereupon his companions in the dialogue, shouting encouragement,
urge him to "leaue this big thunder of words" and begin (III, 40, 20).
Nashe promises them "a continuat *Tropologicall* speech" (III, 41, 7–

8). When they appear surprised at the word *tropologicall*, he tells them that it was coined by Dick Harvey in the *Lamb of God*.

Importuno replies that he would enjoy a sample of Doctor Harvey's style, which he has heard generally commended. Nashe, as Respondent, quotes the extravagant praise given it by a "red bearded thridbare Caualier" at an ordinary "as he sat fumbling the dice after supper," who immediately afterward shrugged his shoulders, talked of going to a brothel, and recommended to young gentlemen "two or three of the most detested loathsom whores about *London*" (III, 42, 5–6). Thus by the juxtaposition of these two preferences expressed by this disreputable "Caualier," Nashe conveys to the reader his idea of the only type of people who could possibly admire Harvey's style. Now he plans to compose a "short Oration" made up of "most of the ridiculous senseles sentences, finicall flaunting phrases, and termagant inkhorne tearmes throughout his Booke" (III, 42, 17–19).

VII   *Nashe's Oration Composed in Harvey's Style*

As Nashe delivers his oration, his companions hilariously comment. When Importuno interrupts to ask why he has not prepared marginal notes for each of his disjointed excerpts, the "orator" reminds them that he has already discussed Harvey's neglect of pagination. As Nashe continues, Don Carneades breaks in to remark that if Harvey were pleading in the law courts he would be more entertaining than one of Lyly's comedies played by the Children of Pauls. Then Don Carneades himself tries his hand at inventing an imaginary legal address containing the same unusual words that Nashe has just used, which, as the speaker points out, would require an interpreter in the courtroom.

After Don Carneades has finished, Nashe resumes his oration with frequent derisive interruptions from the rest. When he mentions the name of Sir Philip Sidney, they express the opinion that because of its ill-chosen language Harvey's intended praise of this nobleman actually dishonors him. For example, in discussing the wit of Sidney and Spenser, Harvey uses the word *Tuscanisme*,[8] which had appeared in the satirical sketch of the Italianate Gentleman that had offended the Earl of Oxford.[9]

As the oration continues in this fashion, Nashe quotes Harvey's allusions to the "arte of figges" and to "Saint Fame" (III, 52, 30–36). Grand Consiliadore identifies the former expression as directed at Lyly and the latter at Nashe, who had invoked Saint Fame at the end of the

prefatory letter in *Strange Newes*. Nashe ends his improvised oration
with a final paragraph of jargon and asks, "Haue not I comprehended
all the Doctors workes brauely, like *Homers Iliads* in the compasse of
a nut-shell?" (III, 54, 16–17).

VIII   *Nashe's Satirical Biography of Harvey*

With his parody of Harvey's bizarre style completed, Nashe turns to
the man himself. He tells his friends that he is going to "set downe"
Harvey's life "from his infancie to his present" (III, 55, 15–16). A comparison between this biography and the earlier biography of Penry in
An Almond will show how expert Nashe has become in the use of
satire. Filling his account with humorously applied Latin quotations
and classical allusions, he sets to work.

Harvey was born about forty years ago in Saffron-Walden, the son
of a ropemaker, "a true subiect, that paid scot and lot in the Parish
where he dwelt, with the best of them, but yet he was a Ropemaker"
(III, 56, 2–3). When Grand Consiliadore interrupts in order to request
that Nashe not upbraid his opponent with his birth, which he could not
help, Nashe replies that it is Harvey himself who in his pride scorns his
own origin. In fact, Harvey had told some of Nashe's friends that his
only reason for anger was that Nashe had called him and his brothers
"the sonnes of a Rope-maker." Moreover, Harvey has been very careful not to mention the word except once when he asked, "And may
not a good sonne haue a reprobate to his father?"[10] With feigned per-
plexity Nashe confesses that he was unaware that *reprobate* was the
"Periphrasis" for *ropemaker* (III, 57, 12–15). He then enumerates several of his own references to the elder Harvey's trade which the son
pointedly ignores so as not to have to mention the word *ropemaker*.

Of a more humble spirit was the elder Harvey, who, "in gratefull
lieu and remembrance of the hempen mysterie that hee was beholding
too, and the patrons and places that were his trades chief maintainers
and supporters," selected the names of his sons so that the first letters
"should allude and correspond with the chiefe marts of his traffick, &
of his profession & occupation; as *Gabriell*, his eldest sonnes name,
beginning with a G. for Gallowes, *Iohn* with a I. for Iayle, *Richard*
with an R. for Rope-maker; as much to say as all his whole liuing
depended on the Iayle, the Gallowes, & making of Ropes" (III, 58, 8–
18).

Accordingly, instead of despising their father's trade the sons should constantly keep reminding themselves of it. For instance, they should "haue a salt eele, in resemblance of a ropes end, continuallye seru'd in to their tables." If they could not afford that, a "two-penny rope of onions" would do. To these suggestions Nashe adds, "Were I a Lord (I make the Lord God a vow) and were but the least a kin to this breath-strangling linage, I would weare a chain of pearle brayded with a halter, to let the world see I held it in no disgrace, but high glorie, to bee discended howsoeuer" (III, 59, 1–5). These armorial bearings Nashe would flaunt before the entire world: " . . . from the plough harnesse to the slender hempen twist that they bind vp their vines with wold I branch my alliance, and omit nothing in the praise of it, except those two notable blemishes of the trade of rope-makers *Achitophel* and *Iudas*, that were the first that euer hangd themselues." To Domino Bentiuole's objection that to these two exceptions "Rope-makers were but accidentally accessarie," Nashe, parodying the logician, replies that "in manie things *causa sine qua non* is both the cause and the effect . . . a halter including desperation, and so desperation concluding in a halter." Hence, "it is hard to distinguish which is most to be blamed, of the cause or the effect."

Passing on to young Gabriel's education, Nashe states that the boy "ran through *Didimus* or *Diomedes* 6000. bookes of the Arte of Grammer" and "learnd to write a faire capitall Romane hand" (III, 60, 11–13). These accomplishments were certainly more than "a copy-holder or magistrall scribe, that holds all his liuing by setting school-boies copies," could boast of and might serve "to keepe him out of the danger of the Statute against wilfull vagabonds, rogues, and beggers." "In his Grammer yeares," however, "he was a verie gracelesse litigious youth" and "a desperate stabber with a pen-kniues," which caused his father to prophesy great things of him. His mother, on the contrary, was fearful for his future because of a number of dreams that she had had before his birth, which Nashe interprets as foretelling the boy's highly dubious literary accomplishments. Nashe then recounts the ridiculous prodigies that accompanied Harvey's birth.

His childhood, according to this satiric biography, was distinguished by the composition of ballets and doggerel verse. His early interest in literature grew during his years at Cambridge. This period of his life Nashe sets forth in the form of a letter supposedly written by Harvey's tutor to his father. First, the tutor praises the young student for inventing "strange vntraffiqu't phrases" such as *incendarie* for *fire*, *illuminarie* for *candle and lant-horne*, *indument* for *cloake*, and *vnder foote abiect* for *shoe* or *boot* (III, 65, 31 ff.). Next in the letter are reported the "Epistles and Orations" earlier composed, in which the writer ends every sentence with *esse posse videatur,* with the result that some of his friends gave him that Latin phrase as a nickname. Later on, after beginning the study of logic, he used *ergo* so often that "he was cald nothing but *Gabriell Ergo* vp and downe the Colledge" (III, 67, 1–2). On one occasion he defended the rat as a rational animal until he became a general laughing-stock. His skill in poetry was demonstrated by poems written in the forms of "a paire of gloues, a dozen of points, a paire of spectacles," and other odd objects. He particularly enjoyed reading popular ballads.

Turning from virtues to vices, the tutor reports that the young fellow seems to have had designs on the daughter of his laundress, whom he attempted to seduce with some religious tracts and suggestive Latin epigrams. Furthermore he is exceedingly vain about his personal appearance. He is also quarrelsome. Finally he is addicted to stewed prunes (a euphemism for brothels) and to swearing. With the implication that these are only a small number of his faults the tutor closes the letter.

Continuing as Respondent, Nashe tells of Harvey's exploits in pamphleteering. Beginning with a few obvious exaggerations, he again brings up the letters to Spenser, in which Harvey wrote his "short but yet sharpe iudiciall of Earth-quakes" and "came very short and sharpe vppon my Lord of *Oxford* in a ratling bundle of English hexameters" (III, 69, 32–34). Next he turned to almanacs. Although no almanac by Harvey is extant, Nashe ascribes to him the almanacs written under the name of Gabriel Frend. As evidence for this ascription, Nashe first points out that among Harvey's friends he gave the impression that he possessed an intimate knowledge of Frend. Accordingly, Nashe laughingly concludes, since "euery man is the best *Frend* to himself" Harvey in concealing the identity of Frend must himself be Frend (III, 70, 6 ff.). Second, since no one knows how he makes a living, it must be that he writes almanacs under the assumed name of Gabriel Frend. From now on, Nashe assures his reader, he will be on the lookout for almanacs either by Frend or by Harvey.

Here Nashe digresses in order to inform his readers that though Harvey has sought honor in many ways there was a time when he "would have tooke foule scorne that the best of them all should haue out-faced him" (III, 73, 7–8). When he participated in the disputation in honor of the queen's visit to Audley End, he "came ruffling it out, huffty tuffty, in his suite of velvet," for which he went into debt and which he patched and repatched twice a year before every bachelor's and masters' commencement for the next fourteen years. Whenever it went to the tailor at any other time, it was a sure sign to the university that "the Doctor had some ierking Hexameters or other shortly after to passe the stampe," for he never went to London for any other reason except recently to quarrel with his sister-in-law. Moreover, he still wears what remains of the velvet suit, which he plans to have hung as a "monument" over his tomb. This account of his attachment to his velvet suit reminds Nashe of another story, the truth of which he will not vouch: a certain gentleman lent Harvey an old velvet saddle, out of which he made a doublet that he has worn ever since.

Then Nashe returns to the episode at Audley End. After the Cambridge scholar had finished his oration, he was permitted to kiss the queen's hand. Because she complimented him by saying "that he lookt something like an Italian," he immediately began to play the part by imitating Italian accents and manners (III, 76, 20). He even went so far as to snub Sir Philip Sidney and another knight. Later in the evening, when the courtiers withdrew to the residence of the Countess of Derby for the ball, they arranged it so that Harvey, who had followed them there, would dance with the ugliest lady-in-waiting of the Countess. Finishing the dance, he kissed his repulsive partner and rushed home to write his poem entitled *Aedes Valdinenses* in commemoration of the occasion.

For a moment Nashe pauses to jeer at this poem. Then he again recalls the difficulties into which another poem by Harvey in his letters to Spenser, *Speculum Tuscanismi,* had plunged him. First, by taking sides in a quarrel between two noblemen, perhaps Sidney and the Earl of Oxford, he had been forced to find refuge in the house of the lord whom he had supported (IV, 340). Since in these same letters he had made derogatory remarks about Dr. Perne under the name of the "olde Controwler," Sir James Croft, controller of the queen's household and privy councillor, thinking the remarks were aimed at him, took umbrage and had Harvey arrested. After apologizing and explaining his ambiguous allusion, he was permitted to return to Cambridge, where he boasted of his experience with such success that he was recalled to the court as a secretary. There he cut such an absurd figure that his patron advised him to return to the university and then sent for another secretary from Oxford.

Upon his return to Cambridge he was ridiculed in the comedy

Pedantius, which contained fragments from his writings. Nashe also mentions two other plays, one satirizing the three Harvey brothers and one satirizing only Richard, who became so angry that he broke the college windows and had to be placed in the stocks by Dr. Perne.

According to Nashe, Harvey was always falling in love. His first hexameters were written to celebrate his love for Kate Cotton, presumably his laundress's daughter, and for the wife of the butler of St. John's College. His brother Richard, on the contrary, was always hating somebody or something—Aristotle or the Great Bear or religion. And John, who was a notorious wencher in the vicinity of Queen's College Lane, finally ran off with the daughter of Justice Meade, in whose house he was acting as schoolmaster. It is John's wife who is now in court accusing Gabriel of attempting to cheat her of all her possessions.

Speaking of lechery, Nashe recalls that Richard once attempted to seduce a certain milkmaid. Nashe solemnly urges him to mortify the flesh and to pray or to try some other remedy for "temptations of the petticoate" (III, 82, 18). Again referring to Richard's disgrace caused by his false prognostication, Nashe digresses to express his own distate for astrology and particularly for the almanacs of Richard Harvey. Here he again sums up all his reasons for despising Richard, many of which he has already mentioned in *Pierce Penilesse* and in *Strange Newes.*

Now that he has thoroughly roasted Richard, he returns to Gabriel, whose pretense to fame as a lawyer he considers absurd. Yet since Harvey has no other employment, rumor has it that he is planning to turn the whole body of the law into English hexameters. This statement reopens the subject of Harvey's interest in the hexameter, the composing of which, Nashe maintains, was his main occupation until he entered the controversy.

Nashe next informs his reader that Harvey in his mad desire for revenge remained at the home of the printer John Wolfe in London during the worst days of the plague "inck-squittring and printing" against him (III, 87, 7). As a result he ran into debt, first with one man and then with another. Wolfe let him work off his debt by writing plague bills and by advising regarding the literary merits of the various pamphlets offered for print. The second office he performed so poorly that as his debts piled up Wolfe finally began to rebel. At first Harvey put him off, but after a while in his flowery rhetoric promised to settle as soon as his rents came in. Nashe, however, expresses strong doubt that Harvey had any rents.

Here he again digresses to tell the story of a friend of his who had recently called on Harvey in order to see how he was reacting to Nashe's attacks. This friend was forced to wait two hours while Harvey dressed himself and practiced his gestures before the mirror. When he finally appeared, he overwhelmed Nashe's friend with "amplifications and complements" (III, 91, 32). Indeed, the Cambridge scholar's manner was so affected that his guest at first mistook him for an usher in a dancing school. As an illustration of his fulsome compliments Nashe cites two lines to Sidney from Harvey's *Gratulationes Valdinenses*, wherein he courted Sidney "as he were another *Cyparissus* or *Ganimede*" (III, 92, 10–11).

In order to emphasize Harvey's insincerity Nashe recalls a chance stopping at an inn in Cambridge a few months earlier when Harvey was there. Apparently he made overtures to Nashe. But since Nashe had already offered a public apology to him in *Christ's Teares* and had been rebuffed, he had no desire for a private reconciliation.

Then Nashe draws a verbal caricature of his opponent—his swarthy complexion, his emaciated wrinkled face, his gray hair, his stooped, gaunt figure. After thus describing his personal appearance, Nashe presents instances of his parsimony: his quarrel with the hostess of an inn in Cambridge, where he stayed a fortnight without spending a penny; hiring horses in Saffron-Walden for three days and keeping them fifteen; dressing in ill-fitting garments the country bumpkin whom he had employed as an attendant. Characteristic of his proud nature were his boasts to Wolfe that he was the most learned man in England. His vindictiveness appears in his threats against any nobleman who might side with Nashe against him, in his incensing the Lord Mayor against Nashe, and finally in his persuading a preacher to preach against both Nash and Lyly at Paul's Cross.

Nashe now comes to the last event in his satirical biography, the publication of *Pierce's Supererogation*. Since Harvey was unable to pay Wolfe the thirty-six pounds owed him for printing this pamphlet and for his living at the printer's establishment, he told Wolfe that he had to go back home in order to collect the money from his tenants. Accordingly Wolfe furnished him with horses, money, and a serving man, one of Wolfe's apprentices. As soon as Harvey and his man were out of London, Harvey persuaded the apprentice to desert his master and to serve him instead. After about six months, when Wolfe was about to arrest them both, the apprentice, who had never been paid, gave notice. Harvey thereupon dismissed him and sent him back to the printer with promises of payment. Wolfe employed a friend, Scarlet, with some bailiffs to seek out Harvey and arrest him. As a decoy Scarlet delivered a letter from the printer concerning the lawsuit of John Harvey's widow. Then, as Harvey and Scarlet were commiserating over this piece of ill luck, Scarlet gave the bailiffs the signal to arrest his companion and take him to Newgate.

Upon arriving at the prison he put on a dreadful scene when he was ordered to hand over his weapons. Finally the jailor's wife, in the absence of her husband, took pity on him and tried to calm him. When he promised to surrender if she would dismiss her servants, she agreed to his request. He immediately closed the door, turned on her, and threatened to kill her. At her screams her servants burst in, disarmed her assailant, and put him into the stocks. After begging forgiveness of the jailor's wife on his knees, he was released and invited to dinner. Because he was not permitted to sit at the head of the table, he flounced back into his cell and refused to eat. Later, when the pangs of hunger became too much for him, he wrote a note to his hostess, begging for food. She persuaded her husband to take him to the tap-house beside the prison and get him a meal, which, incidentally, the jailor had to pay for. Finally a minister also named Harvey but not related to Gabriel paid for him, freed him, and assisted him in finding lodging with a sergeant, who along with the minister bonded himself for Harvey's appearance in court. The latter, running into debt with Wolfe, stole away to Saffron-Walden, where he remained in secrecy until Nashe met him at the inn in Cambridge.

IX Nashe's Rebuttal of Specific Statements in Harvey's Pamphlet

At the conclusion of this satirical sketch Nashe's friends are convinced of its subject's shortcomings. Senior Importuno expresses the opinion that Harvey "swarmeth in vile Canniball words" (III, 102, 11). However, he adds that "there is some good matter" against Nashe in *Pierce's Supererogation.* Nashe agrees to draw up an "Abridgement or Inuentorie of all the materiall Tractates and Contents of hys Booke," which he hands to Senior Importuno to read. At this point, then, he returns to the method of analysis used in his first reply.

First, to Masters Barnabe Barnes, John Thorius, and Anthony Chute, Harvey has expressed his gratitude for their courteous letters and commendatory sonnets *"write to him from a farre."* That is, comments Don Carneades, *"out of the hall into the kitchin at* Wolfes, *where*

altogether at one time they lodged and boorded" (III, 102, 33–35).
Then with many effusive compliments Harvey has urged Barnes to be
a poet like Spenser or a soldier like Sir Thomas Baskerville. Nashe, as
Respondent, interrupts with a slighting remark aimed at Barnes. Don
Carneades adds an anecdote about Barnes's request to be excused from
military service in France.

Next, Harvey has bidden Thorius to be "the many tungd linguist"
like the preacher Lancelot Andrewes or "the curious Intelligencer" like
Sir Thomas Bodley (III, 105, 6–8). Since Thorius has already made his
peace with Nashe, the latter refuses to comment except to say that
Andrewes is above comparison with anyone else and that both Thorius
and Bodley would be insulted at being called *intelligencers*, a term
suggesting treachery.

Harvey has advised Chute to be "the flowing Oratour" and to
remember his "Portugall Voyage" (III, 106, 27–29). Unfortunately
Chute is now dead and beyond Nashe's vengeance. Yet although Chute
had "kneaded and daub'd vp" a comedy about tobacco, he knew no
Latin and had been notably unsuccessful on certain occasions at public
speaking. Furthermore he had served only as a cabin boy on the voyage to Portugal. The fact of the matter is, writes Nashe, that since
Harvey could get no one else to commend his work he chose three
unimportant men. By comparing them with important people, he
hopes to create the illusion that they too were important. And again
Nashe praises Andrewes and Baskerville in order to make up for what
he considers Harvey's slight in naming them with inferior persons who
would never have appeared in print except for Harvey's efforts on their
behalf and who had become infected with their sponsor's "owne spirit
of Bragganisme" (III, 109, 22).

Next Nashe discusses the mysterious "Gentlewoman" whom, Don
Carneades points out, Harvey calls "his patronesse or rather champio-
nesse in this quarrel" (III, 110, 16–17). Domino Bentivole offers the
suggestion that Harvey "thinkes in his owne person if hee should raile
grosely, it will bee a discredit to him, and therefore hereafter hee
would thrust foorth all his writings vnder the name of a Gentlewoman;
who, howsoeuer shee scolds and playes the vixen neuer so, wilbe borne
with" (III, 111, 9–13). Grand Consiliadore agrees. After a few
moments of fun at Harvey's expense, Senior Importuno flatly states his
opinion that the Gentlewoman is merely a fiction. Accordingly Nashe,
as Respondent, refuses to confute the sonnets supposedly composed by
her. Moreover, he adds that if Harvey under her name writes a comedy

on Nashe as he threatens, then Nashe in return will have one ready for which he gives a series of possible titles, all of them absurd. Harvey's derisive epithet "Danter's Maulkin,"[11] or slattern, originally directed at Nashe's patroness, Saint Fame, Nashe deliberately misconstrues as an insult to the wife of his printer, John Danter. But he is sure that Mrs. Danter will be a match for Harvey (III, 114, 32 ff.).

Nashe then scoffs at Barnes's epistle with its sonnet, at the foot of which, as Senior Importuno describes it, "like a right Pupill of the Doctors bringing vp" he has inserted his "post-script or correction of his Preamble with a Counter-sonnet" in which he sneers at Nashe for railing at a friend of Bodin and Sidney (III, 115, 33–36). Nashe explains that Sidney has always cherished anyone showing the least ability in any art and perhaps has written some letters to encourage Harvey. The latter, however, has carried himself so proudly that Sidney has begun "to looke askance on him, and not to care for him" (III, 116, 19–20). Bodin's commendation was merely his reply to a complimentary letter from Harvey. Now, alas, all of Harvey's friends have abandoned him.

Taking up the "Printers Aduertisement to the Gentleman Reader," Nashe, by this time thoroughly suspicious of his opponent's habit of ascribing his own compositions to other people, maintains that the use of the words *preambles* and *postambles* in the third line sounds like Harvey himself. Nashe also laughs at his reference to the "third learned French Gentlemans verses" at the end of the pamphlet (III, 117, 3–15).

Coming to the main text of *Pierce's Supererogation,* Nashe, as Respondent, divides it into four parts: one against himself, one against Lyly, one against the Martinists, and one against Dr. Perne. Moreover, these parts are not separately organized but jumbled together. First taking his own part, he discounts Harvey's complaint that he dislikes entering a quarrel like this. Nashe reminds him that after all he not only began it but even refused to be reconciled. Nashe then takes up the accusation that as a modern Apuleius he has stamped and trodden underfoot "the reuerentest old and new Writers," has opposed himself to "Vniuersities, Parliaments, and generall Councells," and is a "changer, an innouator, a cony-catcher, a rimer, a rayler" (III, 118, 25–28). Nashe challenges him to cite passages supporting each of these assertions. Cannot a man, he asks, write against Gabriel and Dick Harvey without oppugning "vniuersities, Parliaments, general Councells"? Or it may be that Harvey, who boasts of his vast reading and his commencements at two universities, identifies what he has learned with the sources of his knowledge and therefore believes that any attack on him is an attack on these sources.

Don Carneades breaks in with the suggestion that Harvey is merely using "a Rhetoricall figure of amplification" (III, 120, 2). Yet, continues Don Carneades, rhetoricians are "Arithmetique figurers," who are also "jugling transformers, lying by Addition and Numeration, making frayes and quarreling by Diuision, getting wenches with childe by Multiplication, stealing by Substraction." He concludes with the assertion that if in these humors they "haue consumd all, and are faine to breake," they resort to the use of fractions (III, 120, 2–23). Whereupon Nashe replies that he himself is going to teach his opponent "Fraction or breaking" since he knows all the other arithmetical processes, especially multiplication now that he has a "Gentlewoman." Here again Nashe minimizes her threats to attack him.

He then points out that Harvey has stolen many of his opponent's railing "termes." Similarly, suggests Nashe, he may have stolen all his quotations from other authors in order to decorate his attack. Just because Nashe would not let himself be set upon, Harvey likens him to all of the evil people about whom he has read. At this point Nashe plays his trump card. Harvey's pamphlet, he states, was not originally directed at him and therefore is as stale as his attack on Lyly entitled "An Aduertisement for Papp-hatchet and Martin Mar-prelate." All that Harvey did was to substitute either "Nashe" or "Pierce Penilesse" for the original names in the text without adding anything new (III, 124, 18 ff.). Only about "a dozen of famisht quips" could possibly apply to Nashe's criticism of Harvey in *Strange Newes*. These Nashe specifically enumerates and reiterates his original reasons for making them.

Although Harvey frowns upon Nashe's high praise of Aretino, Harvey himself in his letters to Spenser had expressed a similar admiration for the Italian satirist. If Harvey resents being questioned about his doctorate, Nashe retorts that better doctors than Harvey had expressed grave doubts about the authenticity of his degree. In reply to Harvey's objection to Nashe's calling him "a fawne-guest messenger" between Bird and Demetrius, Nashe asks why then had he spoken in a familiar manner about Mistress Demetrius.

This rebuttal Nashe interrupts in order to point out that for the most part his opponent merely repeats the accusation made against him in the first place without answering it, "like Sophisticall Disputers that only rehearse, not answere." Even if Harvey pretends to reply, what he has to say is beside the point. For example, Nashe charges that he uses such "carterly derisions and milk-maids girds" as "Good beare, bite not" and "a man's a man thogh he hath but a hose on his head." Domino Bentivole impatiently brushes aside Harvey's defense that these clichés are classical ironies.

Nashe requests him to be explicit concerning Harvey's new accusation that Nashe has "derided and abused the most valorous Mathematicall Arts" (III, 126, 9–11). In addition Nashe ridicules Harvey's suggestion of atheism, which seemingly was made because Nashe criticized Richard Harvey's *Lamb of God.* The next new complaint is that Nashe shows little regard for such eminent men as Bird, Spenser, Bodin, Watson, all of whom have praised Harvey. Singling out Watson, Nashe states that it was he who first pointed out Harvey's vanity and who composed satiric hexameters on him.

Here Nashe becomes temporarily confused. In *Strange Newes* he had attributed these particular hexameters about Harvey's alleged imprisonment to William Butler (I, 300, 12 ff.). Furthermore Nashe refers to Harvey's "welwillers Epistle" as appearing in *Foure Letters* whereas actually it had been prefixed to his *Three Proper and wittie Familiar Letters* published fifteen years earlier (III, 127, 12–13; IV, 365). Regarding this epistle Nashe states that the compositor who had set it swore that it had come to him in Harvey's own handwriting. Finally in this confusion Nashe assumes that Harvey's reference to "the Preamble" before *Pierce Penilesse* is directed at his letter to the printer in his second and third editions. But Harvey apparently is referring to the short epistle to the reader signed "R. I." in the first edition. These few inaccuracies seem to bear out Nashe's many hints of increasing boredom with the entire affair.

Continuing with the list of Harvey's charges, Nashe takes up the reference to his poverty. To this he replies with something of his old form that his father "put more good meate in poore mens mouthes than all the ropes & liuing is worth his [Harvey's] Father left him, together with his mother and two brothers" (III, 127, 29–32). Moreover Nashe's father had sent him and another young man to Cambridge. Harvey's contemptuous comment that Nashe derives his living from the printing house he considers irrelevant since the universities and all the learned scholars who publish do likewise. He receives money for his publication whereas Harvey has to pay for his. In fact, the printer Danter has sworn to get even with Harvey for his slurs upon the press.

At this point Nashe wearily complains that it would be like cutting off Hydra's head to "run throghout all the foolish friuolous reprehensions & cauils he hath in his Booke" (III, 128, 30–35). Ending with a bit of gossip about Harvey's "baudy sister" Mercy (III, 129, 24–33), he categorically states that all of the names that he has heretofore given Harvey he "will still perseuer and insist in" (III, 130, 2–5). He protests his love for the Queen and his reverence for the city of London. He denies that he has ever detracted from "anie generall allowed moderne Writer." He blames the beginning of the quarrel on the Harveys. He also repeats that he had once praised Harvey in his preface to Greene's *Menaphon* just as Harvey had praised him in "his first butter-fly Pamphlet against *Greene*" (Harvey's second letter—a statement which McKerrow interprets to mean that it was first separately issued before the publication of *Foure Letters*—IV,368). Then, after railing against Nashe in the third letter, Harvey had again included him among the great writers of the day.[12]

Next Nashe denies the allegation that he had ever abused Marlowe, Greene, or Chettle. As proof he encloses a note from Chettle absolving him. For a moment, then, Nashe again digresses in order to point out that Harvey never substantiates his accusations. As far as traducing or imitating Greene's style, Nashe denies both counts and asks Harvey to contrast his with Greene's. On the contrary, Nashe asserts, Harvey himself "hath purloyned" something from him and thus improved his own style in confuting (III, 132, 29–31).

Before concluding, Nashe requests the patience of his reader for a few more jests at Harvey's expense. First he parodies his opponent's attempts at poetry both in *Pierce's Supererogation* and in *A New Letter*. Regarding Harvey's threat to use physical violence, Nashe reminds him that he had his opportunity when they stopped at the same inn in Cambridge. Now in a ribaldly humorous fashion he returns the challenge and in addition promises to steal from his opponent all of his best patrons.

He then returns to the items appended to *Pierce's Supererogation* consisting of letters and poems by John Thorius and Anthony Chute, a poem in French by a French scholar, the printer's postscript, a sonnet signed "Shore's wife," and three sonnets by Harvey himself.[13] Instead of criticizing Thorius's compositions, Nashe inserts a letter of apology from Thorius, protesting that when he composed certain verses in Harvey's commendation he had read only five or six sheets of his pamphlet and now flatly denies that the sonnet with his name subscribed is his. Regarding Chute, now dead, Nashe repeats that he never would have mentioned him except that his friend is alive to answer for him. As far as the Frenchman is concerned, Nashe urges that he be declared a fugitive from England, as he already is from his own country.

At this point Nashe expresses his desire to write a word or two in defense of Dr. Perne and John Lyly, both of whom Harvey has constantly maligned. Of Perne, first, Nashe maintains that "the Vniuersitie had not a more carefull Father this 100. yeare," distinguished as he was for his hospitality, his wit, and his learning (III, 137, 23–31). As for Lyly, he is quite able to answer for himself and plans soon to be at Harvey's chamber windows. In response to Harvey's assertion that as an anti-Martinist confuter Bishop Cooper would have done better than Lyly, Nashe asks why Lyly and others had to come forward in order to silence Martin. Here Nashe apparently cannot resist a triumphant verbal allusion to his authorship of the pamphlet that succeeded in bringing the Marprelate controversy to an end. It will be recalled that on the title page of this pamphlet, *An Almond,* Nashe had issued the warning, "Therefore beware (gentle Reader) you catch not the hicket [hiccough] with laughing" (III, 339). Now in deriding Harvey's smug boast that some people had identified him as Martin, Nashe writes, "I haue a laughing hickocke [hiccough] to heare him saye, *he was once suspected for* Martin, when there is nere a Pursiuant in England, in the pulling on his boots, euer though of him or imputed to him so much wit" (III, 138, 15–18). Whereupon Nashe selects for ridicule a few of Harvey's comments on the bishops and clergy of the Church of England, which in his opinion represent "the bangingest thinges" which he might have used in religious controversy.

With a brief statement of faults escaped in printing Nashe abruptly ends his second and final reply to Harvey. All that remained was for the authorities of Church and State to step in.

CHAPTER 11

Nashe's Lenten Stuffe

I *Summary*

NASHE dedicated his final pamphlet to Humfrey King, variously nicknamed Lustie Humfrey, little Numps, Honest Humfrey, King of the Tobacconists. In the author's opinion King was as able a poet as the "H. S." whom McKerrow identifies as the editor of Sidney's *Arcadia* (1593) and the writer of its prefatory epistle (IV, 375). Humfrey, indeed, excels all those soldiers of fortune, carpet knights, and men about town who render only promises or excuses in return for a fine dedication. Because King is both a king by name and a king of good fellows, this encomium to the king of fishes was destined to be his from his infancy.

The dedication is followed by an epistle to his readers "hee cares not *what they be*" (III, 151, 1–2). In it he explains that he entitles his pamphlet "Lenten-stuffe" because he spent most of his last Lent composing it. If anyone by chance were to compare it to a recently published book about the red herring's tail, he maintains amid a glittering series of puns that his tale will not "turne taile" to any man but will provide his reader with "Head, body, taile, and all of a redde Herring" (III, 151,18). He promises that in a short time he will compose an answer to the anonymous *The Trimming of Thomas Nashe* that will make everyone laugh. This "light friskin" of his wit praising the red herring is intended to demonstrate that it is cleverer to write of insignificant than of great matters. His "true vaine," he adds, is to be a *"tragicus Orator,"* employing a satirical style like that of Aretino (III, 152, 8).

In the opening lines of the pamphlet-proper Nashe expresses regret at being forced to leave London because of his connection with the ill-fated play *The Isle of Dogs*, of which he admits writing only the induction and the first act. His main concern is not so much that his banishment has taken away his livelihood but that it has given his enemies free rein to criticize him. However, he threatens sooner or later to get back at them. In fact he is already planning his reply to *The*

Trimming of Thomas Nashe, which he intends to call *The Barbers warming panne*.

Nevertheless his forced exile has not been altogether unfortunate because it introduced him to the hospitable city of Yarmouth, where he has spent some six long weeks. Now that he learns that his escapade may be pardoned providing he appeal it, he has decided to write in praise of and thanksgiving to the city that took him in when he was little more than a beggar. He compares himself to Homer rejected by one city and taken in by another which he made famous.

Yarmouth stands as a bulwark against the sea. What seems like a narrow harbor running two miles from the sea will easily accommodate 600 fairly good-sized ships from all nations making as inspiring an appearance as the Spanish Armada even if they are smaller than the Spanish ships. After a storm, when they spread their sails again, they make a beautiful sight. In spite of their number Yarmouth feeds both them and her own citizens without showing any sign of scarcity and without raising the price of food. For fear of displeasing the city fathers, Nashe forbears to discuss the "royal magnificence" of the municipal government (III, 159, 1). Instead he plans to present a complete history of Yarmouth from her very beginnings.

Until about A. D. 1000 Yarmouth was just a marsh. The harbor which ran two miles up to Castter, or Old Yarmouth, has since been filled in. The Saxons constructed a second city of Yarmouth on the site of what is now the nearby village of Gorlstone. Finding the environment unattractive the inhabitants pulled up stakes and moved to the present site. Although according to Camden this city had seventy inhabitants in the reign of Edward the Confessor, a Latin document hanging in the Guild Hall states that at that date the land was still partly under water.

Situated sixteen miles east of Norwich between the ocean and the bay, the city has a plentiful supply of drinking water. In the days of Harold and William the Conqueror people used to gather on Yarmouth sands and set up tents where they sold fish. During the reign of William Rufus, the Bishop of Norwich built a chapel there. Between the times of Henry I and Richard I the sands gradually joined the mainland at Eastflege, where a royal provostship was established that lasted until the reign of John. Then the Bishop of Norwich decided to pull down the chapel and build the cathedral of Saint Nicholas. In the year 1209 the King declared Yarmouth a town and bestowed many privileges on it. By 1240 it was large enough to be governed by bailies and strong enough that its ships and men took on its rivals, defeated them, and forced them to appeal to King Henry II. The King consequently placed a fine on Yarmouth of 1,000 pounds, later removed.

Edwards I and II increased the privileges of the city and changed it from a borough to a port town with a customs house. Henry III gave it two more charters and permitted fortifications to be built. At the same time he named two lord admirals over the English navy, one of whom was John Peerbrowne, burgess of Yarmouth, in control of the northern navy. For his splendid record, especially in destroying the French navy of 400 ships, Peerbrowne was reappointed by Edward III. As a reward for his victory the King joined Kirtley Road with Yarmouth and raised the price of their privileges. Richard II confirmed the liberties of Kirtley Road. Henry V permitted the city to build a bridge over the harbor. Succeeding rulers likewise have been generous.

Of course Yarmouth has suffered from the plague like other towns, most notably that of 1348 when in one year 7,050 people died. The new building at the west end of the church, begun in 1330, proved too costly for completion. Instead the people have installed wooden galleries which provide as much room as the proposed west end would have given.

Next Nashe describes the architectural plan of the city. The walls forming a quadrangle bordering on the harbor are 2,180 yards from south to north and boast sixteen towers and three mounts fortified with cannon. Nashe gives elaborate measurements for the third and newest mount. The city possesses ten gates, 140 lanes, and three streets as long as sixty London streets. It also owns liberties on fresh water ten miles in each direction.

Originally Nashe had considered giving similar descriptions of all of England's coastal towns lest the reader think that he is praising Yarmouth in this manner because he knows no other port. Furthermore, he had planned to discuss the interest taken by William the Conqueror in the welfare of the people of Kent. Instead he will restrict his subject to economic conditions in Yarmouth.

Wealth in the city is evenly distributed. Two hundred citizens are worth 300 pounds each—a decided contrast to other cities, where one or two have everything. The city acts as a defense to Suffolk and Norfolk counties. It provides fresh herring and salted fish for the entire realm. In the spring when food is most expensive it relieves its own section by furnishing forty boatloads of mackerel. Later in the year it supplies ships for herring and for commercial purposes. The fishing industry, in turn, provides work for poor women and children who braid nets and spin twine. And for the comfort of the people working on the nets the city sets apart a pleasant green park near the seashore. The vigilant care given the harbor improves the marshes and lands along the rivers and makes them more valuable. Not only are Norwich and other towns furnished with fish, but they have their provisions brought to their very doors. Nashe gives the statistics for the cost of maintaining the harbor, of naval action, of losses from foreign attack, of other municipal expenses, and finally of the annual provision of fish for the Queen. If other coastal towns were as industrious as Yarmouth, the world would be as prosperous as it was prior to the Reformation. Moreover, the buildings of the city are more beautiful than those in other port towns. Finally, the citizens themselves are honest, courageous, and law-abiding.

Bidding farewell to Yarmouth, Nashe comes to his praise of the red herring, the Sultan of the sea. He admits that had he not visited Yarmouth he would never have thought of the herring. Nor would he have thought of comparing that fish to the Persian monarch if he had not learned that William Harborne, the first English ambassador to Turkey, was born in that city. Even though the streets of Yarmouth are not crowded with swaggering sea captains as in other English ports, Nashe happened one day to meet an acquaintance who told him that it is the red herring that has made Yarmouth a wealthy city. Indeed, the red herring has built the magnificent walls of the city; it maintains the haven; it defrays all the taxes to the Queen; it dresses the city magistrates in royal robes. Consequently this friend urged Nashe to celebrate the glories of this beneficial creature.

Nashe prefaces his encomium with the apology that in his hasty flight from London he had left all of his notebooks and reference books behind him. Hence the reader must not expect too much of him. In order to defend his choice of subject he cites a long list of other trivialities celebrated in print. Then without further ado he begins. The red herring is the most precious of all English merchandise—more than wool, grain, lead, tin, iron, or dairy products, each of which can be matched elsewhere. The English red herring, however, has no equal. Hosted, roasted, toasted, powdered, salted—it furnishes food and employment for thousands. As a medium of exchange it brings foreign produce into the country. The herring fleets are the training schools for the sailors of the Royal Navy. Although they may not have to endure as great hardship in the former as in the latter, they have no easy life. The fishermen must search for herring sometimes in the sands, sometimes in the roaring seas. Once the fish is caught it must be transported to far-off countries. Therefore anyone depreciating the skill of the sailors of Yarmouth is mistaken.

Another benefit derived from the red herring is as a solace during Lent, when it becomes the chief article of diet everywhere. The herring has launched more ships than Helen's face or the pilgrimage to Rome in King Edward III's day. All sections of England, especially the seaport towns, play an active part in bringing in the catch. Nashe compares the crowds involved to those bidding farewell to a great hero leaving for the wars. The red herring, however, is a harbinger of peace. In satirical pseudo-Scottish dialect Nashe cites the translation of herring from the waters around Scotland to Yarmouth because of a feud in which many deeds of violence were committed. As proof of the truth of this story he humorously refers to the confessions of 600 Scottish witches executed during the past year. Envying Yarmouth for its prosperity, these witches stirred up great storms in the waters near the city. But envy is a universal failing. Nashe is certain that all the smiths in the large cities would be envious of the smith living in Yarmouth who fashioned a tiny lock and key and an equally tiny chest containing a pair of knit gloves.

During the herring season the sun dances for joy. If the skin of the red herring, saffron-colored like the sun, is removed, the taste of the fish is ruined. In order to illustrate the relative nutritive value of various meats Nashe tells a story of a king who for a year and a day had four men fed, respectively, beef, pork, mutton, and veal (III, 190, 7 ff.). The man fed beef became as fat as an ox and cried nothing but "Biefe, Biefe, Biefe." The swine-eater likewise fattened gasped, "Porke, Porke, Porke." The "sheepe-biter" light as a feather cried, "mitton, mitton, mitton." Finally, the calf-eater, thin and pale with shunken calves—a rebuke to physicians who recommend veal for invalids—was barely able to whisper, "veale, veale, veale." Had the king given another man only herring, Nashe comments, he would have cried, "Hurrey, Hurrey, Hurrey," as if the resulting increase in physical strength had given him courage to scatter his enemies.

When the herring is first caught, he is pale in color. Then he is smoked for three or four days until he becomes the color of gold—a treasure sought after by all countries, even distant Turkey. Nashe suggests that the Sultan's pleasure derived from devouring herring stems from his desire to imitate King Midas, who, if the truth were known, actually ate herring instead of gold. When troubled with indigestion, he prayed to Bacchus, who favored him because he had befriended Silenus. The meaning of Bacchus's advice —namely, to wash in the river Pactolus—was that Midas should wash down his herring with wine. When the river turned into gold, the significance of the event was that nothing but golden cups should be used for this wine. Explaining the fable of Jupiter's appearance in a golden coat to Dionysius, Nashe informs his reader that the supposed Jupiter was really a golden-coated red herring which Dionysius had beheaded, skinned, and eaten. For this indignity King Dionysius was dethroned and forced to become a schoolmaster. The Persians who were said to worship Mortus Alli actually worship "*mortuum halec,*" or the dead red herring (III, 195, 4).

In order to explain how the herring came to be a fish and eventually king of the fishes, Nashe in a mock-heroic vein recounts the epic love story of Hero and Leander celebrated first by "Musaeus" and later by "Kit Marlowe." Because of a family feud Leander and Hero were forced to live separated by "an arme of the sea," the Hellespont (III, 195, 24). Leander had to swim by night to the tower where Hero was imprisoned with only one companion, her old nurse. One night, swimming to her in a storm, he was drowned. About to embrace his dead body she saw it swept from her by the waves. Overcome with grief she leaped in after it and was drowned. Leander was transformed into the fish known as the ling. And from the loins of Hero, pregnant at the time, stemmed the race of the noble herring. Her old nurse, who died from grief at the loss of her charge, was changed into mustard-seed. Ever since that tragic day she always accompanies the two fishes at the dinner table. Every year Hero, in memory of her beloved, makes a pilgrimage to the coast near Yarmouth. If, however, the townspeople are at odds there as in recent times, she may come in farther north.

Next Nashe relates the story of a mock-war between the birds and the fishes. A falcon being brought over from Ireland broke loose from the falconer's fist and striking at a fish was snapped up by a shark. The "Kings fisher" carried the news of this murderous act to the land fowls, all of whom prepared for war (III, 201, 23). Since they were unable to swim, they made a covenant with the seafowls. The puffin, "halfe fish halfe flesh," revealed this conspiracy to the fishes (III, 202, 28). The larger ones jeered, but the smaller decided to elect a king. After a long campaign they chose the herring, who ever since has worn a coronet on his head.

As for the outcome of the war between the birds and the fishes

Nashe, now bored with the entire affair, intends to leave it to some other inventor of fables. All that he will add is that from that time on the herring has traveled in armies. It has become customary for fishermen to catch their scouts or advance sentinels, "swinge" them about the main mast, bid them bring in "so many last of Herrings as they have swinged them times," and then throw them back into the sea (III, 204, 5–6).

Bidding farewell to the king of fishes, Nashe continues with an explanation of how the herring happened to change his color. In the early days of Yarmouth a fisherman lacking room in his shed for his entire catch hung the rest in his garret. Since the weather was cold, he made hot fires. In four or five days the herring, white when first hung up, had turned red. Regarding it as a miracle, the fisherman presented a red herring to the king then visiting at "Borrough" (Burgh) Castle, two miles from Yarmouth at the junction of the Jerus and Waveny rivers. On the island thus formed is situated "Leystofe" (Lowestoft), where Nashe was born. Because of his personal interest in the locality Nashe digresses and gives a history of the Castle, formerly a monastery.

When the king heard the fisherman's story, he licensed him to carry and show the red herring everywhere as a rare monster. After making as much money as he could in England, the owner of the fish decided to travel to Rome. On the way he was robbed of everything he possessed except three of his herrings. Arriving in Rome, he polished them and placed them on display in the marketplace. When the Pope's caterer desired to purchase them, the fisherman asked 100 ducats for only one. At the caterer's refusal the fisherman ate the fish. The caterer hurried to the Pope, who demanded that the king of fishes be bought for him. Returning to the marketplace the caterer offered 100 ducats. The fisherman, however, demanded 200. The caterer again refusing to pay, the fisherman ate the second herring. Hearing what had happened, the Pope was furious, but he ordered his caterer to return and buy the third herring. The fisherman not only sold it for 300 ducats but gave instructions how to prepare and cook it.

Then the Pope's cooks made great preparations. Although by now the herring was almost a year old and gave off such a foul odor that everyone fled from it, it was carried with great ceremony to the Pope. However, the stench was so dreadful that it overcame even the Pope himself. Therefore the cardinals, deciding that it must be an evil spirit, unsuccessfully attempted to exorcise it. Finally they concluded that it must be the soul of some drowned king who, unrelieved in Purgatory by the prayers of the Church and bearing with him the foul smell of his sins, had returned to beg their aid. Accordingly they asked the Pope that he might be given Christian burial, have Masses sung for him, and be canonized. The Pope granted these requests. As a result, the herring became Saint Gildarde. His feast day was set for April first. In commemoration of the embers upon which he was cooked, ember weeks were ordained for fasts. When Madame Celina Cornificia, the most famous of the Roman courtesans, heard of the wonderful fish, she pawned all her jewels in order to buy it. However, her purveyor came too late. All that he found were the two "cobs," or heads, of the herrings eaten by the fisherman. These he bought for his mistress at the price of fourscore ducats.

Some people may doubt this tale of the origin of the red herring. The citizens of Norwich, for example, maintain that the first gilding of that noble fish occurred when Castor, a town two miles away, now Norwich Castor, was called Norwich and was the chief seaport. But Nashe dismisses their claim as being as absurd as those of the man who said that the red herring came from the Red Sea or of the Cambridge scholar who after tying a herring with a bell around its neck to his hook told all the simple country folk passing by where he was fishing that he had just caught it.

On the subject of credulity Nashe complains that some people will believe anything. In fact, he himself has been subjected to great misinterpretation—an echo of the trouble caused by his allegory of the Bear and the Fox and his *Christ's Teares*. He severely criticizes lawyers who have found false meanings in his writings. Then just to give these interpreters more riddles to solve, he tells the story of the herring who wooed Lady Turbot. As a consequence of her refusal the fish was sentenced to be boiled and pickled. Nashe defies any so-called interpreter, wishing to terrify his prince so that he can pretend to be his protector, to interpret this tale. He knows that these busybodies will use any chance remark made by any harmless person for their advancement. Nashe promises to refrain from further riddling but admits that his own riddle has as much sense as it should have.

Continuing with his discussion of the red herring, he states that he never used to believe in alchemy. Now, however, the change in color of the herring's skin "from his duskie tinne hew into a perfit golden blandishment" has convinced him (III, 220, 34–35). The skin of a red herring can be used to draw hounds to a scent. Its head can be ground up as a preventive against the stone.

Nashe next explains some of the vocabulary associated with the herring industry. The phrase *to cade herrings*, meaning to pack them in kegs, comes from the rebel Jack Cade, who first hit upon this method of handling them. The *swinging of herrings* as they are being caded recalls the hanging of the rebellious inventor of the process. Another rebel, Jack Straw, the first man to pack herrings in straw, also has a process named after him. Nashe mentions a few uncomplimentary proverbs that, he insists, refer to herring coming from other coastal towns or from Scotland, not from Yarmouth. There the white herring, which travels better than the red, is treated like a lord. Every year during Lent the sheriffs of Norwich send twenty-four herring pies as homage to the nearby Lord of Caster, who, in turn, sees them conveyed in style to the court, where they are received in state. Indeed, the white herring is "meate for a Prince" (III, 223, 11).

Because of the clean diet of the herring, it should have received more attention from classical writers than it has. Nashe boasts that he is the first writer to praise any fish or fisherman. Quoting several unflattering literary references to that industry, he counters by calling fishermen the predecessors of the Apostles, "sonnes and heires of the Prophet Ionas," "Caualiers and Gentlemen" or courtiers, since they are subjects of the king of fishes, and Friars Observants for keeping fasting days (III, 225, 2 ff.). In return for his prayers for them he requests them to defend his pamphlet from the sort of critic who will complain either that Nashe was hard up for a subject or that he might as well have written about a dog's turd. Replying to both scornful criticisms, he concludes with a final string of sparkling epithets in praise of the red herring.

II   *Critical Commentary*

Nashe informs his reader that he began work on his final pamphlet during Lent 1598 (III, 151, 11). As McKerrow points out, it was not finished until the late autumn of that same year (IV, 371). It was published in 1599. It is divided into two distinct parts: first, a historical description of the city of Yarmouth; second, an original tour de force in praise of the red herring providing that city with its main staple of commerce. The immediate sources for the first part were Camden's *Brittania* (1594 edition), a "Chronographycal Latine table" hanging in the Guild Hall in Yarmouth, along with a possible English translation of that table, and a manuscript in English supposedly written about

1562 by Henry Manship and belonging to his son Henry, town clerk from 1579 to 1585 (IV, 372 ff.). Hibbard adds that as in previous writings Nashe also consulted such authors as Cornelius Agrippa and Hakluyt (p. 238). The inspiration for writing the pamphlet sprang from Nashe's deep gratitude to the city that had received him upon his banishment from London for his share in the composition of the allegedly treasonous play *The Isle of Dogs.*

Hibbard calls *Lenten Stuffe* "quite the most idiosyncratic and, in some ways, also the most brilliant and witty of all Nashe's writings" (p. 236). In this farewell to the world of letters, Hibbard adds, Nashe "carries his manner and method to their logical conclusion" and finally achieves his objective of "creating a recognizable literary personality." Seeking a literary classification for the pamphlet, Hibbard assigns it to the genre of the "mock encomium," of which Erasmus's *Encomium Moriae* is the best-known example in the period (p. 239). Again, however, this attempt to classify a work of Nashe according to conventional literary forms is unsatisfactory, for over a third of the pamphlet comprises a history of Yarmouth.

Referring to the mock encomium, Hibbard explains that Nashe relies for his effect on "a comic contrast between low matter and a high-faluting style." Two more recent scholars have given special attention to this important characteristic of Nashe's writing. Quoting Kaula's theory that for the purpose of satire Nashe alternates between a "high heraldic style" and a "low style,"[1] Davis adds that in both *The Unfortunate Traveller* and *Lenten Stuffe* Nashe deliberately strives for an effect of "surprise, sudden shifts in the bases of probability."[2]

Both Hibbard and Davis consider Nashe's original version of the myth of Hero and Leander the real achievement in the pamphlet. Hibbard terms it "the high-light of *Lenten Stuffe*" (p. 247). Again borrowing Kaula's stylistic approach, Davis is convinced that "Nashe's attitudes toward romance, myth, the high style, and even the entire rhetorical tradition behind the high style, are most completely developed in *Lenten Stuffe*," particularly in the Hero-Leander tale.[3] This tale, which is—to quote Davis—"a mock oration in praise of the insignificant red herring," or a "burlesque,"[4] at first treating the herring in the high style, exalts it by myth and at the same time attacks romance through parody. The "playful myth" thus begun in the high style ends in the colloquial style with Hero jumping into the Hellespont and leaving work for Musaeus and Marlowe, with the comic treatment of the sorrow of the gods and with Nashe's new ending to the myth, namely, that Hero and Leander were changed into a herring and a ling, respectively, and would in the future meet at dinner parties on week ends.[5]

Hibbard's principal objection to Nashe's accomplishment is that "the effort to spin out the trivial is painfully obvious" in the two comic tales of how the herring became the king of fishes (p. 247). The first of these, the war between the birds and the fishes, in Hibbard's opinion, "fizzles out in a rather inconclusive fashion" when Nashe decides to leave the account of the actual battle to a professional maker of fables. However, it must be noted that Nashe really accomplishes what he had set out to do, namely, "to tell howe the Herring scrambled vp to be King of all fishes" (III, 201, 7–8). And the last sentence of his fable, then, announces the outcome of the election for the crown:

None woone the day in this but the Herring, whom al their clamorous suffrages saluted with *Viue le roy*, God saue the King . . . and the Herring euer since weares a coronet on his head, in token that hee is as he is. (III, 203, 19–25)

At this point, indeed, Nashe falls back on one of his "extemporall" devices: instead of a formal conclusion he merely expresses his boredom with the subject. Nevertheless in adding that ever since the war the herring travels in armies and in bidding a formal farewell to him, "King, by your leaue, for in your kingshippe I must leaue you" (III, 204, 7–9), Nashe actually has a more clear-cut transition than usual to his next subject, the "camelionizing" of the herring.

Hibbard's main objection to the second comic tale is that it is "little more than a bit of pope-baiting" (p. 247). Undoubtedly Nashe the satirist is not handling the canonization of the red herring in a reverent manner. In the first place, the absurdity of the idea presumes irreverence. Second, he is a staunch member of the Church of England and hence as opposed to Roman Catholicism as to Puritanism. But his humor in telling how the overripe red herring ended as St. Gildarde, with his feast day on April Fool's Day, and in embroidering his account of the canonization with allusions to the liturgy is as merry a piece of fooling as he produced out of the academic exercises of the University of Wittenberg in *The Unfortunate Traveller*.

CHAPTER 12

Nashe's Place in English Literature

I Nashe's Reputation in His Own Time

DURING the years immediately following his death Nashe was regarded somewhat differently from the brilliant journalist described in the preceding chapters. Of course the average Elizabethan reader probably read his pamphlets at the time of their publication for the same reason that we today read our newspapers, namely, for information and entertainment. But the literary critics of the 1590s and the next hundred years were not concerned with the passing scene but rather with classical learning, legend, and history. As a result they compared Nashe with the satirists of ancient Rome. During the first half of the seventeenth century, then, Nashe was remembered chiefly as a satirist—the author of *Pierce Penilesse*, the witty opponent of the Cambridge scholar Gabriel Harvey, and the champion of the Church of England against Martin Marprelate.

Of his masterpiece, *Pierce Penilesse*, he himself proudly boasted that it had passed through "at the least . . . sixe Impressions" between 1592 and 1596 (III, 35, 19). Three of these "Impressions," or editions, came out between August 8, 1592, the date of its first entry in the Stationers' Register, and the end of the same year. The first significant posthumous reference to this pamphlet appears in *The Blacke Book*, by T. M. (probably Thomas Middleton), in 1604. According to its author, the Devil in answer to Pierce's supplication visits London in disguise in order to check on his affairs. He frequents taverns and brothels. He also calls on Nashe, whom he finds dying in extreme poverty in a London slum. McKerrow believes that this imaginary interview between the Devil and Nashe is responsible for the rumor, otherwise unsupported, that the satirist was atill alive "as late as 1603" (IV, 82). Before the Devil departs, he leaves Nashe a legacy of the "tythe of all Vaulting Houses" (brothels) in the city.

Two years later, in 1606, another anonymous "reply" to Nashe's pamphlet appeared. It was entitled *The Return of the Knight of the*

Poste from Hell with the Diuels aunswere to the Supplication of Pierce Penilesse, with some Relation of the last Treasons. In its preface the author tells of his intimacy with Nashe and explains how he came to write his reply. He refers to Nashe's pamphlet as a "moral and wittie Treatise" (IV, 84). Recalling that Nashe in his epistle to the printer had promised to write the "*Deuils* answer to the *Supplication*" (I, 154, 5–8), the author of the reply states that Nashe had confided to him the contents of the proposed sequel. Since death had interfered with Nashe's plan, his friend is going to carry it out for him. First apologizing for the inferiority of his own wit as compared with Nashe's, he goes on to explain that he had met the same knight of the post who had carried Pierce's supplication to Hell and now is returning with the Devil's answer. In composing this answer the author follows Nashe's original plan of the Seven Deadly Sins.

Although Thomas Dekker's *Newes From Hell; Brought by the Diuells Carrier* (1606) was obviously inspired by Nashe's pamphlet, it is not a direct answer. However, it contains many reminiscences of Nashe's work. For example, the headline for its text is entitled "The Deuill let loose, with His Answere to Pierce Pennylesse." Its running title is "The Deuils Answere to Pierce Pennylesse." Nashe himself is addressed as follows:

... thou sometimes Secretary to *Pierce Pennylesse*, and Master of his requests, ingenious, ingenuous, fluent, facetious *T. Nash*: from whose aboundant pen, hony flow'd to thy friends, and mortall Aconite to thy enemies. . . . (v, 151–52)

In these years immediately following Nashe's death there also occur references to his satirical replies to Harvey. In *Father Hubburd's Tales or the Ant and the Nightingale*, published in 1604 by T. M. (again probably Middleton), is a poem containing the line, "Or if in bitternes thou raile like Nashe," and breaking off with " . . . here I began to rayle like *Thom. Nash*, against *Gabriell Haruey*" (V, 150–51).

In Dekker's *Newes From Hell* Nashe is also acclaimed the victor in the controversy with Harvey: " . . . thou that madest the Doctor a flat Dunce, and beat'st him at two sundry tall Weapons, Poetrie, and Oratorie: Sharpest Satire . . . " (V, 152). John Davies of Hereford, in his *Scourge of Folly*, published in 1611, also comments on Nashe's satire in both *Pierce Penilesse* and in his replies to Harvey (V, 153).

Other more general references to Nashe's satiric genius have been discovered in the literature of the first quarter of the seventeenth century. For example, in *A Knight's Conjuring* (1607) Dekker depicts a scene at the well of the Muses when Nashe meets his fellow University Wits:

... whil'st *Marlow*, *Greene*, and *Peele* had got vnder the shades of a large *vyne*, laughing to see *Nash* (that was but newly come to their Colledge,) still haunted with the sharpe and *Satyricall spirit* that followd him heere vpon earth: for *Nash* inueyed bitterly (as he had wont to do) against dry-fisted Patrons. . . .(V, 152)

And in *Rub, and a Great Cast, Epigrams*, published in 1614, Thomas Freeman writes an epigram *Of Tho. Nash*, in which he mentions Nashe's use of "bitter gall in Inke" (V, 153). Finally, Michael Drayton in 1620, in his *Elegy to Henry Reynolds, of Poets and Poesie*, praises Nashe's satirical ability (V, 154).

About 1640, when the tension between the Church of England and the Puritans was rapidly approaching the climax marked by the executions of an archbishop and a king, supporters of both sides turned back to the Marprelate controversy of 1588–90. One of Martin Marprelate's pamphlets, *Hay any worke for Cooper*, was published as Puritan propaganda.[1] In retaliation the defenders of the Established Church apparently looked to see what the anti-Martinist writers had produced. At this point Nashe emerges as the champion of the Establishment. Yet since all of the pamphlets in the controversy were issued under pseudonyms, his own contribution even then was difficult to ascertain.

He himself in *Strange Newes* alludes to his membership in the group (I, 270, 20). His comments, however, are so ambiguous that his exact connection is never specifically stated. Noting that the references to Nashe as the outstanding anti-Martinist writer do not begin to appear until the 1640s, McKerrow nevertheless concedes that the evidence for some connection is "fairly strong" (V, 45).

The first reference to Nashe as an anti-Martinist appears in the title of a tract by John Taylor, in which he names the satirist as a defender of the Established Church: *Differing Worships, Or, The oddes, betweene some Knights Service and God's. Or Tom Nash his Ghost (the old Martin queller) newly rous'd and is come to chide and take order with Nonconformists, Schismatiques, Separatists, and scandal-*

ous Libellers (V, 45). Although no mention of Nashe is made in the tract itself, the title may have inspired an anonymous pamphlet published in 1642 entitled *Tom Nash his Ghost. To the three scurvy Fellowes of the upstart Family of the Snufflers, Rufflers, and Shufflers; the thrice Treble-troublesome Scufflers in the Church and State, the onely Lay Ecclesi-Ass, I call Generalissimos . . . Written by Thomas Nash his Ghost, with Pap with a Hatchet, a little revived since the 30. Yeare of the late Qu. Elizabeths Reign, when Martin Mar-Prelate was as mad as any of his Tub-men are now.* In this pamphlet Nashe, described as "a poore *Poet*," is complimented for his "yerking, firking, jerking veine," which "made the Nests of *Martins* take their flight" (V, 45–46). Thus he is given entire credit for routing Martin Marprelate. Here also begins the attribution to him of other anti-Martinist pamphlets today generally recognized as the products of other pens. In this pamphlet he is credited with authorship of *Pappe with a Hatchet* now believed to be written by Lyly.

Satisfaction that a mere reference to Nashe's ghost in the title of a pamphlet could call forth a response apparently stimulated Taylor to try again in 1644. In a second pamphlet, *Crop-eare curried, or Tom Nash His Ghost,* he introduces a fairly lengthy address supposedly delivered by the Ghost, who admits possessing a "yerking, firking, jerking Satiricall and Poeticall veine" (V, 46–47). He also comments on the helplessness of the divinity scholars who with serious theological arguments tried to reply to Martin's railing pamphlets. Taylor emphasizes that nothing availed until Nashe "put some *Aquafortis* and *Gall*" into his "Inckhorn" and wrote two tracts, namely, "a delicate discourse of *Martin Mar tone* and *Mar to ther*" (probably Richard Harvey's *Plaine Percivall,* the complete title of which includes the phrase "to botch vp a Reconciliation between Mar-ton and Mar-tother") and *Pappe with a hatchet,* neither of which is attributed to Nashe today. Taylor's main point, however, is that Nashe singlehandedly put to flight "the Nest of Mischievous, Malevolent, Malignant *Martins*."

In 1665 Izaak Walton in his *Life of Hooker* credits the defeat of Martin Marprelate to Nashe's "sharp wit" and "scoffing, Satyrical merry Pen" (V, 47–48). Like his predecessors, Walton names Nashe as the author of *Pappe with a Hatchet.* However, he is the first scholar to attribute *An Almond* to its rightful author. Jeremy Collier in 1717 likewise gives Nashe entire credit for the victory of the anti-Martinists. Moreover, he attributes not only *Pappe with a Hatchet* but all of the Pasquil tracts to Nashe (V, 48).

Over a century later, as the Marprelate battles became even more remote and confused, Charles H. Cooper in *Athenae Cantabrigienses* (1861) credits Nashe, who by this time had become little more than a legend, with most of the anti-Martinist pamphlets already doubtfully assigned to him by other scholars, along with pamphlets by the Harveys, Dekker, and other writers (V, 137).

II   *A Twentieth-Century Interpretation*

The modern reader who expects to find in Nashe a typically sixteenth-century writer is in for a surprise. Sidney, in *The Defense of Poesy*, which epitomizes the literary aesthetic of the Renaissance, argues for the superiority of poetry (or literature) over history and astronomy on the basis of its antirealism. The poet, according to Sidney, is concerned with a world far better than the one perceived by the senses, or at least vastly different from it.[2] Nashe, on the contrary, has far more in common with the satirical American journalists Art Buchwald or Russell Baker than with Sidney and his numerous followers during the seventeenth and eighteenth centuries. Unlike Spenser and Milton he had no ambition to write the great English epic or to please the fit though few. Instead, like the columnist of today he was the interpreter of his own time for the understanding and enjoyment of his reader.

The stylistic quality which he cultivates for this purpose is his spontaneity—his "extemporall veine," as he terms it. In keeping with the apparent casualness of his composition as displayed in his frequent digressions and his lack of interest in logical form, he never tires of repeating that he is, as it were, writing "off the cuff." At the same time he pretends to scoff at the triviality of his material. For example, he refers to *Pierce Penilesse* as "this endlesse argument of speech" (I, 245, 15), to *The Terrors of the Night* as "wast paper" (I, 382, 21), and to *Lenten Stuffe*, the very title of which like the titles of some of Shakespeare's comedies suggests its lack of serious purpose, as "a light friskin of my witte" (III, 151, 23).

Throughout my study I have used the analogy of the daily newspaper as a clarification of the puzzle of Nashe's unusual style. Yet even the newspaper does not possess the spontaneity for which Nashe seems to be striving. On the front page the news is almost always at least a day late. If perchance that paper is a "late edition," its contents follow the events by several hours and hence are not truly "extemporall." Similarly in the on-the-spot reporting of television the news is a trifle stale. After a fatal airplane crash the viewer sees nothing but the wreckage scattered about and listens to interviews with onlookers or survivors. Only in a rare instance is the viewer part of the news in the making such as, for example, the broadcast on television after the assassination of President John F. Kennedy when Jack Ruby stepped from the crowd surrounding the prisoner Lee Harvey Oswald and shot him.

Nashe's sense of immediacy is also analogous to that of the novelists of our own day who have come to realize that the perfect work of art as defined by Aristotle with a formal beginning, middle, and end is an artistic ideal not consonant with reality. In recounting an unusual historical event one contemporary school of journalist-novelists is interested in the interrelationship of all the seemingly disconnected happenings surrounding that event in time. And their plot is determined by time: for instance, the day when their protagonist died. This same preoccupation with time marks the most original novel of the twentieth century, James Joyce's *Ulysses*. In this novel, indeed, time is so important that the day of the year chosen for Bloom's odyssey around Dublin has been designated as "Bloomsday"—a tribute to the protagonist whose choice of action determines the events that occur.

Nashe's similar interest in time is not one of his debts to Martin Marprelate. Even in his writings before *An Almond* it is apparent. In the seeming formlessness of *The Anatomie of Absurditie* he demonstrates his awareness of it. By eliminating the conventional introduction, body, and conclusion and by ignoring transitions he gives a sense of immediacy to his account of the absurdities of his day. In his preface to *Menaphon* he exclaims, "Giue me the man whose extemporall veine in any humour will excell our greatest Art-maisters deliberate thoughts" (III, 312, 24–26). Both of these pamphlets were composed before he had begun to imitate Martin's satiric style. Then, after learning the effectiveness of railing and the use of epithets, puns, and allusions from the author of the *Epistle,* his writing achieved a brilliancy that made him rather than Martin the foremost satirist of the Elizabethan era.

Moreover, in spite of a seeming lack of logical development, all of his pamphlets possess a unity that comes not from form but from content. The unity of *The Anatomie of Absurditie* results from the fact that Nashe's subject is the castigation of the vices and follies of the day. The two prefaces, of course, are concerned with literary criticism.

Although *An Almond* seems to lack form, it consists of scurrilous anecdotes intermingled with occasional references to religious differences, all intended to point out the absurdity of Puritanism. Like *The Anatomie of Absurditie*, *Pierce Penilesse* is a satiric attack on the social ills and eccentricities of Elizabethan London. In *Christ's Teares* Nashe is dealing with what today would be called the relativity of time. The events in the first part of the pamphlet occurring long ago in far-away Jerusalem prefigure what is happening in sixteenth-century London. In *The Unfortunate Traveller* Nashe again ignores historical time. Instead he lets Jack Wilton's itinerary determine the concatenation of events. Although the episodes recounted in the pamphlet supposedly begin in 1513 and end in 1520, the reader is never conscious of the passing of time. As a result Nashe is able to insert such unrelated occurrences as the Anabaptist uprising of 1534 and the romantic adventures of the Earl of Surrey, who was not born until 1517.

Similarly, the unity in each of his pamphlets against Harvey is achieved by the content. Here Nashe's aims are, first, to satirize the pedantry, the pompousness, and the egotism of his opponent and, second, to refute all of Harvey's criticism of himself and his friends. Then, in order to give the illusion of spontaneity, he proceeds to ignore all the usual rules of formal logic. If the reader is willing to recognize Nashe's conscious artistry in letting events control logic, he can enjoy each verbal tour de force as it comes along.

III *Conclusion*

In the final chapter of *Thomas Nashe: A Critical Introduction* Hibbard confesses that he feels that he has done little to solve the puzzle that is Nashe. On the contrary, merely in recognizing that Nashe's "bent was for journalism and, perhaps, for the novel which was ultimately to grow out of journalism" (p. 251), Hibbard, in my opinion, has approached the solution. Just because—as he puts it—"the literary forms in which Nashe might have excelled did not yet exist" (p. 251), there is no reason for assuming that the flair for journalism is strictly a twentieth-century phenomenon. An interest in the force of gravity was revealed by thinking men—Aristotle and Galileo, for instance— before the legendary apple fell on the head of Sir Isaac Newton and caused him to formulate the laws of falling bodies. Shakespeare in his great tragedies showed himself an expert in diagnosing neuroses—by

other names, of course—300 years before Sigmund Freud developed
the science of psychoanalysis. Similarly, satirical geniuses have always
felt an urge to extol the virtues and scoff at the absurdities of their
fellow men and women for the benefit of society in general. If we look
at Thomas Nashe as a sort of sixteenth-century Henry L. Mencken with
all of that American journalist's love of words, then I believe the "puzzle" is finally solved.

Appendix:
An Analysis of Nashe's
"Extemporall Vayne"

I His Epithets

NASHE'S chief contribution to English prose style is what he him-self calls his "extemporall vayne" (I, 199, 5–6; III, 312, 25)—an informal, seemingly casual prose sprinkled with invective, colloquial-isms, and startling neologisms. Most of his epithets in his noncontrov-ersial pamphlets are decorative or evocative rather than open to literal interpretation. For example, in *Pierce Penilesse*, the first of the Devil's titles, senior (or signior) *Belzibub*, is instantly recognized as another name for Satan. McKerrow has more difficulty with Laurence Lucifer. He nevertheless ventures the suggestion that in coining this epithet Nashe may have had in mind that St. Laurence's Day falls on August 10 "in the hottest part of the year" (IV, 108). This psychological approach to an analysis of Nashe's style resembles the contemporary technique of interpreting the vocabulary of James Joyce, an artist who like Nashe is in love with words. Had McKerrow used the same method in interpreting the epithet *Nicalao Maleuolo*, he might have discov-ered that it suggests more than just "some vague reference to Niccolò Macchiavelli" (IV, 112). Since Nashe in *Pierce Penilesse* identifies hypocrisy with "all Machiauilisme" (I, 220, 14), he expects his reader to associate the arch-hypocrite with the Italian writer, who to the Eliz-abethans personified treachery.

Similarly, endeavoring to gloss *Diotrephes Diuell*, McKerrow notes that though *Diotrephes* is the title of a dialogue on the *State of the Church of England* written by the eminent Puritan minister John Udall, he finds "little point in the use of the name here" (IV, 127). But the anti-Martinist writer here is identifying hypocrisy, which both in *An Almond* (III, 345, 31 ff.) and in *The Anatomie of Absurditie* (I, 22, 9 ff.) he had termed the besetting sin of Puritanism, with this par-ticular Puritan who had been one of the three principal suspects in the Marprelate incident. The title "You goodman wandrer about the world" may allude to Satan's reply to the Lord's query, "Whence comest thou?" in the *Book of Job*: "From going to and fro in the earth, and from walking up and down in it." "Doctor Diuell" recalls the legend of Doctor Faustus, who sold his soul to the Devil. For "Master *Os foetidum*," for which McKerrow can offer no explanation (IV, 116), Nashe may have been associating the superstition that the appearance of the Devil is accompanied by a foul smell with the fact that the plant asafetida has a strong, not particularly pleasant, odor. But even using this technique of interpretation, reminiscent of the glossaries for *Finnegans Wake*, it is impossible to interpret all of Nashe's epithets. The reader must rely on his own subconscious mind if he wishes to appreciate Nashe's mercurial wit.

As might be expected, Nashe reaches the high point in his use of invective in his controversial pamphlets against Gabriel Harvey. Either through alliteration or connotation his epithets strike the emotional keynote of their context, whether it is insulting or mock-heroic. For example, in *Strange Newes* "Gamaliel Hobgoblin," immediately followed by a reference to the "Poet Hobbinoll" (I, 289, 24 ff.), may refer to Harvey's playfully ambiguous remark to Spenser in *Three Proper and wittie Familiar Letters*, on which Nashe in this same pamphlet makes several other satirical comments. Harvey, whom Spenser dubs Hobbinol in the *Shepheardes Calendar*, is expressing his own preference for a poem by Spenser still in manuscript rather than for the *Faerie Queene*: "If so be the *Faerye Queene* be fairer in your eie than the *Nine Muses*, and *Hobgoblin* runne away with the Garland from *Apollo*: Marke what I saye, and yet I will not say that I thought, but there an End for this once, and fare you well, till God or some good Aungell putt you in a better minde" (*Harvey*, I, 94–95). From this verbal confusion Nashe extracts his epithets.

Each of Harvey's other "nicknames" McKerrow strives to annotate for the reader's benefit. With certain words obviously associated with ropemaking his task is fairly easy. For example, of "Himpenhempen" he writes, "Perhaps suggested—with doubtless a side-allusion to ropemaking—by an expression attributed to Robin Goodfellow" (IV, 329). But whether or not Nashe had Robin Goodfellow in mind is debatable. On the contrary, what McKerrow terms a "side-allusion" is probably Nashe's main allusion. Of a similar epithet, "Archibald Rupenrope," McKerrow writes, "Apparently a mere nonce-name" (IV, 334). Perhaps for the scholarly reader he adds Moore Smith's humorless comment that "there may be more point than a mere allusion to the

Harvey's [*sic*] 'rope-making business.'" But what that "point" may be neither Moore Smith nor McKerrow makes clear. Again, "hangtelow" suggests the common use for ropes. In short, Nashe's main purpose in coining these epithets seems to be to keep his reader aware of the Harvey family background. It must be remembered that Nashe opens his attack on Harvey with a brilliant punning allusion to his father's trade based on the ancient admonition *"Respice finem"*: " . . . what a hell it is for him, that hath built his heauen in vaine-glory, to bee puld by the sleeue and bidd *Respice funem*, looke backe to his Fathers house" (I, 268, 27–29).

Before most of these amusing epithets—derisive as they are to the point of open insult—McKerrow is forced to admit defeat. Two of them, *Dagobert Coppenhagen* and *Heggledepeg*, he discards as "mere" nonce-names (IV, 339, 312). Of one, *Gilgilis Hobberdehoy*, he writes that Gilgilis was one of the "obscure names" mentioned in Agrippa's *De Incertitude et Vanitate* as used by alchemists and that "hobberdehoy is a form of 'hobbledehoy,' an abusive term of somewhat indefinite meaning" (IV, 179). In this last phrase, however, McKerrow arrives at the essence of Nashe's epithets: they are chosen not to convey a definite meaning, but to *suggest* one or more words which will amuse the reader and conjure up in his mind a ridiculous picture of Harvey.

Several epithets point up characteristics of the Cambridge scholar particularly offensive to Nashe. McKerrow notes that *Timothy Tiptoes* and *Pumps and Pantofles* allude to Harvey's alleged vanity regarding his personal appearance (IV, 168, 169). Following McKerrow's lead, we might interpret *Frigius Pedagogus* as an allusion to Harvey's obvious pedantry. *Phobetor geremumble tirleriwhisco or what you will* and *Tapthartharath* hint at Harvey's wordiness. *Gibraltar* points at his heaviness of style. Since he has already published three volumes of letters, *infractissime Pistelpragmos* might mean "incorrigible letter writer." But it is both impossible and unnecessary to seek for a definite meaning in any of these epithets. The reader must listen to the overtones of the consonant sounds in Nashe's alliteration and *feel* his irony.

In keeping with his professed aim to write in the "extemporall vayne," all of the names give the impression of being invented on the spur of the moment. Several begin with a *D* (for Doctor), a *G* (for Gabriel), an *H* (either for Harvey or hangman), an *R*—and include numerous internal *r*'s—(for ropemaker). Then using a process of free association Nashe coins words suggesting Harvey's vanity concerning his scholarship, his sensitiveness regarding his family background, or—like *Heggledepeg* (higgledy piggledy) and *Heyderry derry*—silly Mother Goose rhymes.

II *Other "Extemporall" Devices*

Another characteristic of Nashe's style that has a definitely twentieth-century, or "Joycean," quality, is his association of seemingly unrelated words, in order to interpret which the reader must combine them into a new meaning not implicit in each word separately. Not only is this "punning" technique used in his invention of epithets, but it also sparkles through his synonyms. For example, in *Pierce Penilesse* he refers to the work of shoemakers as "the gentle craft (*alias* the red herrings kinsmen)" (I, 201, 9). Glossing "the gentle craft" as shoemakers, McKerrow adds, "I cannot explain why they are called 'the red herrings kinsmen'" (IV, 125). But Nashe here is alluding to a colloquialism which appears a few pages further on in the same pamphlet, referring to the use of the red herring as an appetizer or hors d'oeuvre: " . . .to haue some shooing horne to pul on your wine, as a rasher of the\,coles, or a redde herring" (I, 207, 13–25). With this colloquialism he then associates another, namely, "a *last* of herring," which in its ordinary sense he uses at the close of the Epistle Dedicatorie of *Lenten Stuffe*, "Yours for a whole last of redde Herrings" (III, 150, 13–14), glossed by McKerrow as "12 *barrels, or* 10 *to* 13 *thousand*" (V, 292). At once perceiving the relationship between the "shooing horne" and the "last," on the one hand, and the "gentle craft" or shoemaking, on the other, he wittily combines the two into "the gentle craft (*alias* the red herrings kinsmen)." And he expects his reader to exert a little imagination in order to enjoy the pun.

Another distinctive characteristic of Nashe's style, though not in itself truly stylistic except as Nashe intentionally uses it in order to give an "extemporall" flavor to his writing, is his tendency to misquote (IV, 215, 468, 469). The purpose of this seeming carelessness is to avoid the appearance of pedantry.

Related to Nashe's intentional misquotation is his pretended misspeaking and mistranslation for humorous effect. In order to produce the effect of casualness he stumblingly alludes to a *Hamlet* extant in 1589: " . . . hee will affoord you whole Hamlets, I should say handfuls of Tragicall speeches" (III, 315, 33–34).

In his later writings this conversational casualness is evident in most of his translations. In *Pierce Penilesse* the Latin proverb *cucullus non facit monachum* becomes a satiric allusion to baldness caused by syphilis—a common Elizabethan joke: " . . . tis not their newe bonnets will keepe them from the old boan-ach" (I, 182, 6–7). Another Latin phrase *quicquid in buccam venerit* he translates as "as fast as my hand can trot" (I, 195, 19–20). And the Latin passage *plenus venter nil agit libenter, & plures gula occidit quam gladius* is modernized into "it is as desperate a peece of seruice to sleep vpon a full stomacke, as it is to serue in face of the bullet" (I, 201, 10–13).

The translations of classical allusions in the rollicking pages of *Strange Newes* become even more far-fetched. The Latin phrase *diù viuas in amore iocísque* is mistranslated as "whatsoeuer you do, beware of keeping diet" (I, 256, 26–27). As has been mentioned, the traditional warning *respice finem* is transformed into an allusion to the elder Harvey's trade of ropemaking: "*Respice funem*, looke backe to his Fathers house"(I, 268, 29). The phrase *valete humanae artes*, translated according to its sound in English, becomes "heart and good will," to which Nashe ruefully adds, "but neuer a ragge of money" (I, 301, 28–29).

Notes and References

Chapter One

1. Alexander B. Grosart, ed., *The Works of Gabriel Harvey, D. C. L.* (Privately printed, 1884–85; reprinted New York: AMS Press, Inc., 1966), III, 68.
2. *Harvey*, III, 67.
3. *Harvey*, III, 68.
4. *Harvey*, I, 199; see also McKerrow, IV, 184–85.
5. J. Dover Wilson, "The Marprelate Controversy," *The Cambridge History of English Literature* (New York:Macmillan, 1939), III, 450.
6. Wilson, III, 450–51.
7. *Harvey*, I, 170.
8. D. J. McGinn, "A Quip from Tom Nashe," *Studies in English Renaissance Drama*, ed. by Josephine W. Bennett, Oscar Cargill, and Vernon Hall, Jr. (New York:New York Univ. Press, 1959), pp. 172–88.
9. C. G. Harlow, "Nashe's Visit to the Isle of Wight and His Publications, 1592–4," *Review of English Studies* 14 (1963):229.
10. "Nashe's Visit to the Isle of Wight," p. 228.
11. "Nashe's Visit to the Isle of Wight," p. 241.
12. "Thomas Nashe, Robert Cotton the Antiquary, and *The Terrors of the Night*," *Review of English Studies* 12 (1961): 7–23.
13. "Nashe's Visit to the Isle of Wight," pp. 240–41.
14. *Harvey*, I, 272 ff.
15. "Nashe's Visit to the Isle of Wight," p. 233.
16. "Nashe's Visit to the Isle of Wight," pp. 236 ff.
17. "Nashe's Visit to the Isle of Wight," p. 235.
18. "Nashe's Visit to the Isle of Wight," pp. 238–39.
19. "Nashe's Visit to the Isle of Wight," p. 240.
20. *Harvey*, III, 43.
21. *Harvey*, III, 50 ff.

Chapter Two

1. Don C. Allen, "*The Anatomie of Absurditie*: A Study in Literary Apprenticeship," *Studies in Philology* 32 (1933): 170–76.
2. "Thomas Nashe and the Satirical Stance," *Cahiers Elisabéthains* 9 (1976):3.

3. William Pierce, *The Marprelate Tracts, 1588, 1589* (London:James Clarke, 1911), p. 101.

4. Pierce, pp. 30–32.

5. "Nashe's Share in the Marprelate Controversy." *PMLA* 59 (Dec. 1944):952–84.

Chapter Three

1. "Thomas Nashe and the Satirical Stance," p.4.

2. "The Allegory of the 'Beare' and the 'Foxe' in Nashe's *Pierce Penilesse*," *PMLA* 61 (June 1946):431–53.

Chapter Four

1. Robert J. Fehrenbach, "Thomas Nashe," *The Predecessors of Shakespeare*, ed. Terence P. Logan and Denzell S. Smith (Lincoln: Univ. of Nebraska Press, 1973), pp. 114–17.

2. "The Low Style in Nashe's *The Unfortunate Traveller*," *Studies in English Literature, 1500–1900* 6 (1966):43–57.

3. *Seven Types of Ambiguity* (London:Meridian, 1956), pp. 25–26.

4. "Nashe's 'Brightnesse falls from the ayre,'" *Renaissance News* 12 (1959), 167–69.

5. "The Practice of Historical Interpretation and Nashe's 'Brightnesse falls from the ayre,'" *Journal of English and Germanic Philology* 66 (1967):506 ff.

6. Trimpi, pp. 512–13.

7. *Sewanee Review* 66 (1958):90–91.

8. Norman Mailer, in *The Armies of the Night* (New York:New American Library, 1968), pp. 21 ff.

9. (New York:Dial, 1964), pp. 41–46.

Chapter Five

1. Kaula, pp. 49 ff.

Chapter Six

1. *Complaint and Satire in Early English Literature* (Oxford:Oxford Univ. Press, 1956), p. 60.

2. "Verbal Tensions in Thomas Nashe's *The Unfortunate Traveller*," *Language and Style* 8(1975):213.

3. *English Literature in the Sixteenth Century* (London:Oxford Univ Press, 1954), p. 414.

Chapter Seven

1. "Thomas Nashe and the Picaresque Novel," *Humanistic Studies in Honor of John Calvin Metcalf, University of Virginia Studies* (Charlottesville, Va.:Univ. of Va. Press, 1941), I, 12–27.

2. Bowers, I, 26.

3. Bowers, I, 25.

4. Bowers, I, 27.

5. *An Introduction to the English Novel* (London:Hutchinson Univ. Lib., 1951, reprinted London:Hutchinson Univ. Lib., 1954, 1957, 1959, 1961, 1963, 1965), I, 24.

6. Kettle, I, 25.

7. Kettle, I, 22.

8. *The English Novel: A Panorama* (Boston:Houghton Mifflin Co., 1960), p. 25.

9. *The History of the English Novel* (London:Witherby, 1929), II, 168.

10. *The Unfortunate Traveller* (Boston:Houghton Mifflin Co., 1920), p. xii.

11. Stevenson, p. 25.

12. *The English Novel: A Short Critical History* (New York:E. P. Dutton and Co., 1954), p. 13.

13. *The Unfortunate Traveller* (New York:Putnam, 1960), p. 7.

14. *Idea and Act in Elizabethan Fiction* (Princeton:Princeton Univ. Press, 1969), p. 216.

15. Davis, p. 219.

16. Davis, p. 234.

17. "Tom Nashe and Jack Wilton: Personality as Structure in *The Unfortunate Traveller*," *Studies in Short Fiction* 4(1967):201.

18. Lanham, p. 204.

19. Lanham, p. 201.

20. Lanham, pp. 208, 216.

21. Lanham, p. 215.

22. Davis, p. 216.

23. *Antecedents of the English Novel 1400–1600* (London:Oxford Univ. Press,1963), p. 206.

24. "Artistic Coherence in *The Unfortunate Traveller*," *Studies in English Literature 1500–1900* 14(1974):37.

25. Leggatt, p. 40.

26. *Thomas Nashe: Selected Writings* (Cambridge, Mass.:Harvard Univ. Press, 1965), p. 18.

27. Schlauch, p. 214.

28. "Polemic, the Rhetorical Tradition, and *The Unfortunate Traveller*," *Journal of English and Germanic Philology* 63(1964):418 ff.

29. "Satire on Literary Themes and Modes in Nashe's 'Unfortunate Trav-

eller'" *Essays and Studies by Members of the English Association,* (London, 1948), p. 85.

30. Latham, p. 88.

31. Latham, p. 86.

32. Latham, p. 87.

33. Latham, p. 100.

34. "The Low Style in Nashe's *The Unfortunate Traveller*," *Studies in English Literature* 6(1966):43.

35. Kaula, p. 45.

36. Kaula, pp. 49–50.

37. Kaula, p. 55.

38. Kaula, pp. 51 ff.

39. Kaula, p. 55.

40. Kaula, pp. 43, 48, 50, 55.

41. "Verbal Tensions in Thomas Nashe's *The Unfortunate Traveller*," *Language and Style* 8(1975):215.

42. Friederich, p. 212.

43. Friederich, p. 213.

44. Friederich, p. 215.

45. Friederich, p. 216.

46. Gibbons, p. 409.

47. Friederich, p. 217.

48. Friederich, p. 218.

Chapter Eight

1. *Harvey,* I, 31.

2. *Harvey,* I, 31–32.

3. *The Poetical Works of Edmund Spenser,* ed. J. C. Smith and Ernest de Selincourt (London:Oxford Univ. Press, 1926), pp. 416, 419. In addition to the dedication and the postscripts E. K. prepared the notes at the end of each month of the *Calendar*. His professed knowledge of Spenser is further evidence for identifying him as Harvey.

4. *Harvey,* I, 38.

5. *Harvey,* I, 8.

6. *Harvey,* I, 92.

7. *English Works of Roger Ascham,* ed. W. Aldis Wright, M.A. (Cambridge Univ. Press, 1904), p. 229.

8. "Robert Greene and the Harveys," *Indiana University Studies* 18 (September 1931):43 ff.

9. *Complete Works of John Lyly,* ed. Richard W. Bond (Oxford: Oxford Univ. Press, 1902), III, 400.

10. *Harvey,* I, 183–84.

11. *Harvey*, II, 122.
12. *Harvey*, I, 180.
13. See p. 19.
14. *Harvey*, I, 162.
15. *Harvey*, I, 171–72.
16. *Harvey*, I, 172.
17. *Harvey*, I, 170.
18. *Harvey*, I, 192 ff.
19. *Harvey*, I, 194, 201.
20. *Harvey*, I, 204.
21. *Harvey*, I, 215–16.
22. *Harvey*, I, 217–19.
23. *Harvey*, I, 208.

Chapter Nine

1. *Harvey*, I, 161.
2. *Harvey*, I, 160.
3. *Harvey*, I, 155.
4. *Harvey*, I, 155.
5. *Harvey*, I, 160.
6. *Harvey*, I, 161.
7. *Harvey*, I, 162.
8. *Harvey*, I, 162.
9. *Harvey*, I, 27.
10. *Harvey*, I, 174–75.
11. *Harvey* I, 188.
12. *Harvey*, I, 70.
13. *Harvey*, I, 200.
14. *Harvey*, I, 202.
15. *Harvey*, I, 202.
16. *Harvey*, I, 215–16, 233.
17. *Harvey*, I, 230.

Chapter Ten

1. See p. 21.
2. *Harvey*, II, 122–23.
3. *Harvey*, II, 275.
4. *Harvey*, II, 319 ff.
5. *Harvey*, I, 276 ff.
6. *Harvey*, II, 145.
7. *Harvey*, II, 36.

8. *Harvey*, II, 50–51.
9. *Harvey*, I, 84.
10. *Harvey*, I, 208.
11. *Harvey*, II, 229–30.
12. *Harvey*, I, 218.
13. *Harvey*, II, 335–46.

Chapter Eleven

1. Davis, pp. 232–33.
2. Davis, p. 234.
3. Davis, p. 212.
4. Davis, pp. 212, 214.
5. Davis, p. 214.

Chapter Twelve

1. Edward Arber, *An Introductory Sketch to the Martin Marprelate Controversy, 1588-1590* (*The English Scholar's Library of Old and Modern Works, No. 8*) (London:Privately printed, 1875), pp. 17–18.
2. Sir Philip Sidney, *Defence of Poesy*, ed. Albert S. Cook (New York:Ginn and Co., 1890), pp. 7 ff.

Selected Bibliography

PRIMARY SOURCES

BERRYMAN, JOHN, ed. *The Unfortunate Traveller*, New York: Putnam, 1960.
BRETT SMITH, H. F., ed. *The Unfortunate Traveller*, Boston: Houghton Mifflin Co., 1920.
GROSART, A. B., ed. *The Works of Gabriel Harvey, D. C. L., Huth Library*, 3 vol. London: Privately printed, 1884–85; reprinted New York: AMS Press, Inc., 1966.
MCKERROW, R. B., ed *The Works of Thomas Nashe*, 5 vol. London: A. H. Bullen, 1904–10; reprinted (with additional notes) Oxford: Blackwell, 1958. Contains:
   An Almond for a Parrat, or Cutbert Curry-knaues Almes, 1590.
   A Pleasant Comedie, called Summers last will and Testament, 1600.
   Christ's Teares Ouer Ierusalem, Wherunto is annexed a comparative admonition to London, 1593.
   Haue with you to Saffron-Walden, or Gabriell Harueys Hunt is vp ..., 1596.
   Nashes Lenten Stuffe Containing the Description and first Procreation and Increase of the towne of Great Yarmouth in Norfolke ..., 1599.
   Pierce Penilesse his Supplication to the Diuell Describing the ouerspreading of Vice and suppression of Vertue ..., 1592.
   Somewhat to reade for them that list (Preface to *Syr P* [hilip]. *S* [idney]. *His Astrophel and Stella*), 1591.
   Strange Newes of the intercepting certaine Letters and a Conuoy of Verses as they were going Priuilie to victuall the Low Countries, 1592.
   The Anatomie of Absurditie: Contayning a breefe confutation of the slender imputed prayses to feminine perfection with a short description of the seuerall practises of youth and sundry follies of our licentious times ..., 1589.
   The Choise of Valentines, or the Merie Ballad of Nashe his Dildo, 1899.
   The Terrors of the night, or A Discourse of Apparitions, 1594.
   The Tragedie of Dido Queene of Carthage, 1594.
   The Unfortunate Traveller, or The Life of Iacke Wilton, 1594.
   To the Gentlemen Students of Both Vniuersities (Preface to R. Greene's *Menaphon*), 1589.
WELLS, STANLEY. *Thomas Nashe: Selected Writings*. Cambridge, Mass.: Harvard Univ. Press, 1964.

SECONDARY SOURCES

ALLEN, DON C. "*The Anatomie of Absurditie*: A Study in Literary Apprenticeship." *Studies in Philology* 32 (1935): 170–76. In order to impress
the reader Nashe in his first pamphlet relies upon compendiums (collec-
tions of classical allusions and quotations). Yet in his mature writings he
condemns their use.

ALLEN, WALTER. *The English Novel: A Short Critical History*. New York: E.
P. Dutton and Co., 1954. *The Unfortunate Traveller* does not meet the
modern specifications for the novel.

BAKER, E. A. *The History of the English Novel*, II. London: Witherby, 1924–
36. Although *The Unfortunate Traveller* possesses realistic elements, it
cannot be considered either an imitation of the Spanish picaresque tale
or an "anti-romance." Actually Nashe is presenting "the romance of
actuality."

BEST, MICHAEL R. "Nashe, Lyly, and *Summer's Last Will and Testament*."
Philological Quarterly 48 (January 1969):1–11. The odd structure of this
play and a number of its stylistic peculiarities may result from Nashe's
reworking and expanding a brief "show" originally written by Lyly.

BOWERS, FREDSON T. "Thomas Nashe and the Picaresque Novel." *Humanistic Studies in Honor of John Calvin Metcalf, University of Virginia
Studies I*, Charlottesville, Va.: Univ. of Virginia Press, 1941, pp. 12–27.
Questioning McKerrow's statement that Jack Wilton fails to meet the
principal specification of the picaresque tale, namely, that its hero must
be a rogue, Bowers considers Jack to be an English version of that type
and the narrative the first English picaresque novel.

DAVIS, WALTER R. *Idea and Act in Elizabethan Fiction*. Princeton, N.J.:
Princeton University Press, 1969. *The Unfortunate Traveller* cannot be
termed the first historical novel. Davis's references to the "travelogue
frame" of the narrative suggest that he places it nearer the pamphlet
than the novel.

DREW, PHILIP. "Was Greene's 'Young Juvenal' Nashe or Lodge?" *Studies in
English Literature 1500–1900* 7 (1967): 55–56. Contrary to the general
assumption that Greene is alluding to Nashe, Drew argues in favor of
Thomas Lodge on the ground that Greene had in mind a writer known
for his plays and satirical verse rather than for his prose satire. The particular "comedie" upon which Greene collaborated with "Juvenal" then
would probably be *A Looking Glasse for London*.

EMPSON, WARREN. *Seven Types of Ambiguity*. London: Meridian, 1950.
Nashe's "Brightnesse falls from the ayre" is an example of ambiguity by
vagueness suggesting a variety of things.

FEHRENBACH, ROBERT J. "Thomas Nashe," in *The Predecessors of Shakespeare*, ed. T. P. Logan and D. S. Smith. Lincoln: University of Nebraska
Press, 1973, pp. 107–24. The most recent and most informative bibliography on Nashe.

FRIEDENREICH, KENNETH. "Nashe's *Strange Newes* and the Case for Professional Writers." *Studies in Philology* 71 (1974): 451–72. Nashe's first reply to Harvey's *Foure Letters* formulates the case for the professional writers against Harvey, who was attacking them for squandering their talents in producing sensational commercial literature. In *Strange Newes* Nashe is writing as a journalist simply embellishing details for effect.

FRIEDERICH, REINHARD H. "Verbal Tensions in Thomas Nashe's *The Unfortunate Traveller*." *Language and Style* 8 (1975): 211–18. Nashe is "an extraordinarily language-minded writer." As a result a conflict frequently arises between his plot and his interest in rhetorical display. In fact his verbal extravagancies frequently overshadow his emotional effects so that the literary experience precedes the visual.

GIBBONS, MARINA. "Polemic, the Rhetorical Tradition, and *The Unfortunate Traveller*." *Journal of English and Germanic Philology* 63 (1964): 408–21. Throughout *The Unfortunate Traveller* Nashe displays his polemic bent whether he is openly reporting such orations as those of Vanderhulke, Heraclide, and Cutwolfe or more subtly in his sermon-oration on the Anabaptist uprising and his attacks on Italians, Spaniards, Roman Catholics, and Jews.

GOHLKE, MADELON S. "Wits Wantonness: *The Unfortunate Traveller* as Picaresque." *Studies in Philology* 73 (1976): 397–413 Lyly's distinction in *Euphues, the Anatomy of Wit* between wit and wantonness, on the one hand, and true wisdom, on the other, is exemplified in the picaresque tale of the adventures of Jack Wilton.

HARLOW, C. G. "Nashe's Visit to the Isle of Wight and His Publications of 1592–4." *Review of English Studies* 14 (1963): 224–42. By correcting McKerrow's dating of Nashe's visit to the Isle of Wight, Harlow alters the chronology of nearly all the events in Nashe's life between 1592 and 1594 and thereby clarifies many puzzling features in his publications during his most productive period.

———. "Thomas Nashe, Robert Cotton the Antiquary, and *The Terrors of the Night*." *Review of English Studies* 12 (1961): 7–23. From Nashe's comment in *The Terrors of the Night* about visiting a house some sixty miles from London during a February between 1592 and 1594 Harlow convincingly demonstrates that Nashe was the guest of Robert Cotton, the antiquary, at Conington in February 1593. This discovery revises McKerrow's dates of composition and publication of this pamphlet.

———. "Thomas Nashe and William Cotton, M. P." *Notes and Queries* 8 (1961): 424–25. Harlow disputes the theory that the William Cotton, whose patronage Nashe once solicited, was a socially unimportant person.

HIBBARD, G. R. *Thomas Nashe: A Critical Introduction.* Cambridge, Mass.: Harvard University Press, 1962. This is the only complete critical study of all of Nashe's pamphlets hitherto published. Hibbard's biographical

summary and his chronology of Nashe's writings must be corrected by
C. G. Harlow's two articles on Nashe's activity between 1592 and 1594,
which appeared after the publication of his book. Since Hibbard regards
journalism as strictly a post-Elizabethan activity, he hesitates to call
Nashe a journalist but compromises with the title "pamphleteer."

KAULA, DAVID. "The Low Style in Nashe's *The Unfortunate Traveller*."
Studies in English Literature 1500-1900, 6 (1966): 43-57. The chief distinction of Nashe's narrative is discovered in the stylistic dexterity with
which he parodied current rhetorical modes. For this purpose he
employed two distinct styles: conventional passages of elaborately ornamental rhetoric satirizing a particular illusion and low, or colloquial, passages conveying Jack Wilton's, and hence his own, response to reality.

KETTLE, ARNOLD. *An Introduction to the English Novel.* London:Oxford
Univ. Press, 1965 (reprint). *The Unfortunate Traveller* is "perhaps the
most remarkable picaresque story" in English. Jack Wilton possesses "all
the characteristics of the outcast rogue."

LANHAM, RICHARD A. "Tom Nashe and Jack Wilton: Personality as structure
in *The Unfortunate Traveller*." *Studies in Short Fiction* 4 (1967): 201-
16. While acknowledging Nashe's narrative to be a novel, Lanham is
dissatisfied with this classification. Since Nashe seems to identify with
Jack Wilton, Lanham prefers the term "a fictional autobiography."

LATHAM, AGNES M. C. "Satire on Literary Themes and Modes in Nashe's
'Unfortunate Traveller.'" *Essays and Studies by Members of the
English Association* (London, 1948): 85-100. Although *The Unfortunate Traveller* may have begun as an early example of the historical
novel, it ended as a parody of popular literary themes and styles. Rather
than being a popular journalist pandering to public taste, Nashe seems
to be parodying the stock commonplaces of Elizabethan journalism.

LEGGATT, ALEXANDER. "Artistic Coherence in *The Unfortunate Traveller*."
Studies in English Literature 1500-1900 14 (1974): 31-46. Because
Jack Wilton is not a "developing character," he is not the hero of a typical novel but rather a series of effects that change with every new
situation.

LEWIS, C. S. *English Literature in the Sixteenth Century Excluding Drama.*
London:Oxford Univ. Press, 1954. The use of the "keyword" as a motif
in Nashe's oration in *Christ's Teares Over Jerusalem* resembles a leitmotif in musical composition.

MACKERNESS, E. D. "*Christ's Teares* and the Literature of Warning." *English
Studies* 33 (1952): 251-54. *Christ's Teares Over Jerusalem* is classified
as belonging to the literature of warning, which, following the mirror
convention, a recognized literary mode, uses history for moral and
didactic purposes.

———. "Thomas Nashe and William Cotton." *Review of English Studies*
25(1949):342-46. Nashe's correspondence in the autumn of 1596 with

this servant of Sir George Carey seems to suggest that he was in financial difficulty.

McGINN, D. J. "A Quip from Tom Nashe." *Studies in the English Renaissance Drama*, ed. Josephine W. Bennett, Oscar Cargill, and Vernon Hall. New York: New York Univ. Press, 1959, pp. 172–88. Because of the similarity in style between Nashe's writings and the attack on the Harvey brothers in *A Quip for an Upstart Courtier* by Greene, this pamphlet is identified as the "Comedie" which Greene admits to writing with "young Juvenal," or Nashe. Furthermore Greene's so-called "social pamphlets" disclose other resemblances to those of Nashe, suggesting further collaboration between the two pamphleteers.

————. *John Penry and the Marprelate Controversy.* New Brunswick, N.J.: Rutgers University Press, 1966. In order to support the author's earlier identification of Martin Marprelate as John Penry he presents a comparison of Penry's signed writings with the Martinist pamphlets. Their similarity in style rules out any other suspects.

————. "Nashe's Share in the Marprelate Controversy." *PMLA* 59 (December 1944): 952–84. The style and content of *An Almond for a Parrat*, along with contemporary references to this pamphlet, designate it as Nashe's principal contribution to the anti-Martinist attack. It also furnishes the stylistic link between Nashe's early publications and his successful *Pierce Penilesse*.

————. *The Admonition Controversy.* New Brunswick, N.J.: Rutgers University Press, 1949. For students of the Marprelate controversy in particular and of English Puritanism in general this study of the first Puritan-Episcopalian controversy presents an account of its causes and its principal contenders along with pertinent excerpts from the various pamphlets published on either side.

————. "The Allegory of the 'Beare' and the 'Foxe' in Nashe's *Pierce Penilesse.*" *PMLA* 61 (1946): 431–53. Nashe's allegory possesses a twofold significance: a political satire involving Robert Dudley, Earl of Leicester, and a religious commentary on the two main figures in the Puritan controversies, Thomas Cartwright and John Penry.

————. "The Real Martin Marprelate." *PMLA* 58 (March 1943): 84–107. From the depositions of the various suspects in the Marprelate controversy, supported by Nashe's statements in *An Almond for a Parrat*, John Penry is identified as Martin Marprelate.

McPHERSON, DAVID C. "Aretino and the Harvey-Nashe Quarrel." *PMLA* 84 (October 1969): 1551–81. Although both Harvey and Nashe admired Pietro Aretino for different reasons, Nashe's successful imitation of Aretino's invective was responsible for his superiority over Harvey in their literary feud.

MORRIS, HARRY. "Nashe's 'Brightnesse falls from the ayre.'" *Renaissance News* 12(1959): 167–69. Hamlet's reply to Polonius's question, "Will you walk out of the air, my lord?" suggests a possible explication of this line from Nashe's poem, implying that beauty must eventually be buried in the grave.

PERCY, WALKER. "Metaphor as Mistake." *Sewanee Review* 66 (1958): 79–99. If "ayre" in Nashe's "Brightnesse falls from the ayre" is a misreading for "haire," as McKerrow suggests, it is adequate but less beautiful than "ayre," which seems to refer to a lovely moment in a summer evening.

SCHLAUCH, MARGARET. *Antecedents of the English Novel 1400–1600.* London: Oxford Univ. Press, 1963. If not a novel, *The Unfortunate Traveller* may be considered a precursor to that form. Influenced, or at least inspired, by *Lazarillo de Tormes*, it could be classified as a picaresque adventure story written in autobiographical form and heavily indebted to medieval rhetorical precepts. Its only unity is supplied by Jack Wilton.

STEVENSON, LIONEL. *The English Novel: A Panorama.* Boston: Houghton Mifflin Co., 1960. Written in a "picaresque vein," *The Unfortunate Traveller* may be classified as the first historical novel.

TANNENBAUM, SAMUEL A. and DOROTHY. *Elizabethan Bibliographies,* VI. Port Washington, N.Y.: Kennikat Press, 1967.

TRIMPI, WESLEY. "The Practice of Historical Interpretation and Nashe's 'Brightnesse falls from the ayre.'" *Journal of English and Germanic Philology* 66 (1967): 501–18. Although most scholars have concentrated on the interpretation of the word "ayre," the key to unlock the meaning of this line is to be found in the word "brightnesse." A study of classical works on astronomy and meteorology suggests that the proper synonym for it is "lightning," which could signify either the natural phenomenon or the plague, both of which would have been evident in October 1592, when Nashe's play was performed at Croydon.

WELLS, STANLEY. "Thomas Nashe and the Satirical Stance." *Cahiers Elisabéthains Etudes sur la Pre-Renaissance et la Renaissance Anglaises* 9 (1976): 1–7. Both particularity and generality are essential to satirical writing. Overparticularity results in unintelligibility, as in Nashe's preface to *Menaphon*. Absence of particularity, on the other hand, destroys satire, as in his allegory to *Pierce Penilesse*. The effectiveness of Nashe's satire on Harvey results from the writer's strong personal feeling, but its particularity tends to make it trivial.

Index

189